YOU CAN'T WIN ANYTHING WITH KIDS

'

**ERIC CANTONA, MANCHESTER UNITED
AND THE INCREDIBLE 1995/96 SEASON**

WAYNE BARTON

EMPIRE
PUBLICATIONS

First published in 2016

EMPIRE PUBLICATIONS
1 Newton Street, Manchester M1 1HW
© Wayne Barton 2016

ISBN: 9781909360419

CHAPTERS

To Freddy,
Dream of the impossible

ACKNOWLEDGEMENTS

I would like to thank the following people for their time and help with this project; Dan Burdett, who, as always, has been invaluable; Dave Murphy for his support; Cal Gildart for his creative input; Danny Taylor at *The Guardian* and Ian Herbert at *The Independent* for their help; the players who agreed to be interviewed: Darren Anderton, Brian Deane, Stuart Pearce, and last but not least, Andrei Kanchelskis (and a big thank you to Andrei Jr., too). Thanks also to Jasmine Shaw for proofreading the finished book so expertly.

Finally, as always, thanks to my wife and family – without their love and support none of this would have been possible.

INTRODUCTION

THE DATE IS 31ST MARCH, 1995. The venue is the courthouse on Altyre Road in Croydon, South London. In the gallery a young teenager wearing the new change strip of his favourite football team observes his hero and passes him a card that reads 'Good luck'. Details of an appeal are read and decided upon.

Shortly afterwards, a man enters a room to be greeted by the nation's media and the din of cameras and flash photography. He is followed by solicitors and other representatives as they take their seat at a table at the head of the room. There is a hum of expectancy and a hubbub of conversation which betrays the common truth – all are gathered to hear this man break his silence.

"When the seagulls..." starts the man, teasingly, before picking up a small glass of water and pensively taking a short drink, "... follow the trawler... it is because they think sardines... will be thrown in to the sea. Thank you, very much."

With that he stands, shaking the hand of a man to his left, and makes his exit to the sound of a suddenly raucous room that now sounds like the type of arena the man is more accustomed to.

The handshake grasp is still warm in the palm of Maurice Waktins, the solicitor acting on behalf of Eric Cantona and Manchester United, who is tasked with the duty of explaining to a bemused media the meaning of his client's latest pronouncement. 'It was an obscure thing to say,' Watkins admits. 'He just does not want to stay here and meet you and answer questions because he has had enough. I think he has been under tremendous strain.'

Cantona had just won an appeal to have a custodial sentence reduced to one hundred and twenty hours of community service following what was commonly referred to as a 'kung fu' attack on Crystal Palace supporter Matthew Simmons. "It was a kick that reverberated around the world, but I never even saw it," Manchester United manager Alex Ferguson would tell the *Mail on Sunday* on July 16th, 1995 in an interview promoting the serialisation of his book 'A Year in the Life – The Manager's Diary'.

Yet for United fans, the crime itself was of secondary importance. They were still reeling from the news that their star man would be absent for the rest of the season. The importance of Eric Cantona to the rise of their club was incredible. Before him, the club had limped along in the shadow of the great teams of the 50s and 60s of titles and trophies won in black and white. The Frenchman's arrival had brought United technicolor glory: two league titles and an FA Cup, including the prestigious Double. Now he would be gone and United would end up potless for the first time in the 1990s.

★

On Monday 21st September 1992, as the first team prepared for a League Cup game at Brighton and Hove Albion, United's reserves were at Rotherham United. The starting line up read: Pilkington, G Neville, Switzer, Butt, Carey, Casper, Beardsmore, Beckham, McKee, Scholes. Seven of these players had featured in the team that lifted the FA Youth Cup back in May, while Paul Scholes would forever be included within that same group of players who broke through, as would Gary's brother Philip. The reserves won 3-2 that day, a clear sign of the maturity they had acquired after racking up goals in the youth, A and B teams.

The match was a quiet pre-cursor for a far more noteworthy event exactly two years to the day later. United played away at

The 'Class of 92'

Port Vale in the first leg of their second round League Cup tie where Neville, Butt, Beckham and Scholes again took to the field, joined by fellow Youth Cup winners Keith Gillespie and Simon Davies. Chris Casper missed out through injury and so Roy Keane was drafted in to play at centre half. Of course, as most know, United went on to win that game 2-1, with both goals coming from Scholes. Yet the team selection by Sir Alex Ferguson caused such unrest and disappointment that Port Vale supporters took their complaints as far as the House of Commons.

Now, to say that you were one of the 18,605 in attendance that evening gives you the prestige of attending one of those 'I was there' moments - you could ask a pretty penny (and some do) for a ticket stub that some were once tempted to rip up and discard out of rage. The kids had done more than alright. They had saved their manager from considerable embarrassment.

The orthodox (hindsight driven) history of this period would have you believe that Ferguson's confidence in these youngsters was shared by a support brought up on the triumphs and tragedies of previous generations. Yet nothing could be further from the truth. Despite securing the club's first league title in 26 years and becoming the fourth club in the 20th century to win the League and Cup double, the manager was under fire. The loss of the title on the final day in 1995 was the prelude for a summer of disruption at Old Trafford and unease among supporters. A *Manchester Evening News* poll conducted in July 1995 indicated that the vast majority wanted the manager sacked. It seems inexplicable now so what had happened in those few months that had provoked such a drastic change in support?

Eric Cantona's suspension was widely seen as the turning point of the 1994-95 season. Yet after that 1-1 draw at Selhurst Park in January, United were second on 54 points after 26 games played, five points behind league leaders Blackburn Rovers. A difficult four weeks in the autumn had seen United lose three consecutive league games at Leeds, Ipswich and Sheffield Wednesday, but they had recovered sufficiently to stay in touching distance. A thrilling win over Blackburn at Ewood Park was followed by a victory over Newcastle United – by the time that double header came back around in mid-January, the Reds were well placed for a title push, with many of their players in peak form. Cantona was imperious and Andrei Kanchelskis was arguably at the peak of his powers in a United shirt. In between, United registered a 2-0 win at a blustery Bramhall Lane in the FA Cup in which both Mark Hughes and Cantona scored and before United's trip to St. James' Park in the league in January, Ferguson broke the British transfer record for Andy Cole of Newcastle United, the £7m deal included Keith Gillespie going the other way. By the evening of 25th January 1995, Blackburn had scored ten more goals than United after boosting their frontline with their own British record signing Chris Sutton for £5m.

Ferguson hadn't counted on fate giving him the best examples of his senior forwards ability to score right before they were stolen from him – Hughes netted in a draw at Newcastle with a typically brave effort but was hurt in scoring, in a collision with the goalkeeper. No matter, United had Cole. But when Cantona was sent off at Crystal Palace after scoring the decider against Blackburn at Old Trafford, United were left short up front. Hughes wasn't out for too much longer but the absence of the Frenchman was felt keenly throughout the side. In twenty-six months he had become the most integral part of the United side and now it was time for others to step up. Invariably, they did.

Cole scored five in a still-record 9-0 Premier League victory over Ipswich Town in early March and when, three days later, Steve Bruce scored a late winner to give Ferguson a happy return to Selhurst against Wimbledon in March; United went top. Blackburn had a game in hand, but United had managed to get three goals in front of them on goal difference.

It appeared as if, despite the absence of Cantona, the form of Andrei Kanchelskis and Andrew Cole might be enough to tip the balance in United's favour. But Kanchelskis' last game for the club turned out to be on March 22nd, 1995, marked with a goal in a 3-0 win over Arsenal at Old Trafford. It was his fourteenth league goal in just twenty-five league starts, underlining his status as, arguably, the team's star performer in a side glittering with quality – and his absence was keenly felt. The two following home games against Leeds and Chelsea were goalless. These were the games that did for United in the end rather than painful defeats, despite the glee Liverpool fans might have garnered from their 2-0 win at Anfield on 19th March. That was only United's second defeat since Christmas and it put them six points behind Blackburn again.

United then went on a run of five wins and three draws from their next eight games, closing the gap and taking it to the wire, and Blackburn almost capitulated under the pressure, losing at home to Manchester City on a sodden pitch and then failing at West Ham.

Perhaps the final day encapsulated that Premier League season. At the death, Blackburn could not control their own destiny, losing late in front of an Anfield crowd who were desperate to see Rovers win. At Upton Park the home support were equally desperate to see the Hammers prevent another Mancunian triumph and threw everything at the visitors. United fought back from a goal down and hammered at the home goal for most of the second half but journeyman goalkeeper Ludek Miklosko wrote himself into the history books with a once in a lifetime performance to defy Cole, McClair and Ince in the dying stages.

The starting line up on that last day of the league season was shorn of Kanchelskis, Cantona, Hughes (who came off the bench) and Giggs (who was battling a hamstring injury to try to get back for the FA Cup Final). Paul Parker, too, was absent from the team that had been victorious in the 1994 FA Cup Final. Gary Neville, Nicky Butt and Paul Scholes all tried their hardest but this was their time to feel disappointment. At least their hard feelings wouldn't be compounded by an over the top media spotlight, unlike Andy Cole, who, after a few efforts were saved by Miklosko, was predictably judged under the harshest spotlight. To compound matters United lost 1-0 to Joe Royle's Everton a week later in the FA Cup final.

Cole may have borne the brunt of the subsequent criticism but there was still enough exposure and emphasis put on United's apparent failure to make the youngsters feel like they had under-performed. It mattered not that they were within inches on a couple of occasions; second was failure. Cole's record of twelve goals in eighteen games was impressive but became seven in seventeen excluding the Ipswich drubbing. Despite scoring crucial goals in two of the previous three games against Coventry City and Southampton, it was his failure to net against West Ham that would be remembered in the summer of 1995.

And so the post-Cantona record of ten wins and four draws in sixteen games – thirty four points from forty-eight available, or approximately 80% of the points available (form that, over a season, would have brought them one hundred points) – was dismissed and United were characterised as a team in free fall and dependent on their talismanic French captain. Their return to the top of the English tree had been brief and was, apparently, over.

Their form during Cantona's suspension should have been a solid indication of how well United had actually done. The damage had actually been done before that kick at Selhurst Park. What we did learn is that the kids were alright. It was this form that convinced Ferguson that, if forced, he would be okay without Kanchelskis, for one. His young stars were ready - perhaps more through accident than design - and he couldn't hold them back. There would be little room for Mark Hughes once Cantona was back and Cole's form in the run-in had shown that he had enough to hold his own. Likewise, Roy Keane's performances had gone from strength to strength and although he hadn't always been used in central midfield, it was obvious that he should be deployed there as the heartbeat of this young team. It was the driven determination once (and still only recently) so prevalent in the leadership of Paul Ince.

Ince had become expendable because Ferguson had disliked the way his ego had bloomed - some might have thought understandably - as he completed the transition into midfield kingpin following the departure of Bryan Robson the previous year. His sale for £7.5m to Inter Milan shocked many. It was a huge fee that Ferguson was able to use as justification but the truth, clear to everyone, was that the dressing room was no longer big enough for the both of them, and speculation about the fractured relationship between the pair raged until it was confirmed in a documentary three years later.

Granada TV had cameras in the Old Trafford dressing room before a crucial game against Ince's new team Liverpool in the run-in towards the end of the 1997/98 season. "If he tries to bully you, he will fucking enjoy it," Ferguson tells his team, "don't ever let him bully you, right! You just make sure you are ready for him. That's all you need to worry about. He's a fucking big-time Charlie." The name stuck. Ten years later Ferguson was preparing to face Ince who had become manager of Blackburn. Taking into account the fact that we all say things in the heat of the moment and Ferguson's words were clearly used to motivate his side, he backtracked significantly in 2008. "I regret saying that," he admitted. "That was a mistake. We let a camera into our dressing room, which we had never done before, and it won't happen again. It wasn't a personality issue with Paul. With Paul you could not have a honeymoon all the time, because he was such a volatile character, but he never let us down."

Another high profile exit that summer was, if anything, even more of a shock. Mark Hughes was a firm fan favourite, a hero to a generation of fans dating back to his spectacular promotion from the youth team in the mid-1980s. A scorer of spectacular and important goals, his game mixed tough hold up play with subtle flicks and volleys that were often out of this world. If there was a big game, Sparky wouldn't hide, in fact he'd be in the front-line leading the charge. In 1986 when United were riding high at the top of the First Division, his sale (allegedly insitgated by chairman Martin Edwards who received a percentage of all incoming transfer fees) precipitated a collapse. Liverpool went on to win the league and cup double.

In the summer of 1988 Ferguson, still finding his feet at Old Trafford after some high profile departures such as crowd favourites Norman Whiteside and Paul McGrath, re-signed 'Sparky' from Barcelona and later admitted he did it to win back the crowd – attendances during the previous season had hit an all-time post-war low. Hughes went on to play a pivotal role in the FA Cup run in 1990 before scoring twice in Rotterdam helping United lift the European Cup Winners' Cup. He seemed to blossom further with the arrival of Eric Cantona as the pair hit it off instantly, to the detriment of Brian McClair who was shuffled into midfield and later the substitute bench. Still only 31, Hughes seemed to have a few years ahead of him, yet he was allowed to sign for Chelsea for a nominal fee just months after apparently signing a new contract on the pitch before the home game against Aston Villa. Fans were stunned by the decision, although in 2013 Hughes insisted it had been coming. "In truth, my decision to leave was not such a shock as he had already signed Andy Cole as my replacement and I wanted to play," he admitted.

The final departure, that of the flying Russian Andrei Kanchelskis, would be protracted and linger on into the new season with speculation filling gossip columns for months. While the sales were significant, the manager seemed confident in being able to replace them. Crucially, despite the disappointing way in which the Kanchelskis saga unfolded, the manager had been in control of the decisions and it was this which had provoked so many raised eyebrows. What he was unable to control, however, were any incomings. Ferguson had calculated that Hughes and Ince would be surplus to requirements but the impending departure of his number 14 presented an unwelcome headache. Relieving his club of the extra baggage which came with Kanchelskis may have been a positive but replacing the talent would not be straightforward. His ability to beat players at pace and score goals from out wide was a precious commodity. If Ferguson had a crystal ball there was no way Keith Gillespie would have been used as a makeweight and a tentative move to bring the Northern Irishman back to Manchester was dismissed out of hand by Kevin Keegan.

If Andy Cole wasn't singled out as the sole reason United failed to win their third league title on the trot, then the man who broke the bank to sign him was. All that recent success wasn't enough to stop the *Manchester Evening News* running that poll asking whether Ferguson ought to be relieved of his duties. Shortly after the manager's announcement of retirement in 2013, the MEN's Stuart Mathieson recalled the timing of the poll coming soon after he was hired as United's beat reporter for the newspaper.

"Within a month of being appointed the MEN's new United reporter in May 1995, the newspaper ran a poll asking, as the summer of discontent unfolded, whether Fergie should be sacked," recalled Mathieson. "When Alex Ferguson returned from his summer holiday in America, the poll was eventually pointed out to him. I suspect some media rivals did the pointing out in an attempt to wreck the cosy relationship this paper then had with the boss. It worked. Fergie decided he was not going to compromise his position with the daily papers any more in favour of giving the MEN exclusives and toned down his assistance. For a few months I tolerated the new regime, but was finding him more and more difficult and aloof. One day I decided I had had enough and I said to him that I couldn't work this way because I wasn't getting any stories and the paper needed them on a daily basis. He shrugged off my argument and just blamed my predicament on the paper's decision to run the poll."

Ferguson's frosty relationship with the media is not news; even in the run-in to the title win of 1994, there was a growing frustration in the perception of United's aggressive play, particularly when Cantona was sent off against Arsenal in an incident that barely warranted a yellow. United suffered a number of red cards during that period – Peter Schmeichel was dismissed against Charlton in the FA Cup, meaning that he would miss the League Cup Final, Cantona was sent off for a stamp on Swindon Town's John Moncur and Kanchelskis was sent from the field after a handball denying a last minute goal in the League Cup Final. It may well have been true that there was some dramatic over-reaction but it was similarly true that many of those red cards – in fact all but the Cantona one against Arsenal – couldn't really be disputed. The British media tend to love a failure more than a success and United were learning that knives were being sharpened in gleeful preparation for their hoped-for demise.

PRE-SEASON

31ST JULY 1995
FIRST TEAM FRIENDLY / GLAMOIR INVITATIONAL CUP
SHAH ALAM STADIUM, KUALA LUMPAR. ATT: 50,000

SELANGOR SELECT XI 1-4 UNITED

TEAM: Schmeichel, Parker (P.Neville), Irwin, Bruce1, G. Neville, Pallister[1], Scholes (Beckham), Butt[1], McClair, Keane, Sharpe[1]

2ND AUGUST 1995
FIRST TEAM FRIENDLY / GLAMOIR INVITATIONAL CUP
SHAH ALAM STADIUM, KUALA LUMPAR. ATT: 20,000

SELANGOR SELECT XI 0-2 UNITED

Team : Schmeichel (Pilkington), Parker (G.Neville), Irwin, Bruce[1], P.Neville, Pallister, Scholes[1] (Cooke), Butt, McClair (Beckham), Keane, Thornley

7TH AUGUST 1995
FIRST TEAM FRIENDLY
ST. ANDREWS, BIRMINGHAM. ATT: 13,330

BIRMINGHAM CITY 1-0 UNITED

Team: Schmeichel, Parker (Thornley), Irwin, Bruce, Sharpe, Pallister, Butt, Keane, McClair, Scholes, G.Neville

9TH AUGUST 1995
FIRST TEAM FRIENDLY
VALLEY PARADE, BRADFORD. ATT. 13,457

BRADFORD CITY 0-1 UNITED

Team : Schmeichel, Parker, Irwin, Bruce, Sharpe, G.Neville, Butt, Keane[1], McClair, Tomlinson (Scholes), Beckham (Cooke)

11TH AUGUST 1995
FIRST TEAM FRIENDLY
TOLKA PARK, DUBLIN. ATT. 12,500

SHELBOURNE 2-2 UNITED

Team : Pilkington, Parker, Irwin (O'Kane), Bruce (P.Neville), Sharpe, G.Neville, Butt[1] (Beckham[1]), Keane, McClair, Scholes, Cook (Thornley)

13TH AUGUST 1995
JIMMY BONTHRONE TESTIMONIAL
BAYVIEW, EAST FIFE. ATT. 5,385

EAST FIFE 0-4 UNITED

Team : Pilkington, Parker (O'Kane), Irwin (P.Neville), Bruce, Sharpe1, G.Neville, Beckham2, Keane, McClair1, Scholes (Cooke), Thornley

15TH AUGUST 1995
FIRST TEAM FRIENDLY
BOUNDARY PARK, OLDHAM. ATT. 8,766

OLDHAM ATHLETIC 0-2 UNITED

Team : Pilkington, P.Neville, Irwin (O'Kane), G.Neville, Sharpe[1] (Thornley), Pallister, Butt (Tomlinson), Keane, McClair, Davies (McGibbon), Beckham +(Jobson o.g.)

Perhaps the wafer-thin size of United's squad by modern standards caught even those in charge by surprise. Several of the younger players who made the trip to Malaysia (led in the first game by Brian Kidd as the manager was absent with an ear infection) had originally been named in Manchester United Select XI's to play the likes of Blackpool Mechanics and Flint Town.

To further compound matters, not only were United unlikely to bring any new faces in but Ferguson was facing regular headaches about potential new departures. Andrei Kanchelskis was still wanting away and the manager was preparing for life without him when it emerged that Eric Cantona was close to handing in a transfer request too after the FA discovered he had played in a behind closed doors friendly against Rochdale.

United were attempting to get their forward match fit so he would be prepared for first team football as soon as his ban expired on September 30th but the FA deemed the friendly to be a breach of the conditions of Cantona's suspension and considered lengthening it. The Frenchman was outraged and went to the United board amid rumours of a bid from Inter Milan – on the morning of the friendly at Bradford City, the news hit the papers.

From *The Independent*:

CANTONA'S TRANSFER DEMAND STUNS UNITED

Manchester United's summer of discontent took a dramatic turn for the worse last night when it emerged that Eric Cantona, apparently angered by the prospect of further punishment by the Association, had asked for a transfer.

His request was promptly turned down by the United board, and the FA later announced that it would take no action against either Cantona or the club over his appearance in a behind-closed-doors match against Rochdale last month. But the news of Cantona's unrest is sure to alert Internazionale – who made strong overtures to the 29-year-old Frenchman and have already lured Paul Ince from United to Milan – as well as other leading European clubs.

The chances of Cantona leaving Old Trafford appeared to increase substantially when his French lawyer, Jean-Jacques Bertrand, said in Paris that his client would not return to England unless the FA agreed to certain conditions. "Eric Cantona has left England and will not return if the English FA doesn't change, before midnight, 11 August, its decision banning him from taking part in closed-door training matches with his club," Bertrand said. It was not clear last night whether the FA's decision permitted Cantona to take part in future private matches.

However, the latest developments in football's most absorbing soap opera cast the darkest shadow yet over a close season which has seen Mark Hughes follow Ince out of Old Trafford and Andrei Kanchelskis make a protracted attempt to do likewise, to the anger of many supporters.

Cantona, whose ban followed his "kung-fu" attack on a Crystal Palace supporter in January, was expected to learn tomorrow whether he faced another FA inquiry into his appearance in the private practice match against Rochdale.

Instead, evidently in response to reports of Cantona's request to be released from his contract, the FA issued a statement which indicated that it had already accepted United's explanation as to the nature of the fixture, played before a dozen spectators at the Premiership club's training ground. "Yesterday, the FA received a response from Manchester United in regard to our inquiry about Eric Cantona. We are entirely satisfied with their explanation and we have conveyed that to the club," Mike Parry, an FA spokesman, said.

United contended that it was merely a training game, and as such did not breach the terms of Cantona's seven-month worldwide ban. The fact that it was against another club rather than his team-mates complicated the matter, which had raised the possibility that Lancaster Gate would either fine the player and/or United, or even increase his suspension.

That prospect, although now removed, clearly deepened Cantona's feeling that he was being victimised in English football, leading to his asking to be released from his contract. In a statement on behalf of the club, United's press officer, Ken Ramsden, said: "Cantona was very upset at the recent inquiry by the FA concerning his involvement in the training session of 25 July. He told Martin Edwards [United's chairman] that he felt he had little future in the English game and that his career would be best served by a move abroad. The board has considered the request very carefully but is not prepared to agree to it, believing that it is in the best interests of both the club and player that he remains with United."

The Independent closed with an update on United's unsettled winger,

Meanwhile, the destiny of Kanchelskis remains uncertain after the breakdown of talks between United and Everton. The Merseyside club yesterday faxed a request to the Premier League to adjudicate within a week on the dispute over Kanchelskis' £5m move - so he can play in their Cup Winners' Cup first-round match.

One player definitely leaving was Gary Walsh; the goalkeeper who had been highly rated but denied the opportunity of making a real impact at Old Trafford due to a succession of injuries and illness. He had been given a run of games after an injury to Peter Schmeichel in the autumn of 1994 and would have qualified for a Premier League winners' medal had United won the league. That taste of first team football had whetted his appetite for more and now, at the age of 26, Walsh was signed by Middlesbrough, now managed by former United legend Bryan Robson, who had been promoted to the FA Carling Premiership.

Two days after the final friendly of the pre-season, it emerged that the club had vetoed the proposed move of Kanchelskis to Everton.

"Manchester United yesterday called off the £5m transfer of Andrei Kanchelskis to their Premiership rivals Everton after failing to resolve a financial wrangle whereby the player's former club was due a slice of any sell-on fee," reported *The Independent*.

"The refusal of UEFA, Europe's governing body, to extend the European Cup Winners' Cup registration deadline in order to allow Kanchelskis to play in the opening rounds of the competition only further complicated the Ukranian's transfer after his former club, Shaktyor Donezts, demanded a £1.1m cut. Kanchelskis had already been paraded at Goodison Park in front of the cameras, having vowed never to play for Alex Ferguson, the United manager, again after a long-standing disagreement.

"Outlining the facts behind the on-off transfer Martin Edwards, the United chairman, said in a statement: 'Original negotiations proceeded after a fax was received by Manchester United from Shaktyor Donezts, procured by a representative of the player and signed apparently by a vice-president of Donezts, waiving their rights to 30 per cent of any transfer fee above the total monies already paid to them. On the basis of the above waiver, the player then negotiated his terms with Everton. Manchester United subsequently received a further fax from Donezts, this time signed apparently by the president of Donezts, maintaining their claim to the 30 per cent payment. The effect of this demand would reduce the net payment to Manchester United by the sum of £1.14m.

"'Under these circumstances, Manchester United have been forced to withdraw from the negotiations with Everton. This matter is very much regretted. No blame can be attached to Everton.'"

Ironically, Kanchelskis was now registered with United for the opening rounds of the UEFA Cup. The breakdown of the transfer revived interest from Middlesbrough, whom Kanchelskis rejected in favour of Everton, and champions Blackburn. It seemed that United were still, nonetheless, resigned to losing the man who had illuminated the right wing and were hunting for alternatives.

From that same *Independent* report: "The United manager failed in an attempt to land Tottenham's Darren Anderton as a replacement and has been put off by Ajax's £10m valuation of the Dutch international Marc Overmars. They are now reported to be keeping tabs on the 21-year-old Nigerian striker Tijiani Babangida, currently playing for the Dutch club Roda JC Kerkrade. He has a maximum sell-on fee of £2m written into his contract."

There were mixed reports of how far that interest in Anderton went and who pulled the plug. The July 10th *Manchester Evening News* quotes Alex Ferguson as saying "I understand that Alan Sugar is out of the country at the moment. But he is expected back within a few days and once he returns we will be pursuing Anderton more vigorously. He is a terrific young player, he's English, and would be the ideal replacement for Kanchelskis."

In his 2008 autobiography, Anderton himself has shared some of the details. In an interview for this book, he shared the reasons why he didn't make the move despite Sir Alex Ferguson confessing in his 1999 autobiography 'Managing My Life' that the winger was the only player he liked enough to have brought in.

"I'd had a good season and the previous year I had played with Paul Parker for England and I believe Sir Alex had asked him about me," says Darren. "We had played against Sweden (in the 'Umbro Cup') at the end of the '94/95 season and, after the game at the hotel, Pally (Gary Pallister) told me that his gaffer told him to tell me that he wanted me to go there and wanted to know how much my buy out clause was. I was, of course, flattered but went off on holiday. Three weeks later, Pally called me and asked if it was okay to give Sir Alex my number as he wanted to have a chat. He called and basically said they'd had a few problems with Andrei Kanchelskis and he was leaving and wanted me to go there. I said I was willing to go up there and have a look around, but the next day I was called to Sir Alan Sugar's house with Gerry Francis to discuss staying and a new contract."

He signed that contract and Spurs were not remotely tempted to part with their man after losing a number of players such as Nick Barmby and Jurgen Klinsmann, even though United were seemingly prepared to pay something in the region of £10m, unaware that Anderton's release clause was just £4m. One can debate whether or not acquiring the player may have restricted the progress of David Beckham, although it is worth remembering that even following the season of emergence which was to follow, United were persuaded to part with £3.5m for Karel Poborsky. A price of £4m for Anderton seems like a bargain by comparison, and who knows what might have happened? It is reasonably safe to deduce that there is some confusion over how formal discussions over an offer were – after all, this was a time when relations between the clubs were amicable. And so it stands to reason that the clause in Anderton's contract would have been honoured. Although we can probably presume that in those tentative enquiries, United were sufficiently dissuaded to not test the waters. Ferguson can happily claim no regrets missing out on this particular occasion but the player himself wonders what might have been.

"I was very happy at Spurs, and didn't want to leave," he admits, "but in hindsight, with how Manchester United went on to be incredibly successful and how I started to have injury problems because of the poor treatment I received from the medical team at Spurs, then of course there is a bit of regret at not going... especially after how I was treated by Spurs when I finally left after twelve years. I would have loved to have been a part of the success that Manchester United had. But at the time it seemed the right decision."

Anderton had bags of potential with his leggy and languid style, an eye for goal and ability to quickly change pace – he offered something different to Beckham and an established, prominent star name which could have boosted United's stature (an argument worth considering if one is to reason that some of their success was attributable to taking many teams by surprise). Though the winger would get into the Euro '96 squad, he did so on the back of an injury plagued season which saw him play less than ten times for his club. Those injury problems would dog Anderton for the rest of his career, earning him the unfortunate terrace nickname, Sicknote.

"I believe I could have added something to the (United) team, although of course it wasn't lacking with quality or world class players," says Anderton. We will never know, but what is fact is that Anderton was forced to watch, often literally from the sidelines, as United went on to enjoy success after success.

"Apart from missing out on the trophies, as I've said, I missed out on getting the right treatment for my injuries so I am 100% certain I wouldn't have missed as many games as I did from 1996 to 1999," he says. "When United won the treble and we played them in the last game of the season it was tough to take, watching them celebrate winning the league. Still, I spoke to Teddy Sheringham a lot when he went to United and of course I was delighted for him to get the success his talent deserved."

United were dogged by their own injury woes heading into the new season. Not only did they have to line up without Cantona, Hughes, Ince and Kanchelskis, but Steve Bruce, Ryan Giggs and Andy Cole were also absent with injury. Not that these mitigating circumstances would affect the reaction to the result of their game against Aston Villa...

KICK OFF

19TH AUGUST 1995 - FA CARLING PREMIERSHIP
VILLA PARK, BIRMINGHAM - ATT: 34,655

ASTON VILLA 3-1 UNITED

Scorer: Beckham 84

Team : Schmeichel, Parker, Pallister (O'Kane 59), G.Neville, Irwin, P.Neville (Beckham 45), Keane, Butt, Sharpe, McClair, Scholes

UNITED BEGAN THEIR SEASON in a change strip of light and dark grey – later in the season its part in an infamous episode would make it an unforgettable part of the culture of the club and the strip is often derided as the worst ever worn by a Premier League team. What is often forgotten is that this same year, Chelsea also had a variant of the strip with an orange stripe which was arguably even more offensive to the eye.

The grey strip would eventually be associated with invisibility but there was no hiding place for United at Villa Park. They started poorly and, in fact, their first foray forward (a meek attack which saw a cross aimed at Scholes which he was never going to challenge for) provoked an attack from the hosts on the counter. The lively Yorke flashed the ball across goal and it was picked up by Gary Charles on the far side. The right back was in an inexplicable amount of space and he drilled the ball low into the six yard area, where Ian Taylor was allowed to find space and prod home.

The visitors' response was poor but, again, it was from their next attempt to work the ball into the box (after some intelligent work from Keane, Butt and McClair) that Villa countered. Alan

10

Wright won the ball from Phil Neville, playing out of position on the right wing, and played it to Mark Draper. An attack which saw Yorke and then Savo Milosevic work the ball back to Draper ended with the midfielder beating Schmeichel at his near post.

Villa's in-house television commentator remarked that the goalkeeper hadn't been beaten more than twice in any Premier League game the previous season. Less than ninety seconds later, the Dane had brought down Milosevic, giving away a penalty converted by Dwight Yorke. Referee Robbie Hart would have been within his rights to send off the goalkeeper but perhaps took sympathy on the Red Devils. 36 minutes gone – 3-0.

Perhaps Villa boss Brian Little had sympathy for the visitors too, because in the second half the home team offered little going forward. United offered some invention with substitute David Beckham having an effort from range just a couple of minutes before scoring spectacularly. His 25-yard effort was so beautifully hit that it flew over Mark Bosnich, only a couple of yards off his line, into the top corner.

It was a reward for the vocal travelling support but no more than a consolation and the final scoreline of 3-1 flattered Ferguson's team, who might have found themselves on the end of an even heavier thrashing if Villa had been so inclined.

Reports of United's demise may have been greatly exaggerated but the reality seemed to be that United were falling from grace. The half time score sent shockwaves around English football and hyperbolic statements were being uttered by many. Unfortunately, some were caught on film and would be relived time and time again.

On Match of the Day later that evening, supporters of all colours must have been thrilled to hear former Liverpool and Scotland centre-half Alan Hansen rule out a United title challenge after only 90 minutes of action. "I think they've got problems," began the Liverpool legend, "I wouldn't say they've got major

Alan Hansen delivers his verdict

problems. Obviously three players have departed and the trick is always buy when you're strong so he (Ferguson) needs to buy players. You can't win anything with kids. You look at that line up Manchester United had today and Aston Villa, at quarter past two when they get the team sheet, it's just going to give them a lift, and it'll happen every time he plays the kids. He's got to buy players, simple as that."

Host Des Lynam tried to counter with the theory of those absentees such as Bruce, Giggs and Cole returning. "It's just not enough," Hansen insisted, "the trick of winning the Championship is to have strength in depth. And they just haven't got it."

What Hansen thought of his former club's chances of glory was not quite as transparent but they got off to a good start, winning 1-0 at home to Sheffield Wednesday thanks to a goal scored by £8.5m man Stan Collymore, who, of course, had been linked to United prior

OTHER LEAGUE RESULTS:

Blackburn 1-0 QPR

Chelsea 0-0 Everton

Liverpool 1-0 Sheff Wed

Man City 1-1 Spurs

Newcastle 3-0 Coventry

Southampton 3-4 Nott'm F

West Ham 1-2 Leeds

Wimbledon 3-2 Bolton

SUNDAY 20 AUGUST 1995

Arsenal 1–1 Middlesbrough

to Cole's arrival. Liverpool's big spending didn't end there as they splashed out another £4m on Bolton prospect Jason McAteer.

Elsewhere, champions Blackburn defeated Queens Park Rangers by a single goal and big-spending Newcastle United destroyed Coventry City 3-0 to send a message to the rest of the league.

★

It was clear that the manager would face questions. There were obvious things he must address when compiling his notes for the first match programme of the season ahead of United's home game with West Ham.

"Let me make my position clear straight away," he wrote. "I am committed to the cause of Manchester United and I am not the slightest bit interested in anyone who cannot match that commitment... Please think about the word commitment. It's the tone which is important covering everything from loyalty to dedication and concentration. It's a feeling difficult to describe.

"So that is my statement, my philosophy if you like, after a summer of some turmoil which has asked questions of our supporters as well as of our players, and I ask you to think deeply when you consider the events of the close season.

"Perhaps also a few of our fans might pause to consider what they are doing when they open up the debate in public. If they doubt the manager, what chance do we have with our rivals and the media who are looking to slaughter us at every opportunity?

"The departure of three major players from our team must inevitably cause concern. It worries me, too, but sometimes you have to examine a situation and take drastic decisions, however painful.

"Let me just take you through the situations we faced soon after the end of last season," Ferguson continued, with a candidness one might not expect about such matters. "To start with, Mark Hughes had avoided signing his new contract so that when Eric Cantona decided to stay Mark wanted to go and was free to do so. Mark felt that he would not be a first-choice striker so he made a career decision to leave. I am as disappointed as anyone that he chose to go because he is a hero and a legend at Old Trafford. What we should be saying is good luck and thank you for all you have done in your ten years with us. Mark left in the proper way but I am not sure we can say quite the same about the other players who have gone and at the end of the day decisions were taken for what I consider to be the best interests of the club.

"Playing for Manchester United is all about maintaining standards and though Paul Ince has been a marvellous player for us, when I got the vibes that he was looking for a new challenge in Italy, I thought that now is probably the right time for us to take a new look at our engine room. You have to remember that we have some very exciting young players on the scene now and my faith in them is such that we must give them their chance.

"As for Andrei Kanchelskis, I assure you we have tried all means to get him to stay. All the stuff he has come out with about our relationship is exaggerated and quite over the top. I have got to say that money has played a big part in his campaign to leave our club and cash, while important, is not the kind of commitment I have been talking about.

"We could have done without all these problems but I assure you that they will not be allowed to diminish our quest for the honours of the game. I have worked too hard for eight and a half years to allow any slackening in either ambition or commitment. No-one at Old Trafford is accepting anything less than competing for the Premiership in the way we have for the last four years."

"For a club with a strong tradition in the transfer market as buyers, the past few months will have been disconcerting for supporters," admitted Chairman Martin Edwards in his own customary start of season address. "Let me assure you that the decisions taken to release players have been for footballing reasons and the Manager has been fully supported by the Board. We all have favourite players but the game moves on. We too must move on if we are to maintain our challenge for glory and honours."

Edwards' words about 'footballing reasons' related to concerns that the players had been sold to fund the re-development of the North Stand. It had not been completed in time for the new season, which meant that the capacity was significantly reduced, meaning that games at the start of the season would not have any visiting supporters. Elsewhere, the match programme noted the July 1995 passing of James Alan Gibson, the son of James Gibson who saved the club in 1931.

23RD AUGUST 1995 - FA CARLING PREMIERSHIP
OLD TRAFFORD, MANCHESTER. ATT. 31,996

UNITED 2-1 WEST HAM

Scorers: Scholes 50, Keane 68
Team : Schmeichel, G.Neville, Bruce, Pallister, Irwin, Beckham, Butt,
Keane, Sharpe, McClair (Thornley 84), Scholes (Cole 69)

The snack manufacturer Walker's gave away free bags of their new range of 'Double Crunch' potato crisps but the 'crunch' in this game came courtesy of new West Ham striker Marco Boogers who had signed for £1m in the summer. All the goals had been scored – Paul Scholes and Roy Keane giving the hosts the lead either side of a Steve Bruce own goal – before Booger was brought on. He had been on the pitch a matter of minutes before throwing himself into a horrendous challenge on Gary Neville. With both feet off the ground, it was the kind of tackle which might easily have ended a player's career but, mercifully, Neville was relatively unscathed and able to finish the game. The same could not be said for Boogers who was promptly red-carded by Dermot Gallagher and given a four-match ban afterwards.

The story didn't end there for Boogers. It was believed for a number of years that, suffering from homesickness, Boogers went into a depression that was so severe he ended up living in a caravan. Sadly for those who like an unconventional story, it turned out to be a miscommunication from a West Ham press officer. The truth wasn't much better for Boogers – he made just a couple more appearances for the Hammers before being moved on. Manager Harry Redknapp infamously described him as the worst player he signed at Upton Park – and he signed a few!

The incident overshadowed a lively performance from United who had been able to field a more experienced and familiar looking team, including most of their regular defence. Gary Neville was selected in front of Paul Parker and was to become more a regular as the season progressed.

That it went under the radar was probably just fine with Ferguson who could have been excused for wanting a quieter life. If so, he was given further cause to breathe a sigh of relief when the Kanchelskis saga was finally put to bed on the eve of the game against Wimbledon – the winger completing that acrimonious and controversial £7m move to Everton. The ifs and buts about potential replacements can be debated until the end of time but the finalisation of this transfer

OTHER LEAGUE RESULTS:

MONDAY 21 AUGUST 1995
Leeds 1-0 Liverpool
TUESDAY 22 AUGUST 1995
Bolton 1-3 Newcastle
WEDNESDAY 23 AUGUST 1995
Coventry 2-1 Man City
Everton 0-2 Arsenal
Nott'm F 0-0 Chelsea
QPR 0-3 Wimbledon
Sheff W 2-1 Blackburn
Spurs 0-1 Aston Villa

definitively marked the end of the Russian's stay at Old Trafford and with it lingered a bittersweet feeling.

His tremendous form, particularly in the previous 18 months, had seen him rise in prominence and he was arguably as important or influential to the team as Schmeichel or Cantona. One thing lost among the discussion of potential replacements is that none would quite bring the special qualities that Kanchelskis possessed: principal among his attributes was a searing change of pace which had to be seen to be believed. He was probably the fastest player ever to play for the club. Allied to that he had a composure and a clinical eye in front of goal – an asset not always associated with wingers. His natural chemistry with his team-mates was something that could not be manufactured; the number of attacks started by a long throw from Schmeichel to the run of Kanchelskis were too plentiful to mention.

The player would become a cult hero in 18 months at Goodison Park but was soon on the move again to Fiorentina – and later in his career even played for Manchester City, the team against whom he had enjoyed arguably his finest Old Trafford moment.

26TH AUGUST 1995 - FA CARLING PREMIERSHIP
OLD TRAFFORD, MANCHESTER. ATT. 32,226

UNITED 3-1 WIMBLEDON

Scorers: Keane 27,79, Cole 59
Team : Schmeichel, G.Neville, Bruce, Pallister, Irwin, Beckham, Butt, Keane, Sharpe, Scholes (Davies 82), Cole (Giggs 71)

United's strong recovery continued with a convincing performance against notoriously stubborn opponents. Though he was playing as a support striker to Andy Cole, Paul Scholes showed signs of the chemistry with Roy Keane, for which both would become renowned, by linking up with him for United's first goal on 27 minutes.

The young players were showing impressive character. Many thought they might wilt before the self-styled 'Crazy Gang' and physical opponents such as Vinnie Jones, Robbie Earle and Oyvind Leonhardsen. That they passed with flying colours and no little ease should not detract from their achievement on the day, even if Ferguson – who later would describe the task of facing Wimbledon as 'an initiation test' in which players must 'grow up' – preferred to focus on the achievements of Andy Cole: whose tremendous angled drive on the hour mark settled this game. Cole's selection had come late in the day following a thigh injury to Brian McClair but the record signing showed no signs of rustiness. 'Cole's goal was typical and an exceptionally good one,' Ferguson was quoted as saying in the *Sunday Express*. 'He will definitely be in the team for Blackburn on Monday.'

Wimbledon showed signs of their resilience by coming back into the game

OTHER LEAGUE RESULTS:

SATURDAY 26 AUGUST 1995

Bolton W 2-1 Blackburn
Coventry 0-0 Arsenal
Everton 2-0 Southampton
Leeds Utd 2-0 Aston Villa
Middlesbro' 2-0 Chelsea
Nott'm Forest 1-1 West Ham
QPR 1-0 Man City
Spurs 1-3 Liverpool

SUNDAY 27 AUGUST 1995

Sheff Wed 0-2 Newcastle

when Earle scored five minutes after Cole, but Keane's smart second ten minutes from time afforded the manager the luxury of resting Scholes ahead of the titanic fixture against the champions in little over forty-eight hours time.

THE KIDS ARE ALRIGHT

28TH AUGUST 1995 - FA CARLING PREMIERSHIP
EWOOD PARK, BLACKBURN. ATT. 29,843

BLACKBURN ROVERS 1-2 UNITED

Scorers: Sharpe 46, Beckham 72
Team : Schmeichel, G. Neville, Bruce, Pallister, Irwin,
Beckham (Giggs 76), Butt, Keane, Sharpe, Cole, Scholes (Davies 76)

'IT WAS A SUPER PERFORMANCE. It was a performance
full of confidence, full of belief, and a maturity beyond
the age of the side,' purred Andy Gray on Sky Sports after
Manchester United's thrilling victory. As was the case with the
broadcast giant throughout most of the mid-nineties, they were
attempting to revolutionise the way the game was brought to the
viewer and this season they introduced 'Replay 2000' - an on-
screen technology showing degrees of offside and distances from
goal. The reality was nothing other than a harsh red and white line
and text added to the picture but these baby steps marked Sky as
being at the forefront of innovation of this sort.

Instead, our glimpse at the future would come from what
we saw on the pitch - a statement that rang true for both teams.
It shouldn't have been the case that Rovers and United were
undergoing a transition; it was an unusual scenario indeed that saw
both the champions and runners-up from the previous year dealing
with serious change. Kenny Dalglish had moved up to become
Director of Football straight after winning the title and Ray Harford
was appointed the manager. Still, Blackburn had at least managed

to keep hold of their title winning squad – even if their transfer activity in the summer hadn't been all that encouraging. In front of their home fans they would have expected to triumph: particularly as Cantona, Kanchelskis and Hughes – the three scorers for the Red Devils in the previous season's 4-2 win – were all missing for one reason or another.

'...while the newspapers have been full of various stories concerning Old Trafford during the summer months, it won't make any difference to our approach,' Harford wrote in his programme notes. 'We know only too well that, whoever the personnel United send out against us, we will have to be at our best to achieve our objective – another home victory.'

The match programme also commented on the death of former United captain and two time Rovers manager Johnny Carey at the age of 76. He held the distinction of playing in every outfield position for United and even managed a game in goal. This followed a tribute in United's programme against West Ham for Carey, who had at one time been one of the elder statesmen of the United team who saw the 'Busby Babes' come in to the senior side. Much attention was centred on how United's tremendously youthful front six would cope against the champions – even if the programme did refer to Ryan Giggs in the following terms: 'Giggs seems to have been around for so long it is easy to forget that the young Welsh wizard is still only 21.' Giggs, however, could only watch on from the bench as Lee Sharpe was selected to play from the left hand side. It was a selection which would pay off for the manager and his insistence that Cole would definitely play was almost rewarded with a goal but the forward's goal-bound effort was cleared off the line – the closest of a flurry of efforts in the opening period.

Straight after the restart, United got the goal their efforts deserved. Typical of the game, it came after an almighty scramble that saw Tim Flowers deny Nicky Butt, Andy Cole, Paul Scholes and Roy Keane before his save from the latter fell kindly at the feet of the freshly shorn Lee Sharpe. It was a sequence that proved impossible to cope with for the defending champions. Their reaction in this game, however, was stronger than their defence of their title over the season – Alan Shearer's fine left footed effort levelling on the hour after United failed to clear a corner.

United would not be denied. Their response was superb and packed with an energy with which their hosts could not deal and, after another frenzied assault on the Rovers goal similar in speed and disorganisation to the opening goal, Sharpe prodded the ball to David Beckham whose finish from wide left in the penalty area was anything but messy. His effort curled out and then just back inside the post, leaving Flowers helpless again. Ferguson's team held on even after Roy Keane was sent off after receiving a second yellow card for diving. It was a strange decision from David Elleray, even accounting for the constant changing of the rules in the post-USA World Cup era when it was becoming easier for a player to be dismissed.

Andy Gray wasn't the only one impressed by United's performance. 'United's general passing and movement were superior throughout,' enthused *The Guardian*, while *The Sun* proclaimed it to be 'one of the greatest performances turned in by any Manchester United side since Alex Ferguson took charge.' After the over-reaction that accompanied the opening day defeat, caution should perhaps have been exercised; there was some justification for the excitement however as it was the performance more than the three points that got the pulses racing.

Yet, just as stern a test lay in wait after

OTHER LEAGUE RESULTS:

TUESDAY 29 AUGUST 1995
Arsenal 1-1 Nott'm Forest
WEDNESDAY 30 AUGUST 1995
Aston Villa 1-0 Bolton
Chelsea 2-2 Coventry
Liverpool 1-0 QPR
Man City 0-2 Everton
Newcastle 1-0 Middlesbro'
West Ham 1-1 Spurs
Wimbledon 2-2 Sheff Wed
Southampton 1-1 Leeds

the international break, and a reunion nobody was really looking forward to. Plenty has been said and written about Andrei Kanchelskis' move to Everton and after covering all of those points, it's only fair that that the man himself has the final say on one of the most controversial transfers in Manchester United history.

Speaking for the first time about the matter in an exclusive discussion for this book, Kanchelskis' version of events is compelling. "During the summer there were a lot of rumours going around, and, to be honest, it did upset me a bit," he admits. "That is not to say that the paper talk affected me. I still got on with my job. Leading up to my move, I was in my prime and wanted to do my job and when the club labelled me as someone who had become uncommitted in the previous season, it really upset me."

Ferguson had alluded to a clause in Kanchelskis' contract which entitled him to a percentage of any transfer fee if he moved and it has been implied that was a key factor. However, the player suffered an injury over the Christmas period after he scored a fabulous goal in the 1-1 draw with Leicester City that the club disputed.

"The fact is that, during that season, I was suffering from a double hernia and the club did not acknowledge this," Andrei tells me. "Instead, outside physiotherapists diagnosed me when the club didn't really acknowledge it as an injury. This obviously took a toll on my performance and during the season, as I was getting used to the recovery process, the performances faltered."

It is important to note at this point that, while it is often said that 'there are two sides to every story', there can also be more than one version of the truth. Ferguson has described a number of other events of which the player could not have been aware: discussions with agents and so forth. While United may have privately disputed the legitimacy of Kanchelskis' injury, it was sufficient enough to keep him out of a run of fixtures and then gently re-introduced him into the first team as a substitute. He was notably absent for those goalless draws against Leeds United and Chelsea during the run-in. Still, even if Ferguson had already decided that, for whatever reason, he wanted Kanchelskis to leave, the player himself was coming to the realisation that a move would probably be for the best.

"The situation was not ideal for the club or the manager so, in the end, following advice from friends and agents, I thought it was best to move on to another club and prove to all, and most importantly to myself, that I could still play like I did during the majority of my Manchester United career. With this injury and the rumours, alongside advice from various people, yes, I did want to leave. I was still young and wanted to prove myself as a world class footballer and, with relationships turning sour at United, I thought that another club would give me another chance."

The soap opera has been aired in public before but the subject of the dispute has chosen to stay silent over the past two decades. Often, major fallouts come from the most minor of misunderstandings. In his post-retirement years it has been interesting to see Ferguson talk of power and control. This was a perfect example of him making a perfect example; no player was above him, even one as crucial as Kanchelskis. The decision is interesting from a psychological point of view as it could be argued that Eric Cantona 'got away' without punishment he still curried favour with the management. So, was the manager worried he may be perceived as weak? Did he sell Kanchelskis in order to re-assert his power and control?

Of the protracted transfer, Andrei says, "At first, yes it annoyed me because it's never nice to have your life talked about and debated like that. However, after a while, I got used to it and I knew myself that some of the talk was pure fiction and only rumours. I then learnt to ignore it and even laugh it off in the end."

A move, then, was inevitable, particularly with the episode being played out in the press before he'd even agreed a move. The winger's transfer was, arguably, the most distressing of the lot for United supporters; while Cantona had undoubtedly served as the focal point for the club's transformation, the asset of speed that Kanchelskis brought to the right hand side (in a perfect complement to Giggs on the left) was a quality that blew teams away. Describing Kanchelskis as collateral damage may be the most apt thing to do; it was a gamble to give David Beckham his position and it wasn't certain that he would be up to the rigours of a full English season. In fact, despite Beckham's very impressive season, the manager was sufficiently concerned about that right hand side in the summer of 1996 to sign Karel Poborsky on the back of Euro 96. Beckham demonstrated the strength of character which would become one of his trademarks in that blitz of goal of the season contenders in the first few weeks of the 1996/97 season but the point remains that, while United may have been well stocked in areas to replace Ince and Hughes, they didn't have anyone with the ability of Kanchelskis to walk into the team. Consequently, even with Beckham's subsequent rise to prominence, Andrei's departure is one that still causes some United supporters to go misty eyed. When the question "Could you have stayed?" is put to him, he gives a somewhat surprising answer. "Yes of course and in truth the manager and club still wanted me to play for United," he reveals. "However, with the injury saga, advice from various groups of people and my young (to an extent) naivity I thought it was best to move."

That said, it's perhaps not too surprising to learn Kanchelskis regrets leaving. "In hindsight, yes: a part of me does (regret it). That is not to say that I did not enjoy the other clubs I played for and I still like to think that I had a very successful career. However, thinking about it more now, it is hard to imagine me being at United for much longer and be a one club man like Ryan Giggs, Paul Scholes, Gary Neville and co. After all, I really did enjoy my time at United and both me and my family were more than happy with our lives in Manchester. If the injury saga didn't upset me so much, and if I had received different advice, I could have a longer career at United."

It's a strange one. Even having played for Manchester City and the nature of his transfer, United supporters never quite vilified their former hero, despite what seemed to be a campaign to portray him as the villain of the piece and perhaps that warmth from supporters helps shape the player's memories of his time at Old Trafford. "I look back on my time there with fondness, of course!" he emphasises. "It was my first club outside the USSR. It will always be a special time for me and, to this day, I have followed everything United. Due to my time at United, I managed to become a fully committed supporter of the United cause. The supporters during my time were fantastic to me and I really did appreciate their support. The fans were terrific. I remember how Old Trafford used to vibrate with all the emotion the fans gave the team. Home or away, it really didn't matter – the chants were there and the emotion was always portrayed. Off the pitch, the fans were really nice to talk to as well. I am glad that during my time at United I managed to adapt so quickly to the English game and the club really did help me with this. All aspects of the club made my career: from the supporters to the lunch lady, each part made me the player I was at United. I will always be grateful to United for this.'

After more than twenty years, Kanchelskis' warm words of affection are only likely to solidify and enhance his standing amongst those who once worshipped him. However, on 9th September 1995, he was nonetheless the pantomime villain of the day.

PREMIER LEAGUE TABLE - 1ST SEPTEMBER 1995								
1 Newcastle United	3	3	0	0	8	1	9	7
2 Leeds United	3	3	0	0	5	1	9	4
3 Manchester United	4	3	0	1	8	6	9	2
4 Wimbledon	3	2	0	1	7	5	6	2
5 Liverpool	3	2	0	1	4	2	6	2
6 Aston Villa	3	2	0	1	4	3	6	1
7 Arsenal	3	1	2	0	3	1	5	2
8 Nottingham Forest	3	1	2	0	5	4	5	1
9 Middlesbrough	2	1	1	0	3	1	4	2
10 Everton	3	1	1	1	2	2	4	0
11 Coventry City	3	1	1	1	2	4	4	-2
12 Bolton Wanderers	3	1	0	2	5	7	3	-2
13 Blackburn Rovers	4	1	0	3	4	6	3	-2
14 Sheffield Wednesday	3	1	0	2	2	4	3	-2
15 Queens Park Rangers	3	1	0	2	1	4	3	-3
16 Chelsea	3	0	2	1	0	2	2	-2
17 West Ham United	3	0	1	2	3	5	1	-2
18 Manchester City	3	0	1	2	2	4	1	-2
19 Tottenham Hotspur	3	0	1	2	2	5	1	-3
20 Southampton	2	0	0	2	3	6	0	-3

THE KIDS ARE ALRIGHT

9TH SEPTEMBER 1995 - FA CARLING PREMIERSHIP
GOODISON PARK, LIVERPOOL. ATT. 39,496

EVERTON 2-3 UNITED

Scorers: Sharpe 3,49, Giggs 74
Team : Schmeichel, G. Neville, Bruce, Pallister, Irwin, Beckham, Butt,
Keane, Sharpe, Cole (Davies 73), Scholes (Giggs 66)

This trip to the FA Cup holders was the second of three tricky away games (with the UEFA Cup tie against Russia's Rotor Volgograd to follow); it was a real test of character for the players who had been described as 'pups' and 'babes' in the press. Toffees manager Joe Royle refused to believe that United were on the decline. "Alex decided to make one or two changes in the summer but if some people were predicting the fall for an outstanding team, I never thought that for one moment," he wrote in his notes to welcome the visitors. "The man knows what he's doing and he has a record to prove it." Royle appealed for calm in anticipation of an atmosphere even hotter than usual following the acrimonious transfer of Kanchelskis. "He's our player now, let's all be sensible and allow the game to take pride of place," he wrote.

The winger had been given the opportunity to write to his new adoring supporters in the same programme, and addressed the situation with diplomacy. "I spent four marvellous years at Manchester United and was greatly supported there," Kanchelskis said. "I have no regrets about playing for Manchester United, but Everton gave me a fresh challenge and I hope we can have the same success as United have enjoyed over the past few years... the main thing is to play good football for the Everton fans. I know they like good football and I hope to have a good team spirit with my new team-mates and to stay clear of injury."

Famous last words: before even quarter of an hour, Kanchelskis fell victim to a shoulder injury which caused him to be substituted for Andy Hinchcliffe. United supporters had given their former hero a tough ride, as expected, but were relieved that he was withdrawn – particularly as Duncan Ferguson, another serious threat, was also missing from this game through injury.

Everton had defeated United 1-0 in their two previous meetings in 1995 but, by the time Kanchelskis left the pitch, the Reds were already a goal up. Scholes, Cole and Beckham combined in a neat triangle on the right hand side, the latter flashing the ball across the face of goal, Sharpe was in an identical position to the one he'd scored from at Ewood Park and made no mistake this time either. It had taken less than three minutes for Sharpe to justify the manager's decision to name an unchanged side.

Sharpe was already, then, the scourge of the home support, and it was his heavy challenge which caused the injury to Kanchelskis. The home fans may have wondered if it was game up already but they showed the spirit that had saved them from relegation and led them to Cup glory earlier in the year to battle back and equalised through Anders Limpar. Hinchcliffe caught Steve Bruce in possession and Limpar capitalised – slotting the ball past Schmeichel. The goalkeeper wasn't at fault then but almost cost his team a second goal when he came unreasonably far from his goal. Daniel Amokachi was wasteful, shooting straight at him. David Beckham responded with a free kick that rattled the home crossbar. At half time it was 1-1 and the game was already becoming a classic.

The pace of the game was more like a cup tie with both sides going for it on the counter and it was from one such move early in the second half that United grabbed their second. A long punt forward from Schmeichel found its way to Cole, the striker found space with the bouncing ball and was just about to strike when Lee Sharpe, buoyed by the momentum of his run, took over and clinically finished into the corner. He had been booed since the Kanchelskis incident and this latest impact on the game did nothing to endear him to the home support. However, as one of the players who stood to be a direct beneficiary from Kanchelskis' departure from Old Trafford, it was clear that Sharpe was intent on taking full advantage.

Everton remained competitive in a tightly contested game and struck level just five minutes later. Limpar, like Beckham, hit the bar from a free kick, and, just as he had in the FA Cup Final 112 days before, Paul Rideout (possibly only picked because of the Ferguson injury) capitalised to score on the rebound. Still, both teams pushed for the win. United were able to bring on Giggs for Scholes and the winger hadn't been on the pitch for ten minutes when he was presented with a fine opportunity; the Red Devils had pushed high up the pitch, pressing Everton into a mistake, and when David Beckham seized the ball on the edge of the area, his clever pass found Giggs in space dead centre on the edge of the 18 yard box. Giggs' clinical effort would win the goal of the month competition; it was cool finishing associated more with his form during the '93/94 campaign than that of the previous season when he'd struggled to find the net.

United finished strongly but Everton's cause was not helped by the dismissal of David Unsworth although they could barely complain about each of the yellow cards he picked up for ploughing through both Beckham, then Giggs. It wasn't a dirty game and Unsworth's misdemeanours were far from over the top; they were merely an indication of the sternness of the test that United had faced, and passed.

OTHER LEAGUE RESULTS:

SATURDAY 9 SEPTEMBER 1995

Blackburn 1-1 Aston Villa
Bolton 1-1 Middlesbrough
Coventry 1-1 Nott'm Forest
QPR 0-3 Sheff Wed;
Soton 1-0 Newcastle
Spurs 2-1 Leeds
Wimbledon 1-0 Liverpool

SUNDAY 10 SEPTEMBER 1995

Man City 0-1 Arsenal

MONDAY 11 SEPTEMBER 1995

West Ham 1-3 Chelsea

TUESDAY 12 SEPTEMBER 1995

Middlesbro' 0-0 Soton

12TH SEPTEMBER 1995
UEFA CUP FIRST ROUND FIRST LEG
CENTRAL STADIUM, VOLGOGRAD. ATT. 40,000

ROTOR VOLGOGRAD 0-0 UNITED

Team : Schmeichel, G. Neville, Bruce, Pallister, Irwin, Beckham, Butt, Keane (Davies 23), Sharpe, Giggs, Scholes (Parker 70)

The 2,600 mile trip was made by just 140 United supporters to watch a game kindly described as 'fascinating if not thrilling stuff' by the *Daily Telegraph*. With the youth of United's team taken into consideration, it was difficult to be too critical about the disciplined manner in which they approached unfamiliar opponents: particularly as team selection was still restricted by UEFA's foreigners rule.

Ryan Giggs, whose usual comrades on continental forays forward would include the likes of Cantona, Kanchelskis, Hughes, Ince and Robson, led by example as the senior attacker but was unable to provide the breakthrough. The uncertainty of a goalless scoreline away in Europe was made worse when Roy Keane was forced to leave the field with an injury early on. He had been due to miss the following game against Bolton through suspension anyway but there was no doubt that despite the impressive way the youngsters conducted themselves, this tie was very much up in the air.

OTHER SELECTED RESULTS

UEFA CUP
FIRST ROUND FIRST LEG

AS Monaco 0–3 Leeds
Vladikavkaz 1–2 Liverpool
Malmö FF 2–1 Nottingham F

WED 13TH SEPTEMBER 1995

CHAMPIONS LEAGUE GROUP B

Blackburn 0–1 Spartak Moscow

THURS 14TH SEPTEMBER 1995

CUP WINNERS' CUP
FIRST ROUND FIRST LEG

KR Reykjavík 2–3 Everton

16TH SEPTEMBER 1995 - FA CARLING PREMIERSHIP
OLD TRAFFORD, MANCHESTER. ATT. 32,812

UNITED 3-0 BOLTON WANDERERS

Scorers: Scholes 17, 85, Giggs 33
Team : Schmeichel, Parker, Bruce, Pallister, P.Neville, Cooke (Davies 74), Butt, Beckham, Sharpe, Scholes, Giggs

"I think we have all been cheered and encouraged by the performances of our young players who have shown the courage and aptitude to reach the high standards that have been set for this club," Alex Ferguson declared in his notes ahead of the visit of Bolton Wanderers. He went on to praise the players for their performances in each of the three away games but it must (surely) have been hope, rather than expectation, that his youngsters would continue their fine form with the display that followed.

Terry Cooke was given his debut in the absence of Keane, meaning David Beckham moved into his favoured central midfield position and Ryan Giggs played up front alongside Paul Scholes. With Nicky Butt and Lee Sharpe, it was an almost entirely home grown front six and even Sharpe had been included in that group of 'Fergie's Fledglings' that had first broken through in the late 80's.

The 32,812 supporters in attendance were treated to a performance as fine as any that United would put on that season: with the first half, in particular, a show that would live long in the memory for many years. That their reward was just a 2-0 half time lead did not reflect their domination, vibrancy, speed or flair. Paul Scholes scored to give the hosts a deserved lead just after the quarter hour mark but, in the 33rd minute, Ryan Giggs put the finishing touches to a move which was simply outstanding. Beckham, Scholes and Cooke were all involved in a one touch, lightning-fast build up which captured the imagination of all within the stadium. The move provoked Bobby Charlton to say he couldn't remember seeing anything as good and, after Scholes scored a second to rubber stamp this emphatic performance, a third convincing league win was delivered in such style that there was enough reason to start believing that United were the real deal after all.

United had elevated themselves to joint leaders in the league after Newcastle's perfect start had been ended by a 1-0 defeat at Southampton on the same day as the Goodison Park triumph, although the Geordies retained a slight advantage on goal difference. The 3-0 win over Bolton also brought a welcome clean sheet for the first time this season, halting that run

OTHER LEAGUE RESULTS:

SATURDAY 16 SEPTEMBER 1995

Arsenal 1-0 West Ham
Aston Villa 2-0 Wimbledon
Chelsea 3-0 Southampton
Leeds United 1-3 QPR
Liverpool 3-0 Blackburn
Middlesbro' 2-1 Coventry
Newcastle 3-1 Man City
Sheff Wed 1-3 Spurs

SUNDAY 17 SEPTEMBER 1995

Nott'm Forest 3-2 Everton

of eight goals conceded in just five league games (or five in four following the Villa game). If Alex Ferguson thought his defensive concerns were over, he had another thing coming.

20TH SEPTEMBER 1995
COCA COLA CUP SECOND ROUND FIRST LEG
OLD TRAFFORD, MANCHESTER. ATT. 29,049

UNITED 0-3 YORK CITY

Team : Pilkington, Parker, McGibbon, Pallister, Irwin, Beckham, P.Neville (Cooke 46), McClair, Sharpe, Davies (Bruce 56), Giggs

'Oh, the terrible shame and embarrassment of it all,' reported *The Sun*, for once not needing to further sensationalise a result which sent shockwaves throughout the UK.

One can speak of the League Cup and associate United's involvement in it as obligatory rather than committed over the years but that would be to brush over a scoreline that was as staggering as it reads. York City's only previous encounters with Manchester United had come in the 1974/75 season, where the latter spent a year in the Second Division. Tommy Docherty may have had no choice but to field his strongest side with promotion the crucial objective; Alex Ferguson still selected a side that should have been easily strong enough to overcome opponents that were at the foot of the third tier of the pyramid. It wasn't too dissimilar to the team which had seen off Wrexham with ease earlier in the year in an FA Cup tie but the midfield pairing of David Beckham and Lee Sharpe, both more accustomed to playing wide, were unable to cope with the energy and industry of Simon Jordan and Nigel Pepper.

A shock it may have been but by the time York grabbed their lead in the 24th minute through Paul Barnes, the Minstermen had already spurned two gilt edged opportunities. United had come close themselves; Beckham, in a more familiar wide position, whipped in a cross and McClair's effort was tipped over by Dean Kiely but, soon after, Phil Neville was caught in possession and York attacked. Barnes, just outside the area, took a speculative punt. His shot took a huge deflection off Gary Pallister's shin and caught Kevin Pilkington off guard. Pilkington got a hand to the shot but was unable to stop it spinning in. Old Trafford housed visiting supporters for the first time this season due to this being a cup competition, and the York fans behind the goal in the East Stand could barely believe their eyes.

If the goal had come about from misfortune it was a comedy of errors which led to the second early in the second half; Pat McGibbon, on his debut, was turned by Paul Barnes and, in a vain attempt to catch him, upended the forward. It appeared to be outside the box but the referee awarded a penalty. Barnes' successful conversion compounded the fact that United were down to ten men. In their disarray, another free kick was conceded a couple of minutes later; Pilkington came out to claim but was beaten to the ball by Tony Barras. 3-0. Perhaps with damage limitation on his mind, Ferguson brought on Steve Bruce for Simon Davies but the truth was that it barely helped matters. Even with Bruce, Barnes caused so much havoc that he had the ball in the net again, only to have his effort ruled out for offside. York also found themselves down to ten men when Paul Atkin was ridiculously sent off for two very soft yellow cards within the space of three minutes but, even then, with the opportunity to throw Bruce forward, United were unable to redeem any pride.

The most famous victory in York City's history subsequently prompted the question – which Manchester United team should we expect to see for the rest of the season: the team capable of beating the League Champions and FA Cup holders on their own grounds or the team capable of shipping goals to lower league opposition at an alarming rate?

LEAGUE CUP SECOND ROUND, FIRST LEG

TUESDAY 19TH SEPTEMBER 1995

Bolton Wanderers 1–0 Brentford; Bradford City 3–2 Nottingham Forest; Bristol City 0–5 Newcastle United; Cardiff City 0–3 Southampton; Crewe Alexandra 2–2 Sheffield Wednesday; Hartlepool United 0–3 Arsenal; Huddersfield Town 2–0 Barnsley; Leeds United 0–0 Notts County; Oxford United 1–1 Queens Park Rangers; Shrewsbury Town 1–3 Derby County; Southend United 2–2 Crystal Palace; Stockport County 1–1 Ipswich Town; Tranmere Rovers 1–0 Oldham Athletic; Watford 1–1 Bournemouth; Wimbledon 4–5 Charlton Athletic; Wycombe Wanderers 0–0 Manchester City.

WEDNESDAY 20TH SEPTEMBER 1995

Aston Villa 6–0 Peterborough United; Birmingham City 3–1 Grimsby Town; Bristol Rovers 0–1 West Ham United; Coventry City 2–0 Hull City; Leicester City 2–0 Burnley; Liverpool 2–0 Sunderland; Manchester United 0–3 York City; Middlesbrough 2–1 Rotherham United; Millwall 0–0 Everton; Norwich City 6–1 Torquay United; Reading 1–1 West Bromwich Albion; Sheffield United 2–1 Bury; Stoke City 0–0 Chelsea; Swindon Town 2–3 Blackburn Rovers; Tottenham Hotspur 4–0 Chester City; Wolverhampton Wanderers 2–0 Fulham.

THE KIDS ARE ALRIGHT

23RD SEPTEMBER 1995 - FA CARLING PREMIERSHIP
HILLSBOROUGH, SHEFFIELD ATT. 34,101

SHEFFIELD WEDNESDAY 0-0 UNITED

Team : Schmeichel, Parker, Bruce, Pallister, Irwin, Beckham, Butt,
McClair, Davies (Cooke 67), Giggs, Scholes

The immediate answer to that poser was 'neither'. Although there
was some stability back in the team with Schmeichel and Bruce in
from the start and Nicky Butt restored to the starting line up too.

It would be understandable if the likes of Beckham and Davies
had had their confidence diminished or at least challenged by the
defeat to York but it's fair to say that just as many questions were
being asked of United's senior defenders who, just two years ago,
had looked close to impenetrable as the club stormed to a double.

It was that familiar defence which took to the field at
Hillsborough against a Sheffield Wednesday team capable of causing
problems and as the game wore on it appeared to be an exercise in
restoring calm and solidity to the back. "United were composed
and intermittently dangerous for the first
30 minutes," reported *The Independent*,
"but they adopted a much more passive
approach in the middle third of the match,
when attack was less of a concern than
containment."

This largely forgettable affair would
be followed by yet another game from this
relatively short period which would go
down in United's cult history.

OTHER LEAGUE RESULTS:

SATURDAY 23 SEPTEMBER
1995

Arsenal 4-2 Southampton
Aston Villa 1-1 Nott'm F
Blackburn 5-1 Coventry
Liverpool 5-2 Bolton
Man City 0-1 Middlesbro'
West Ham 2-1 Everton
Wimbledon 2-4 Leeds

SUNDAY 24 SEPTEMBER 1995

Newcastle 2-0 Chelsea

MONDAY 25 SEPTEMBER 1995

QPR 2-3 Spurs

26TH SEPTEMBER 1995
UEFA CUP FIRST ROUND SECOND LEG
OLD TRAFFORD, MANCHESTER. ATT. 29,724

UNITED 2-2 ROTOR VOLGOGRAD

Aggregate 2-2 - Rotor won on away goals
Scorers: Scholes 59, Schmeichel 89
Team : Schmeichel, O'Kane (Scholes 26), Bruce, Pallister,
P.Neville, Beckham (Cooke 82), Butt, Keane, Sharpe, Cole, Giggs

There are several players who have made an impact at Old
Trafford only to go on to fade into relative obscurity afterwards
and are only remembered for goals scored at Old Trafford: Paulo
Wanchope, Malcolm Christie and Steven Gerrard, for example.
Vladimir Nidergaus isn't a name probably remembered by anyone
after this game but his goal, which turned this tie on its head in the
16th minute, should be remembered as one of the best scored by
a visiting team in Europe. His clever skill (nutmegging and racing
past Bruce) and one-two with Zernov left him with an open goal
and, all of a sudden, that poser of whether the goalless draw in
Russia was a good result was given a firm answer in the negative.

Bruce was found wanting again when his heavy touch
surrendered possession on the half way line after he had charged
forward to try and reclaim the ball but was caught out and left
his defenders horribly exposed. Oleg Veretennikov advanced and
with no other options, felt secure enough to have a punt from
distance. Schmeichel got a hand to it but only enough of a touch
to push it on to the inside of the post. 2-0 with 24 minutes gone.
United weren't only staring defeat and a second humiliation at Old
Trafford within a week in the face but they were also on the verge
of losing at home in Europe for the first time in their history: a
proud record dating back to 1956.

Ferguson made an instant change following the goal - bringing
John O'Kane off and replacing him with Paul Scholes. It took until
the 59th minute for that substitute to have an impact but when it

duly arrived – Scholes pouncing to convert a Cole shot that had been saved: United were given a way back into the tie.

United's reputation for late comebacks may have still been at an embryonic stage but, with half an hour remaining, it wasn't stretching the realms of imagination to suggest that they could muster up an equaliser to avoid defeat or even the two goals required to secure qualification to the second round. However, it looked less and less likely that an equaliser would arrive as the game moved towards injury time and it would have been impossible to predict the identity of the person who would eventually spare United's blushes.

In the closing stages, United won a corner and goalkeeper Peter Schmeichel advanced up the pitch to help cause confusion as he had done against Blackburn in the dying stages of the 1-1 draw here in the 1993/94 season. Ryan Giggs whipped in a corner and the Dane took a running leap at it, coming in from the left hand side of the box. He met the ball flush with his head and, via the smallest of deflections from the thigh of either Andy Cole or the defender marking him, the ball just went over the line. There was no way that Schmeichel wasn't claiming it.

Alex Ferguson was all smiles as he saw that United's proud European record had been preserved and, although it must be said that the novelty of Schmeichel's goal has, over time, become far more of a positive thing than the dire circumstances in which it was scored, the harsh reality of UEFA Cup elimination to the Russian Cup runners up was a cause for concern: especially as United's record since lifting

OTHER SELECTED RESULTS

UEFA CUP
FIRST ROUND SECOND LEG
Leeds United 0–1 AS Monaco
(agg 3-1)
Liverpool 0–0 Vladikavkaz
(agg 2-1)
Nottingham Forest 1–0 Malmö
(agg 2-2 - Forest won on away goals)

WED 27TH SEPTEMBER 1995

CHAMPIONS LEAGUE GROUP B
Rosenborg 2–1 Blackburn

THURS 28TH SEPTEMBER 1995

CUP WINNERS' CUP
FIRST ROUND SECOND LEG
Everton 3–1 KR Reykjavík

the 1991 Cup Winners Cup now read: played 18, won 5, drawn 10, lost 3. They had been eliminated in the second round of the Cup Winners' Cup to Atletico Madrid in 1991-92, the first round of the 1992-93 UEFA Cup to Torpedo Moscow on penalties, the second round of the Champions League in 1993-94 after losing on away goals to Galatasaray and the first group stage of the Champions League in 1994-95 after defeat in Gothenburg. Clearly, they were still some distance short of being competitive on the European stage, even if UEFA's rules on overseas players remained a burden.

But what of the Russian team that eliminated them? Rotor Volgograd went on to be eliminated themselves in the next round by Bordeaux. The French team went on to lose the final to Bayern Munich. After finishing second in the Russian league in 1997, a multitude of problems began to pile up for Rotor. In 2009, they were eventually declared bankrupt and excluded from competing in the Russian Second Division. In 2010 FC Volgograd was renamed 'FC Rotor Volgograd' and put straight into the 'second level' of the Russian Football National League. More financial problems continued to dog the reputation of the club and in 2015 a new team by the name of 'Rotor-Volgograd' was established and entered into one of Russia's amateur leagues.

For United, after a run of games which had promised so much, it was back to earth with a bang – being knocked out of two cups by second class opposition didn't bode well. Still, all that was quickly forgotten by Eric Cantona's return to first team action…

PREMIER LEAGUE TABLE - 1ST OCTOBER 1995								
1	Newcastle United	8	7	0	1	17	4	21	13
2	Aston Villa	8	5	2	1	12	5	17	7
3	Manchester United	8	5	2	1	16	10	17	6
4	Liverpool	8	5	1	2	15	7	16	8
5	Leeds United	8	5	1	2	14	9	16	5
6	Arsenal	8	4	3	1	10	5	15	5
7	Middlesbrough	8	4	3	1	9	4	15	5
8	Nottingham Forest	8	3	5	0	14	9	14	5
9	Tottenham Hotspur	8	4	2	2	14	11	14	3
10	Chelsea	8	3	3	2	9	7	12	2
11	Wimbledon	8	3	1	4	13	16	10	-3
12	Queens Park Rangers	8	3	0	5	7	12	9	-5
13	Sheffield Wednesday	8	2	2	4	8	11	8	-3
14	Blackburn Rovers	8	2	1	5	10	13	7	-3
15	Everton	8	2	1	5	10	13	7	-3
16	Coventry City	8	1	3	4	7	17	6	-10
17	West Ham United	7	1	2	4	7	11	5	-4
18	Southampton	7	1	2	4	7	14	5	-7
19	Bolton Wanderers	8	1	1	6	8	18	4	-10
20	Manchester City	8	0	1	7	3	14	1	-11

THE KING IS BACK

"**N**ATURALLY I AM DELIGHTED to have him back," wrote Alex Ferguson about the return of the prodigal son. "Nine months without playing League football is a long time for a professional and Eric has been very quiet this week, no doubt making his own personal preparations. There is no point opening up all the rights and wrongs of why he did what he did and the severe punishment he received. All I really want to say is that he has trained hard during his ban and he did well in his community service. He has served his punishment and all he needs now is some football. So on with the show."

The manager did not avoid the embarrassment of the previous week, calling European elimination a 'big blow' though insisting that the second leg was 'crazy', but there was no getting around the fact that Cantona's return was huge news overshadowing recent setbacks.

The career of Eric Cantona had been stop-start to put it mildly. Eric could not be bound by the constraints of an ordinary professional footballer and, in many ways, you could generously argue that his frequent bans were as a result of this fight. He was a performer who had felt misunderstood during his career in France. Now, having found a club equal to his talent and a manager who was prepared to treat him as an adult, it must have seemed as if he had squandered his final chance.

Scouted as a prodigy by Guy Roux's Auxerre, Cantona made his name at Marseille and played a significant role in France's under-21s triumph in 1988 alongside many of the players who would go on to lift the 1998 World Cup. Yet by 1991 his career was in ruins. Immaturity saw him clash with coaches and a nomadic career soon saw him languishing at Second Division Nimes. Salvation came from English clubs looking to add flair to a dull brand of football. A trial at Sheffield Wednesday led to a transfer to Leeds and a significant role in pipping United to the 1991-92 Football League title. But, just as Cantona was earning cult status at Elland Road, he was proving a handful once more for his manager. Howard Wilkinson thought him a disruptive influence, so when that famous enquiry from Martin Edwards was made in November 1992, Leeds were eager to rid themselves of a talented but unpredictable figure who had spent more time back in France of late than at training.

One of Alex Ferguson's best attributes was his awareness that genius plays by its own rules. His reputation as a firebrand was misplaced. Yes, he could blast a player into performing but he could also allow someone like Cantona the freedom to do whatever he pleased if he played by certain rules. From the start it was a match made in heaven. United were still struggling to get over their failure to land the title in April 1992. The club: board, players, manager and fans - were in desperate need of self-assurance and for £1.2m they got it.

At 6'2, Eric had a physical presence but it was the way he carried himself, strutting and strolling around the Old Trafford pitch like a peacock; the lead actor waiting for the support, which made witnessing Cantona in his pomp an event in itself. You never knew what to expect but you knew it would be spectacular. It could be in a win with a tremendous goal. It could be in a nondescript mid-week draw when he was given a red card. He could even create memories in defeats where United failed to score; his half volley from just outside the centre circle at Stamford Bridge which crashed against the crossbar in the 1993/94 season is remembered more than the single goal that decided the game in the home team's favour that day.

From his debut in November 1992 until his two penalties wrapped up United's first League and Cup double in May 1994, he dominated English football. Soon, every club in the top flight was looking for their Eric; a catalyst who could change the course of history.

In the months since, however, there had been problems. Failures in Europe had exposed the limitations of that '93/94 team: they were too open to compete against the great teams of the era. With this in mind, United were shifting to a different, more rigid style and, while Cantona would be central to leading the up and coming kids in the short term, in hindsight it seems obvious he wouldn't see the project through.

1ST OCTOBER 1995 - FA CARLING PREMIERSHIP
OLD TRAFFORD, MANCHESTER. ATT. 34,934

UNITED 2-2 LIVERPOOL

Scorers: Butt 1, Cantona 70 (pen)
Team : Schmeichel, G.Neville, Bruce, Pallister, P.Neville (Scholes 73), Sharpe, Butt (Beckham 46), Keane, Giggs, Cantona, Cole

Cantona was the draw - to the extent that his return overshadowed the biggest fixture in the English game. That didn't stop the other twenty-one players trying to grab the headlines: they put on a terrific show. His entrance was like that of a Roman warrior entering the Colosseum. There was a feverish anticipation whenever he got the ball. Yet, somehow, something had changed. If anything, those nine months had heightened expectations. Absence had only made the heart grow stronger. The sense of excitement belonging to the occasion caused supporters to forget that the other players had won at the home of the current Champions earlier in the season and that only a couple of weeks before they had destroyed Bolton

41

Wanderers, playing a scintillating brand of football.

The first time he received the ball in an attacking position, just wide of the left hand side of the box, those in attendance stood instantly as their hero caressed an inch-perfect, left-footed sweeping pass to the edge of the area and in to the path of the on-rushing Nicky Butt. Butt's contribution should not be diminished as what followed was one of the most smartly taken goals of his career: with a wonderful first touch that completely took out the defender and a conclusive second which flew past David James into the Liverpool goal. On this occasion, however, the goalscorer was merely the subplot. The King had waved his magic wand with just over a minute played. Most ran to Nicky Butt to celebrate – Ryan Giggs was about to but, in a telling moment, turned around and congratulated Cantona.

> OTHER LEAGUE RESULTS:
>
> SATURDAY 30 SEPTEMBER 1995
>
> Bolton W. 0-1 QPR
> Chelsea 1-0 Arsenal
> Coventry 0-3 Aston Villa
> Leeds United 2-0 Sheff Wed
> Middlesbro' 2-0 Blackburn
> Nott'm Forest 3-0 Man City
> Spurs 3-1 Wimbledon
>
> SUNDAY 1 OCTOBER 1995
>
> Everton 1-3 Newcastle
>
> MONDAY 2 OCTOBER 1995
>
> Soton 0-0 West Ham

Yet every protagonist needs an antagonist. Step forward Robbie Fowler. By the start of the 1995/96 season the Toxteth Terror was a goal-scoring phenomenon, having already claimed a hat-trick in under 5 minutes against Arsenal the season before. Now Fowler set out to ruin the party. He found space behind Gary Neville and beyond Steve Bruce just inside the area and unleashed a powerful left footed drive into Schmeichel's top right hand corner. Early in the second half he doubled his tally and gave the visitors the lead. Neville had a nightmare again, this time he was outmuscled on the left; Fowler worked enough space and, as Schmeichel advanced from goal hoping to narrow the space and angle, he steered it around and over him into the unguarded goal to give the visitors the lead.

The King reclaims his crown

All of a sudden the party was being well and truly pooped. Yet, again, cometh the hour, cometh the man. Cantona received the ball in the middle of Liverpool's half and advanced, Giggs raced into the space where the Frenchman played the ball and was brought down by Jamie Redknapp inside the area. David Elleray, the referee who had awarded two penalties for United in the 1994 FA Cup Final, blew his whistle, presenting Cantona with another opportunity to convert the spot-kick. Not only did he take it but he put it in the exact same spot as he had against Chelsea in that final. 2-2, and Cantona was heading for the crowd again, only this time, to spin around the pole supporting the netting on the goal.

Yet the real winners of this pulsating draw were Newcastle United who managed to open a four point gap at the top of the table, giving them breathing space after the weekend's fixtures but days like this are remembered for the occasion first and result second so United supporters weren't too downhearted. The King had returned to claim his crown and few could argue about the instant impact he had made.

"I thought he did well, he was obviously tired towards the end but that's to be expected," said Ferguson afterwards. "The hype's finished now, thank goodness, I don't think it did either team any good today, but at the end of the day they still produced a marvellously entertaining match."

The manager wasn't wrong; the game was even voted number 27 in Liverpool's 'all time Premier League classics' on their own television channel during the Rafael Benitez reign.

Conversely, *The Independent* claimed that the result was an 'anti-climax' for the welcome home party, even taking into account Cantona's equaliser, while the now-defunct *Today* newspaper described Cantona as the 'returning Messiah' who 'didn't disappoint', an apt description considering that United were seeking a minor miracle in the unlikeliest of venues in their next game at York City's Bootham Crescent.

THE KING IS BACK

3RD OCTOBER 1995
COCA COLA CUP SECOND ROUND SECOND LEG
Bootham Crescent, York. Att. 9,386

YORK CITY 1-3 UNITED

Scorers: Scholes 7, 80, Cooke 14
Team : Schmeichel, G.Neville, Bruce, Pallister, Sharpe (P.Neville 67),
Cooke (Keane 53) Beckham, Scholes, Giggs, Cantona, Cole

It proved to be a miracle too far. United got off to the best of starts, scoring twice in the first fifteen minutes through Scholes and Cooke, and really, from there, it ought to have been a formality. Yet a nervous York side hung on and when Scott Jordan, so impressive in the first leg, grabbed a goal just before half time, the entire complexion of the tie changed again.

United huffed and puffed and grabbed a glimmer of hope when Scholes scored a second with ten minutes left on the clock. It was kitchen sink time and Peter Schmeichel was back in the opposition penalty area for a number of late corners, but a resolute display kept York's illustrious opponents at bay and the final whistle was greeted with as much joy as it had been at Old Trafford.

The embarrassing episode was over, though it would have to be relived time and time again; next up was the international break and after that the small matter of the Manchester derby. Even without senior football on the cards, United still managed to get plenty of attention.

LEAGUE CUP SECOND ROUND, SECOND LEG

TUESDAY 3RD OCTOBER 1995

Arsenal 5-0 Hartlepool United (agg: 8-0); Barnsley 4-0 Huddersfield Town (agg: 4-2); Bournemouth 1-1 Watford (agg: 2-2); Brentford 2-3 Bolton Wanderers (agg: 2-4); Burnley 0-2 Leicester City (agg: 0-4); Bury 4-2 Sheffield United (agg: 5-4); Charlton Athletic 3-3 Wimbledon (agg: 8-7); Crystal Palace 2-0 Southend United (agg: 4-2); Fulham 1-5 Wolverhampton Wanderers (agg: 1-7); Grimsby Town 1-1 Birmingham City (agg: 2-4); Ipswich Town 1-2 Stockport County (agg: 2-3); Notts County 2-3 Leeds United (agg: 2-3); Peterborough United 1-1 Aston Villa (agg: 1-7); Queens Park Rangers 2-1

Oxford United (agg: 3-2); Rotherham United 0-1 Middlesbrough (agg: 1-3); West Bromwich Albion 2-4 Reading (agg: 3-5).

WEDNESDAY 4TH OCT 1995

Blackburn Rovers 2-0 Swindon Town (agg: 5-2)); Chelsea 0-1 Stoke City (agg: 0-1); Chester City 1-3 Tottenham Hotspur (agg: 1-7); Derby County 1-1 Shrewsbury Town (agg: 4-2); Everton 2-4 Millwall (agg: 2-4); Hull City 0-1 Coventry City (agg: 0-3); Manchester City 4-0 Wycombe Wanderers (agg: 4-0); Newcastle United 3-1 Bristol City (agg: 8-1); Nottingham Forest 2-2 Bradford City (agg: 4-5); Oldham Athletic 1-3 Tranmere Rovers (agg: 1-4); Sheffield Wednesday 5-2 Crewe Alexandra (agg: 7-4); Southampton 2-1 Cardiff City (agg: 5-1); Sunderland 0-1 Liverpool (agg: 0-3); Torquay United 2-3 Norwich City (agg: 3-9); West Ham United 3-0 Bristol Rovers (agg: 4-0).

7TH OCTOBER 1995 - PONTINS LEAGUE DIVISION ONE
OLD TRAFFORD, MANCHESTER. ATT. 21,502

UNITED 2-0 LEEDS UNITED

Scorers: Cooke, Tomlinson
Team : Pilkington, P.Neville, Casper, Wallwork, Sharpe, Cantona (Baker), Cooke, McClair, Scholes (Mustoe), Tomlinson

Let it never be said that United fans don't turn up in their droves for an occasion. This was a club who still brought in the highest attendances in the country when they were in the Second Division and regularly drew large crowds for reserve and FA Youth Cup Finals. This was just a regular Pontins League reserve game but with a special attraction; Eric Cantona. Now that the Frenchman was allowed to participate in organised games: there was no stopping him and that meant that this fixture had to be moved to Old Trafford from Bury's Gigg Lane.

Not that the second string needed the French forward, they won the division by a convincing 11 point margin, illustrating the calibre of talent they had in back up. Still, once Cantona was named in the team there was only one aim. "The gaffer told us before the game to just give the ball to Eric," laughs Kevin Pilkington.

"A couple of the lads didn't pass to him when he was in a good position. At half time the Gaffer ripped into them, saying it wasn't about them, it was about Eric."

Perhaps the decision to play him backfired. Cantona was brought off in the second half for young Irish forward Des Baker, having picked up a calf injury which would keep him out of the Manchester derby – a fixture in which he had been so prolific.

14TH OCTOBER 1995 - FA CARLING PREMIERSHIP
OLD TRAFFORD, MANCHESTER. ATT. 35,707

UNITED 1-0 MANCHESTER CITY

Scorers: Scholes 4
Team : Schmeichel, G.Neville, Bruce, Pallister, P.Neville, Beckham, Butt, Keane (McClair 76), Giggs, Scholes (Sharpe 63), Cole

"Of course, on paper the result should really only go one way because this is a top and bottom encounter, but I am sure City's plight will serve to inspire them to pull something special out of the bag," Ferguson wrote in his programme notes.

He may have predicted that they would raise their game for the occasion but City had lost eight out of their nine previous games and were low on confidence and when United (fielding, according to the *Sunday Times*, 'their youngest team in memory') took the lead from a set piece in the fourth minute, scored by, one of those youngsters, Scholes, the supporters probably expected a repeat of the 5-0 drubbing they had enjoyed so much the previous season.

However, there was an intensity that

OTHER LEAGUE RESULTS:

SATURDAY 14 OCTOBER 1995

Aston Villa 0-1 Chelsea
Blackburn 2-1 Southampton
Bolton 1-1 Everton
Leeds 0-3 Arsenal
Liverpool 0-0 Coventry
QPR 2-3 Newcastle
Spurs 0-1 Nott'm Forest

SUNDAY 15 OCTOBER 1995

Sheff Wed 0-1 Middlesbro'

MONDAY 16 OCTOBER 1995

Wimbledon 0-1 West Ham

was missing. The nature of the occasion against Liverpool had meant that the fact that there were no official away support wasn't even noticed. But here, it made for a strange atmosphere lacking the spark of a derby fixture; to the benefit of Alan Ball's team, who grew into the game. "Memories are certainly not made of stuff like this," quipped *The Observer*.

Having gleaned just one point from their opening nine games, City would struggle for the rest of the season but shortly after the derby it was announced that Manchester would host the 2002 Commonwealth Games. As part of the bid, a new stadium would be built, which City, of course, inherited. The 1995/96 season would see City disappear from view; it would take over a decade and the unlikely intervention of an Arab potentate to put them back on the map.

United just about edged it on the day with 11 efforts on goal (Cole responsible for almost all of them) but, even with that in mind, the manager expected more. "We didn't play well today," said Ferguson, "I think, at times, our players' inexperience showed. They didn't know whether to keep the ball or penetrate. That will come though."

OTHER SELECTED RESULTS

WED 18TH OCTOBER 1995

UEFA CUP
SECOND ROUND FIRST LEG
    Auxerre 0–1 Nottingham Forest
    Brøndby 0–0 Liverpool
    Leeds 3–5 PSV Eindhoven
CHAMPIONS LEAGUE GROUP B
    Legia Warsaw 1–0 Blackburn
THURSDAY 19TH OCTOBER 1995

CUP WINNERS' CUP
SECOND ROUND FIRST LEG
    Everton 0–0 Feyenoord

THE KING IS BACK

21ST OCTOBER 1995 - FA CARLING PREMIERSHIP
STAMFORD BRIDGE, LONDON. ATT. 31,019

CHELSEA 1-4 UNITED

Scorers: Scholes 3,9, Giggs 78, McClair 85
Team : Schmeichel, G.Neville, Bruce, Pallister, Irwin, Scholes
(McClair 80), Butt, Keane, Giggs, Cantona, Cole

And how it would come! Their return to form owed much to the return of Cantona but if you ever wanted to see an example of how this young team could be transformed by the presence of their talisman just look at the contrast between this game and the preceding fixture.

United were so full of confidence that they looked like a completely different team to the one that had displayed such hesitancy against City the previous week: going for the jugular right from the off this time around. And Scholes, whose early goal had decided matters last time out, was at it again, with two goals in the first ten minutes to put United in complete control. His first, a smartly taken effort from the edge of the box after Cantona let it run, was followed by an emphatic finish after a fine patient passing move. Cantona's prodded through ball found the diminutive Scholes in an impossible amount of space; the youngster kept his composure to slam home his eighth goal in seven games. An effort early in the second half slammed against the crossbar, denying the Ginger Prince a hat-trick.

Ferguson later described the first half performance as the best United had played so far that season and he had a point; there were good performances all over the pitch against a very competitive Chelsea team that were giving everything to get back into the game. This was Mark Hughes' first time playing against his former team and it was he who gave the Blues some hope of a comeback when he found space between Pallister and Bruce to finish with an ease, United fans had seen so many times over the years.

However, that simply prompted the visitors into life and, within moments of the restart, Ryan Giggs had picked up the ball on the left hand side and charged at Steve Clarke. It was a classic case of defenders hating attackers running at the them and Clarke couldn't cope with the pace or movement of the Welsh youngster; Giggs darted past the experienced Scot and poked past Dmitri Kharine in the home goal to restore that two goal advantage. It was Ryan Giggs at his very best.

That provided Ferguson with the opportunity to rest Scholes; one would presume the kid was kicking himself when his replacement, Brian McClair, added a fourth five minutes from time: after smart passes from Cantona and Cole. Four goals from just five shots on target (the other of those efforts deemed to be Scholes' that hit the bar) demonstrated just how clinical United had been. Inflicting Chelsea's first home defeat of the season was impressive enough but the news that Newcastle had smashed six past Wimbledon provided some deflation. As impressive as United had been, it seemed that Newcastle were capable of going two better.

With the Magpies able to call on a big squad, the pool of senior players available to the Manchester United manager was something that was clearly weighing heavily on his mind. "The youngsters have done extraordinarily well for us but one or two of them need a break. They are still developing physically and I have always been sensitive to the dangers of burning out young players," he wrote in the match programme ahead of the visit of Middlesbrough.

The visitors, of course, had just been promoted back to the top division in new boss Bryan Robson's first season in charge,

OTHER LEAGUE RESULTS:

SATURDAY 21 OCTOBER 1995

Arsenal 2-0 Aston Villa

Coventry 0-1 Sheff Wed

Man City 0-0 Leeds

Middlesbro' 1-0 QPR

Newcastle 6-1 Wimbledon

Nott'm Forest 3-2 Bolton

West Ham 1-1 Blackburn

SUNDAY 22 OCTOBER 1995

Southampton 1-3 Liverpool

Everton 1-1 Spurs

and Ferguson was keen to welcome back his former captain, "I just know that he will get a warm and affectionate greeting from United supporters and I would have it no other way. I don't have to spell out what Robbo did for Manchester United in his time here."

OTHER RESULTS: LEAGUE CUP THIRD ROUND - TUESDAY 24 OCTOBER 1995: Barnsley 0-3 Arsenal; Birmingham City 1-1 Tranmere Rovers; Bolton Wanderers 0-0 Leicester City; Watford 1-2 Blackburn Rovers.

WEDNESDAY 25TH OCT 1995: Aston Villa 2-0 Stockport County; Crystal Palace 2-2 Middlesbrough; Coventry City 3-2 Tottenham Hotspur; Derby County 0-1 Leeds United; Liverpool 4-0 Manchester City; Millwall 0-2 Sheffield Wednesday; Norwich City 0-0 Bradford City; Queens Park Rangers 3-1 York City; Southampton 2-1 West Ham United; Stoke City 0-4 Newcastle United; Wolverhampton Wanderers 0-0 Charlton Athletic;

28TH OCTOBER 1995 - FA CARLING PREMIERSHIP
OLD TRAFFORD, MANCHESTER. ATT. 36,580

UNITED 2-0 MIDDLESBROUGH

Scorers: Pallister 43, Cole 87
Team : Schmeichel, G.Neville, Bruce, Pallister, Irwin, Scholes
(McClair 45), Butt, Keane, Giggs, Cantona, Cole

Bryan Robson was given a tremendous reception but that generosity was never going to extend to the gift of points to take back to Teeside. Ferguson had explained his decision to give David Beckham a breather and seemed conscious of the time spent by Paul Scholes on the pitch as evidenced by his half time withdrawal.

It had been a barmy and eventful first half. On the half hour, Roy Keane was involved in a tussle with forward Jan Aage Fjørtoft. The Irishman reacted badly to the challenge and struck out at the Norwegian and there was nothing referee Lodge could do but dismiss the United midfielder. It forced Ferguson into a rethink and Ryan Giggs was forced to tuck in to play in a midfield three. He coped with this new role excellently and it was from his free kick just before half time that Gary Pallister rose to net against his former club. Gary Walsh, in goal on his return to Old Trafford, was unable to stop his old colleague from scoring.

Giggs and Cantona were exceptional in the second half, always giving Robson's team too much to cope with. Cantona was the provider for the late goal that settled any nerves, finding Andy Cole. It was only Cole's second goal of the season and it took a while to find its way to the net, bouncing and bobbling as it moved.

OTHER LEAGUE RESULTS:

SATURDAY 28 OCTOBER 1995
Aston Villa 1-0 Everton
Blackburn 3-0 Chelsea;
LeedsUnited 3-1 Coventry
Liverpool 6-0 Man City
QPR 1-1 Nott'm Forest
Sheff Wed 0-1 West Ham
Wimbledon 1-2 Soton
SUNDAY 29 OCTOBER 1995
Spurs 1-1 Newcastle
MONDAY 30 OCTOBER 1995
Bolton 1-0 Arsenal

All that mattered was that it went in. "Middlesbrough's continuing lack of enterprise was punished again two minutes from the end when Cantona, the game's major creative influence and model of restraint, released Cole with a perfect through pass," said the *Sunday Telegraph*.

A 'Red October' it had most certainly been and the result on the following day - Newcastle's 1-1 draw at White Hart Lane - ended the month on a high.

OTHER SELECTED RESULTS

TUESDAY 31ST OCTOBER 1995

UEFA CUP
SECOND ROUND SECOND LEG

Nott'm Forest 0-0 Auxerre
(agg 1-0)
Liverpool 0-1 Brøndby IF
(agg 0-1)
PSV Eindhoven 3-0 Leeds
(agg 8-3)

WED 1ST NOVEMBER 1995

CHAMPIONS LEAGUE GROUP B

Blackburn 0-0 Legia Warsaw

THURS 2ND NOVEMBER 1995

CUP WINNERS' CUP
SECOND ROUND SECOND LEG

Feyenoord 1-0 Everton
(agg 1-0)

PREMIER LEAGUE TABLE - 1ST NOVEMBER 1995									
1	Newcastle United	10	9	0	1	26	7	27	19
2	Manchester United	11	8	2	1	23	11	26	12
3	Liverpool	11	7	2	2	24	8	23	16
4	Arsenal	10	6	3	1	15	5	21	10
5	Nottingham Forest	11	5	6	0	19	12	21	7
6	Middlesbrough	11	6	3	2	11	6	21	5
7	Aston Villa	11	6	2	3	13	8	20	5
8	Leeds United	11	6	2	3	17	13	20	4
9	Tottenham Hotspur	10	4	3	3	15	13	15	2
10	Chelsea	11	4	3	4	11	14	15	-3
11	Blackburn Rovers	11	4	2	5	16	15	14	1
12	West Ham United	11	3	4	4	10	12	13	-2
13	Sheffield Wednesday	11	3	2	6	9	13	11	-4
14	Queens Park Rangers	11	3	1	7	10	17	10	-7
15	Wimbledon	11	3	1	7	15	25	10	-10
16	Everton	11	2	3	6	12	16	9	-4
17	Southampton	11	2	3	6	11	20	9	-9
18	Coventry City	11	1	4	6	8	21	7	-13
19	Bolton Wanderers	10	1	2	7	11	22	5	-11
20	Manchester City	11	0	2	9	3	21	2	-18

GREY DAYS

4TH NOVEMBER 1995 - FA CARLING PREMIERSHIP
HIGHBURY, LONDON ATT. 38,317

ARSENAL 1-0 UNITED

Team : Schmeichel, G.Neville, Bruce, Pallister, Irwin (McClair 82), Scholes (Sharpe 64), Butt (Beckham 64), Keane, Giggs, Cantona, Cole

NORTH LONDON WAS PROVING to be an unhappy hunting ground for Premier League challengers; having reduced the deficit at the top of the table to one point, United found themselves four points behind again on a day of action which seemed as if it may prove pivotal.

An uncharacteristic error from Denis Irwin (one of a handful in a very long career) was seized upon by Dennis Bergkamp; the £7.5m new signing had taken his time to settle at the Gunners, but made no mistake here.

Arsenal survived a late onslaught described by *The Independent* as "the most precise and relentless of attacks" but David Seaman was equal to all of Andy Cole's efforts. The visitors had found it hard to penetrate a resolute back line of Dixon, Adams, Bould and Winterburn and, even on the occasions when they did, the goalkeeper was rarely troubled enough to put the result in doubt. Meanwhile,

OTHER LEAGUE RESULTS:

SATURDAY 4 NOVEMBER 1995

Chelsea 0-0 Sheff Wed
Coventry 2-3 Spurs
Man City 1-0 Bolton
Middlesbro' 1-1 Leeds
Newcastle 2-1 Liverpool
Southampton 2-0 QPR
West Ham 1-4 Aston Villa

Newcastle's late winner against Liverpool compounded matter; their perfect home record being the key to their growing lead in the table.

OTHER RESULTS:

LEAGUE CUP THIRD ROUND: Reading 2–1 Bury

LEAGUE CUP THIRD ROUND REPLAYS:

Tranmere Rovers 1–3 Birmingham City; Leicester City 2–3 Bolton Wanderers; Middlesbrough 2–0 Crystal Palace; Bradford City 3–5 Norwich City; Charlton Athletic 1–2 Wolverhampton Wanderers

OTHER LEAGUE RESULTS:

SUNDAY 5 NOVEMBER 1995
    Everton 1-0 Blackburn
MONDAY 6 NOVEMBER 1995
    Nott'm F 4-1 Wimbledon
WEDNESDAY 8 NOVEMBER 1995
    Newcastle 1-0 Blackburn

18TH NOVEMBER 1995 - FA CARLING PREMIERSHIP
OLD TRAFFORD, MANCHESTER. ATT. 39,401

UNITED 4-1 SOUTHAMPTON

Scorers: Giggs 1,4 Scholes 8, Cole 69
Team : Schmeichel, G.Neville, Bruce, Pallister, Irwin (P.Neville 45), Beckham, Butt, Scholes (McClair 49), Giggs (Sharpe 67), Cantona, Cole

A response was clearly needed again and it was provided, literally, within seconds against Southampton. Ryan Giggs' recent fine form had seen him arguably outperform Cantona. Of course, in the near-twenty years which would follow, he would set and break numerous more records, and he set one here with a goal after just fifteen seconds. It was a goal made all the more remarkable by the fact that Southampton took the kick off. Paul Scholes won possession on the halfway line and sent a floating ball across to Cantona; the Frenchman was as precise as ever in finding Giggs who met the ball first time with an accurate left foot drive. They'd had just five touches of the ball: one from Scholes to tackle, one to pass, then the chest control of Cantona and the pass which was taken with Giggs' first touch. There weren't even five minutes on the clock by the time Giggs grabbed his second; this time intercepting the pass of a Saints defender and running clear on goal to power past Dave Beasant.

Those in attendance had seen a number of quick starts by United this season but, this time, all inside Old Trafford must have thought they were about to see a scoreline that would better that registered in March's 9-0 destruction of Ipswich Town. When Paul Scholes made it 3-0 in the eighth minute (a goal created again by Cantona's slight flick on a Neville cross),

OTHER LEAGUE RESULTS:

SATURDAY 18 NOVEMBER 1995

Aston Villa 1-1 Newcastle
Blackburn 7-0 Nott'm F
Bolton 0-3 West Ham
Leeds 1-0 Chelsea
Liverpool 1-2 Everton
Sheff Wed 1-1 Man City
Spurs 2-1 Arsenal
Wimbledon 0-0 Middlesbro'

SUNDAY 19 NOVEMBER 1995

QPR 1-1 Coventry

even the manager expected something special. "I got carried away thinking we were going to slaughter them," Ferguson later said. "Old Trafford hasn't seen such a tremendous opening to a match in years," said the *Sunday Telegraph*.

Yet Southampton rallied so as not to capitulate completely. United's only other goal came in the 69th minute when Cole headed in a Beckham corner and the Saints even grabbed a consolation in the 85th minute when Neil Shipperley was the beneficiary of some slow reactions from Steve Bruce to convert an unlikely opportunity.

Was it mercy which caused United to step off the gas? Was the message clear as early as half time, that energy should be preserved? It may be strange to refer to a 4-1 win as an anti-climax yet there is a temptation to consider what might have been possible if the side had wanted to score more. For many, it was a flashback to the days of seeing the likes of Giggs and Butt boss games in the youth and reserve teams, racking up big scorelines against senior professionals.

And if this what they could do in 8 minutes, what could this United team achieve if it were at its best for ninety?

GREY DAYS

22ND NOVEMBER 1995 - FA CARLING PREMIERSHIP
HIGHFIELD ROAD, COVENTRY ATT. 23,400

COVENTRY CITY 0-4 UNITED

Scorers: Irwin 27, McClair 47,76, Beckham 57
Team : Schmeichel, G.Neville (P.Neville 48), Bruce (May 79), Pallister,
Irwin, Beckham, Butt (Sharpe 65), McClair, Giggs, Cantona, Cole

As strong as the temptation must have been to pull in the reins a little bit, sometimes Alex Ferguson must have simply enjoyed watching his team put on a masterclass. It was a young team with apparent teething problems – knowing when to be ruthless and that guile to break through resolute and experienced defences as at Arsenal but they played with such confidence and expression here that they demonstrated all the hallmarks of a potentially great side.

The four goals against Southampton were followed by four more at Highfield Road although, this time out, it was actually Coventry who started the better and threatened to score early on. Bruce, who had been culpable at the weekend, was back to his best to deny former team-mate Dion Dublin a goal which would have given the Sky Blues the lead.

It seemed as if the first goal would prove vital and Denis Irwin got it midway through the first half. Still, it took until the second for the visitors to really stamp their authority on the match. They were inspired, again, by stellar performances from Cantona and Giggs who were singled out by the manager for particular praise. "They all played well tonight but, again, I find myself picking out Cantona and Giggs," said Ferguson in his post-match comments. "They are both having a massive influence this season. Ryan's contribution has been outstanding and Eric just possesses that composure which spreads throughout the side."

The press were keen to shower Giggs with plaudits."Magnificent United, led by the trickery of Ryan Giggs, cut Newcastle's lead to a manageable three points," said *The Express*, while *The Mirror* gushed, "With Ryan Giggs providing the inspiration through his sheer genius, this encounter became increasingly one-sided."

United peppered Steve Ogrizovic's goal with fifteen attempts and the three that were scored in the second half were netted by McClair (twice) and Beckham, with a thunderous drive on the angle. The scale of the defeat put the hosts, managed by Ron Atkinson, bottom of the table on goal difference. United's tally of 31 goals equalled Newcastle's; both had scored eight more than champions Blackburn's 23.

OTHER LEAGUE RESULTS:

MONDAY 20 NOVEMBER 1995
Soton 0-1 Aston Villa

TUESDAY 21 NOVEMBER 1995
Arsenal 4-2 Sheff Wed
Middlesbrough 0-1 Spurs

WED 22 NOVEMBER 1995
Chelsea 3-2 Bolton
Coventry 0-4 Man Utd
Everton 2-0 QPR
Man City 1-0 Wimbledon
West Ham 0-0 Liverpool

With Rovers in the bottom half of the table and eighteen points off the lead, their spell as Champions looked as if it would be brief. The title race looked unpredictable but the official *Manchester United Magazine* tried their hand at predicting the events of 1996 which included the following highlights-

★ The March game between Newcastle and Man Utd would be called off, re-arranged for May. Andy Cole would score an injury time hat-trick to decide the title for his new club.

★ Diana Ross and Chris Waddle to both miss penalties in an opening ceremony for Euro '96 in England.

★ United qualifying for the FA Cup Final and releasing a cup final song which would feature 'Sonia from Echobelly and 1000 bagpipes'

★ Outrage after Eric Cantona 'appears at a fashion show in Milan modelling United's new home shirt as designed by Giorgio Armani'.

★ 'Take That split up after a farewell concert in Glossop.'

A dodgy FA Cup Final song, missed penalties at Wembley,

United to suffer from controversy due to their kit, and Take That to split? Someone should have asked the compiler for the lottery numbers. Even though they got the specifics wrong about the game against Newcastle on Tyneside, they were also right to project the relevant level of importance on to the fixture. Sometimes truth is stranger than fiction.

OTHER SELECTED RESULTS

WED 22 NOVEMBER 1995

CHAMPIONS LEAGUE GROUP B
Spartak Moscow 3–0 Blackburn

UEFA CUP
THIRD ROUND FIRST LEG
Nottingham Forest 1–0 Lyon

However, for United's next game, they could easily have looked to the recent past to make an accurate description.

27TH NOVEMBER 1995 - FA CARLING PREMIERSHIP
CITY GROUND, NOTTINGHAM. ATT. 29,263

NOTTINGHAM FOREST 1-1 UNITED

Scorer: Cantona 66 (pen)
Team : Schmeichel, G.Neville, Bruce, Pallister, Irwin, Beckham (Sharpe 81), Butt, McClair (Scholes 45), Giggs, Cantona, Cole

Stan Collymore may have left the City Ground but the Nottingham Forest team that had taken the Premier League by storm the previous season, finishing third, was proving to be just as competitive this time around. Filling Collymore's sizeable boots was Paul McGregor, a Liverpool-born striker who would score just thirty times in 182 league appearances. It was a modest tally for a player who received more press attention than his talent: perhaps merited due to his role as a lead singer for Britpop band 'Merc'.

Of course, McGregor scored one of those thirty here after nineteen minutes to give Forest the lead. Frank Clark's side were looking as if they were a bogey team for United and, despite an impressive second half turn around (led, of course, by Cantona and Giggs), the visitors couldn't make their pressure pay. Mark Crossley in the home goal was in inspired form and Andy Cole's missed chances would, again, lead to press questions. The *Daily Mail* led the criticism "all the possession in the world grants United nothing if Cole cannot fit more profitably into the passing shapes around him".

It seemed as if the visitors would require some luck to get back into the game and they got it when they were awarded a penalty. The replays suggested it was a generous decision; home supporters claimed that Cantona had dived following a challenge from Steve Chettle. Once the penalty had been awarded, however, there was no doubting the outcome, and Cantona sent Crossley the wrong way.

Ferguson later lamented United's wastefulness although he commended his team for getting back into the game. Even the fact that United now had two consecutive home games that they could use to try and close the gap at the top did not appease the manager, given the identity of the first of those opponents.

OTHER LEAGUE RESULTS:

SATURDAY 25 NOVEMBER 1995

Chelsea 0-0 Spurs
Coventry 3-3 Wimbledon
Everton 2-2 Sheff Wed
Man City 1-0 Aston Villa
Middlesbro' 2-1 Liverpool
Newcastle 2-1 Leeds
Southampton 1-0 Bolton
West Ham 1-0 QPR

SUNDAY 26 NOVEMBER 1995

Arsenal 0-0 Blackburn

OTHER RESULTS:

LEAGUE CUP FOURTH ROUND

TUESDAY 28TH NOVEMBER 1995: Reading 2-1 Southampton

WEDNESDAY 29TH NOVEMBER 1995: Arsenal 2-1 Sheffield Wednesday; Aston Villa 1-0 Queens Park Rangers; Leeds United 2-1 Blackburn Rovers; Liverpool 0-1 Newcastle United; Middlesbrough 0-0 Birmingham City; Norwich City 0-0 Bolton Wanderers; Wolverhampton Wanderers 2-1 Coventry City.

PREMIER LEAGUE AS AT 1ST DECEMBER 1995									
1	Newcastle United	15	12	2	1	33	11	38	22
2	Manchester United	15	10	3	2	32	14	33	18
3	Arsenal	15	8	4	3	21	10	28	11
4	Aston Villa	15	8	3	4	19	11	27	8
5	Tottenham Hotspur	15	7	5	3	22	17	26	5
6	Middlesbrough	15	7	5	3	14	9	26	5
7	Nottingham Forest	14	6	7	1	24	21	25	3
8	Liverpool	15	7	3	5	27	14	24	13
9	Leeds United	14	7	3	4	20	16	24	4
10	West Ham United	15	5	5	5	15	16	20	-1
11	Chelsea	15	5	5	5	14	17	20	-3
12	Everton	15	5	4	6	19	19	19	0
13	Blackburn Rovers	15	5	3	7	23	17	18	6
14	Southampton	15	4	3	8	15	25	15	-10
15	Sheffield Wednesday	15	3	5	7	14	20	14	-6
16	Wimbledon	15	3	3	9	19	33	12	-14
17	Manchester City	15	3	3	9	7	22	12	-15
18	Queens Park Rangers	15	3	2	10	11	23	11	-12
19	Coventry City	15	1	6	8	14	32	9	-18
20	Bolton Wanderers	15	2	2	11	14	30	8	-16

GREY DAYS

2ND DECEMBER 1995 - FA CARLING PREMIERSHIP
OLD TRAFFORD, MANCHESTER. ATT. 42,019

UNITED 1-1 CHELSEA

Scorers: Beckham 60
Team: Pilkington, G.Neville, Bruce, May, Irwin, Beckham, McClair,
Scholes, Sharpe, Cantona, Cole (Cooke 75)

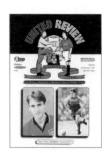

"There's no hiding place for this statistic... Manchester United have a shocking League record against Chelsea at Old Trafford," admitted the manager in his programme notes. Of course, Chelsea had held United to a 0-0 draw in the run-in the previous season and had won 1-0 at Old Trafford in the 1993/94 season, too.

United's matters were not helped by the absence of Peter Schmeichel; the Dane had to have surgery on an elbow problem and it was decided that this was the best time. So Kevin Pilkington, the deputy who had rarely been on the bench and whose previous start had been the infamous York City game, was thrust into the limelight for his full league debut (he had come on for Schmeichel against Palace in a 3-0 win in the 1994/95 campaign). The headaches continued with the imperious Giggs, Gary Pallister and Phil Neville all missing through injury and Roy Keane through suspension. Those absences were categorised as 'mitigation' by *The Telegraph* for what they described as 'listlessness' in United's performance.

Midway through the first half, Cantona chased a ball out of play and his momentum meant he had to carry on over the advertising hoardings and into the East Stand amongst the fans. It brought a huge cheer amongst the supporters stood there who applauded Eric back out of the crowd and onto the pitch as if he had scored a goal. That was as exciting as it got. The thinness of the squad was underlined by the substitute bench on which Cooke, McGibbon and Davies sat so perhaps it was no surprise when Chelsea, bogey team and all, took the lead through Denis Wise just after half time.

The young goalkeeper could do nothing to prevent the goal in an otherwise assured display. It was the contribution of another youngster which saved a point for United when David Beckham's extravagant, chipped effort on the hour mark flew into the top corner.

Suddenly buoyed by this goal, the hosts flooded forward, creating chances – the best of which fell to Andy Cole in the six-yard box. Cole, however, demonstrated the confidence of a man with only three goals in fourteen appearances that season, slicing his effort wide. He was promptly substituted, and the press loved it. "An immediate solution for Andy Cole's desperate lack of self-belief must be found, or the title race is as good as dead," reported the *Sunday Express*.

OTHER LEAGUE RESULTS:

SATURDAY 2 DECEMBER 1995

Aston Villa 1-1 Arsenal
Blackburn 4-2 West Ham
Bolton 1-1 Nott'm Forest
Leeds 0-1 Man City
Liverpool 1-1 Southampton
QPR 1-1 Middlesbrough
Spurs 0-0 Everton

SUNDAY 3 DECEMBER 1995

Wimbledon 3-3 Newcastle

MONDAY 4 DECEMBER 1995

Sheff Wed 4-3 Coventry

5TH DECEMBER 1995 - FIRST TEAM FRIENDLY
WINDSOR PARK, BELFAST. ATT. 22,000

INTERNATIONAL SELECT XI 2-1 UNITED

Scorer: Scholes
Team : Pilkington, Parker, Irwin (McGibbon), G.Neville (Davies), Sharpe (Mulryne), May, Cantona, Beckham (Cooke), McClair, Cole, Scholes

This 'Gala Charity' game was hardly ideal, scheduled at a time when United's squad was thin on the ground, but it was for a good cause and the Red Devils raised well over £150,000 for Co-operation North, which was a non-political organisation working to promote understanding and respect in Northern Ireland.

OTHER SELECTED RESULTS

WED 5TH DECEMBER 1995

CHAMPIONS LEAGUE GROUP B

Blackburn 4-1 Rosenborg

UEFA CUP
THIRD ROUND SECOND LEG

Lyon 0-0 Nott'm F (agg 0-1)

9TH DECEMBER 1995 - FA CARLING PREMIERSHIP
OLD TRAFFORD, MANCHESTER. ATT. 41,849

UNITED 2-2 SHEFFIELD WEDNESDAY

Scorer: Cantona 17,83

Team : Pilkington, G.Neville, Bruce, May, Irwin, Beckham, Scholes
(Davies 53), McClair, Sharpe (Cooke 83), Cantona, Cole

It's fair to say that the confidence of United's younger players was being tested in this period. Manager Alex Ferguson had been described as "the man with the Midas touch" in the match programme for the Belfast friendly but not everything was going perfectly for him in December 1995. Prior to the visit of Sheffield Wednesday, he insisted that in recent games where United had dropped points against Arsenal and Chelsea, they had "played their opponents off the park" - a generous description that was possibly given to boost morale.

Morale was very much the theme of Ferguson's programme notes for the Wednesday game. "I am well aware of the debate about Andy Cole and the fact that I substituted him towards the end of the Chelsea game," he stated, "I make no apology except to say that it is no reflection of my long-term faith in the player who I firmly believe is destined to become a great goalscorer for Manchester United. It's obvious at the moment that Andy is struggling to find the net but that will change... so you might wonder how substituting a player is going to help his confidence but I have been talking about my long-term belief in Andy Cole and there is the short-term to consider as well. I have got to say that I thought the chance he missed just before I decided to bring him off was down to carelessness, and it couldn't be ignored just as I wouldn't tolerate that kind of approach from any other player."

Cole would play the entire game against an experienced Owls side who seemed eager to take advantage of facing a Manchester United team shorn of many of its better players.

"Fergie's babes suffered an attack of the nursery wobbles and were in danger of toppling from their pram with a real crash until big brother Eric came riding to the rescue against slick Wednesday," was *The People's* verdict. Ferguson agreed, stating, "Cantona was the best player on our team today. He was marvellous. He inspired everything we did that was good and I fear that, had he not been on the pitch, we would have lost today."

United had actually led at half time through Cantona's 17th minute goal but Wednesday kept pushing and were rewarded for their strong, second half performance when Mark Bright and then Guy Whittingham scored to turn it around. Whittingham's goal came in the 78th minute and Wednesday might have felt they'd done enough to secure all three points. If they did, they hadn't reckoned with the Tour de Force that was Cantona who scored a precious 83rd minute equaliser after being set up by Beckham.

Elsewhere, Chelsea had continued to influence the title race with a 1-0 win over Newcastle to make United's draw not seem so bad. Yet with the Magpies still top of the table Kevin Keegan was optimistic. "When I get on the bus and I'm taking this team down the country, and I'm on the motorway and we're on a two or three hour journey when we seem to have every time we play away (and sometimes it's five or six hours) I look back, and I look at the players, and I think 'Yeah, I'm proud to take this group of players down there for this game'," he said, "you won't always win but we're very much on par to win something this year, you know, I think the whole country, wherever you go, even if they're Aston Villa supporters or Notts Forest supporters, they say 'If Notts Forest can't win it, or Aston Villa can't win it, we

OTHER LEAGUE RESULTS:

SATURDAY 9 DECEMBER 1995
Bolton 0-1 Liverpool
Chelsea 1-0 Newcastle
Coventry 5-0 Blackburn
Leeds 1-1 Wimbledon
Middlesbrough 4-1 Man City
Southampton 0-0 Arsenal
Spurs 1-0 QPR
SUNDAY 10 DECEMBER 1995
Nott'm F 1-1 Aston Villa
MONDAY 11 DECEMBER 1995
Everton 3-0 West Ham

like the way your team plays and I think we've tried to win in style.'"

Keegan was talking with the good will and confidence that came from his team's fine start to the season, and he was right to reference the wish of the neutral. Newcastle were known as 'The Entertainers' (a rather basic name for an admittedly exciting team) and while they were taking their star names across the country, it was very much the hope and expectation, given United's flagging form, that the quest for Premier League glory was turning into a one horse race.

12TH DECEMBER 1995 - PAUL MCSTAY TESTIMONIAL
CELTIC PARK, GLASGOW. ATT. 37,306

CELTIC 3-1 UNITED

Scorer: Scholes
Team : Pilkington, Parker, O'Kane (Appleton), Bruce, P.Neville, May, Davies, Sharpe, McClair, Cole (Tomlinson), Scholes

McStay was in his penultimate season after a long and successful career at Celtic and this testimonial was a fitting recognition of his service. It was a comfortable win for the hosts, although United did not send a side anywhere near as strong as the one that had just gone to Belfast. Still, with United desperate for a win to lift confidence going into one of the games of the season, it would have been nice to try and generate some momentum. Thankfully, despite the defeat, Ferguson was able to call on some senior players returning for selection ahead of a formidable trip to Anfield.

In the build up to the most heated clash in domestic football, a landmark moment occurred in the European Court of Justice in Luxembourg on Friday, December 15th, 1995.

Belgian player Jean-Marc Bosman had been involved in a legal battle with his former club RFC Liège after he had been prohibited to move following the expiration of his contract. The court ruled that the existing system restricted the free movement of workers and that, as such it, was prohibited by Article 39(1) of the Treaty of Rome.

The ramifications were huge. The most obvious consequence was that players could move clubs at the end of their contract without the new club having to pay a transfer fee. Additionally, the ruling meant that the existing restrictions on foreign players in UEFA competitions must be amended to reflect the free movement of players in the European Union. So 'foreigner' essentially became to mean non-EU players. Edgar Davids, the Ajax midfielder, became the first high profile beneficiary of this change in the transfer system when he moved to AC Milan but the ripple effect in the game would only truly be felt a little later.

17TH DECEMBER 1995 - FA CARLING PREMIERSHIP
ANFIELD, LIVERPOOL. ATT. 40,546

LIVERPOOL 2-0 UNITED

Team : Schmeichel, G.Neville, Bruce, May, Irwin, Beckham, McClair, Giggs, Sharpe, Cantona, Cole (Scholes 53)

Liverpool had won 1-0 against Bolton in their previous game but before that had gone winless in five league games, losing three of them. This, then, was a rare game where both of these giant clubs were out of sorts and desperate for a boost that would revive each side's fading title hopes. "Some pundits were actually writing off Manchester United as Premiership title contenders after their 3-1 defeat at Villa Park on the first day of the season," explained a surprising feature in the Liverpool match day programme, describing that opinion as an "astonishing conclusion".

From one outrageous opinion to another, with new Liverpool goalkeeping coach Joe Corrigan boldly declaring elsewhere in the publication that David James could be better than Peter

Schmeichel. With the benefit of hindsight, it seems a humorous comparison (although James went on to have a very solid career) but it's worth remembering that at the time Liverpool's own young contingent were as highly rated in the press as United's, if not more so. James was part of the 'Spice Boys' group at Anfield which included young stars like Rob Jones, John Scales, Jamie Redknapp, Steve McManaman, Jason McAteer and Robbie Fowler. It was also billed as a battle of the British record signings, with Stan Collymore lining up for the hosts and Andy Cole for the visitors, despite it being their respective strike partners who had made the greater impact in the game between the sides earlier in the campaign.

On the face of it, then, it was the perfect fixture for United's faltering young starlets to turn things around and send a message to all in the league. On this occasion, however, it was the older heads who disappointed just as much as the younger players. United were heading towards half time level, which would have been surprising given their lacklustre performance, when Liverpool were awarded a free kick just outside the area, a perfect position for a left footer from Fowler, and he didn't pass up the opportunity. The returning Peter Schmeichel had been excellent but was helpless to stop it, just as he was helpless to influence his team-mates into a better performance in the second half.

Giggs was the best of a rotten bunch with even Cantona ineffectual; Cole's lack of confidence was so apparent that he was hauled off after just 53 minutes and replaced by Scholes. It was clear that United were missing the bite of Keane or Butt and instead they limped to a defeat that was rubber-stamped by another Fowler goal in the dying minutes. "Rarely can a United team have been so comprehensively out-fought, out-run and outplayed by their most bitter rivals," described the *Daily Mirror*, and it was hard to argue. It had been the exact opposite of the performances at Ewood Park and Goodison Park earlier in the campaign.

"When United come to Anfield I expect them to fight," said

Ferguson afterwards. "They didn't. That was the most lifeless performance from a United team in years. You need passion when you come here. Some of our players haven't played here before but the others have got no excuse." Judging by those comments, a look through the team-sheet identifies experienced outfield players as Irwin, Bruce, May, Sharpe, Cantona, McClair and Giggs, and maybe even Cole, although the immediate post-match words of the manager seemed to absolve Giggs of any blame and his recent comments about Cole would have suggested he too would be spared any direct finger pointing that would be add to the humiliation of another early substitution.

OTHER LEAGUE RESULTS:

SATURDAY 16 DECEMBER 1995

Arsenal 1-1 Chelsea
Aston Villa 4-1 Coventry
Blackburn 1-0 Middlesbro
Newcastle 1-0 Everton
QPR 2-1 Bolton
Sheff Wed 6-2 Leeds
West Ham 2-1 Soton
Wimbledon 0-1 Spurs

MONDAY 18 DECEMBER 1995

Man City 1-1 Nott'm Forest

Ferguson's blast may have been just as much for encouragement and motivation as it was an indication that he had identified players who may not be up to supporting United's cause in the long term. Steve Bruce, never the quickest, was coming up to his 35th birthday and had been given the run around by Fowler all afternoon. The natural end of his playing career was approaching and this performance, although far from an embarrassment, was one of a number of uncharacteristic moments that had occurred so far this season from a hitherto reliable captain and leader.

It was perhaps far more concerning for Lee Sharpe, a player who found himself out of the squad completely the next time United took to the pitch.

OTHER RESULTS: LEAGUE CUP FOURTH ROUND REPLAYS - WED 20TH DEC 1995
Birmingham City 2–0 Middlesbrough; Bolton Wanderers 0–0 Norwich City (3-5 pens)

GREY DAYS

24TH DECEMBER 1995 - FA CARLING PREMIERSHIP
ELLAND ROAD, LEEDS. ATT. 39,801

LEEDS UNITED 3-1 UNITED

Scorers: Cole 28

Team : Schmeichel, G.Neville, Parker (May 71), Bruce (P.Neville 74), Irwin, Beckham (Scholes 74), Butt, Keane, McClair, Cantona, Cole

If the absence of Keane and Butt was something of a contributory factor to United's meek surrender at Liverpool, then their presence barely helped matters here, although Butt was deployed from the left hand side with Brian McClair in the middle, for a game dubbed as 'High Noon' by Sky Sports due to the midday Christmas Eve kick off. Referee Dermot Gallagher handed the hosts an early Christmas present, awarding a penalty when Butt's flailing hand connected with Richard Jobson's header in the fifth minute. Gary McAllister had as strong a reputation as Cantona in such situations and although Schmeichel went the right way, the Scot thrashed the ball into the top corner.

A packed Elland Road were hysterical, as was Peter Schmeichel, but for different reasons. Even amongst the raucous atmosphere, the goalkeeper's dissatisfied yells could be heard as the visitors rocked under the pressure. Somehow, United managed an unlikely equaliser, when Butt, showing fighting spirit, chased down and won a ball on the right hand side and squared for Cole who finished instinctively. His reaction displayed the requisite relief one might expect of a man trying to bear the weight of the world on his shoulders.

His team-mate's reaction was decidedly more sluggish; less than six minutes later Tony Yeboah put Howard Wilkinson's men back in front. Yeboah had earned a reputation for spectacular goals and though it wasn't quite the standard of his long range strikes against Liverpool and Wimbledon earlier in the season, his holding off of Denis Irwin and cool finish past the advancing goalkeeper was still impressive.

United's reaction was game and it seemed as if they may find their way back into it but all hope was wiped out in the 73rd minute. The defence was compact enough and there were plenty of men in the area as Leeds went in search of a goal; the amount of space afforded to Carlton Palmer, Tomas Brolin and Brian Deane, who was allowed a free header, was incredible. Bruce had rushed out to challenge Brolin, an understandable decision taken in the circumstances, and Paul Parker, who was playing at centre half instead of David May, was nowhere near three Leeds players who were all queuing up to score. It was inevitable that it would be Brian Deane who grabbed the goal, considering the number of goals he got against United over the years.

"I can't say why I seemed to score so often (against United)!" Deane said in an interview for this book. "I just really looked forward to it. Those were big games, United were seen as the biggest team to beat and I seemed to have a knack of getting the best of Gary Pallister and Peter Schmeichel. I scored quite often against them for Sheffield United and for Middlesbrough at Old Trafford in 1998 too. Maybe I was just a bogey man! I think our team was built around Tony (Yeboah). We played a 4-3-3 with two out and out forwards at the side of Tony, myself on the left and either Rod Wallace or Noel Whelan on the right. We had a lot of pace in those combinations."

"We are not lacking in confidence. And I don't think Andy Cole is either," Alex Ferguson said afterwards. *The Telegraph*, however, reckoned the manager "must have felt like joining in with Peter Schmeichel's constant chastising" while *The Independent* said "In the space of eight days, the Manchester United manager has seen his team's title credentials look as tatty as last year's tinsel."

Ouch.

Both Bruce and Parker were hauled off immediately after the Deane goal but despite some endeavour, the game was well and truly up. And despite Ferguson's protestations about some improvement, the display was almost as abject as that at Anfield. It was reasonable to dismiss a title challenge. After all, Newcastle would now be ten points clear on Christmas Day after a dismal December with the top two set to face off for the first time this season on the day after Boxing Day.

It is worthwhile taking a look at Leeds considering the importance their involvement to the title race would become as the season wore on. Deane's comments highlight an interesting mindset that Ferguson would discuss publicly towards the end of the season but is it not only natural that sportsmen raise their game when they are faced with an opponent that is considered among the elite? Concentration levels become greater, as do energy and performance levels. Up until recently, these two teams had been battling for the title, and the home supporters were keen to see their own team compete at that level again, guaranteeing a white hot atmosphere in an already hostile derby.

Still, it's hard to shake off the fact that this Leeds United team had, the previous week, lost 6–2 at Sheffield Wednesday. And their form

OTHER LEAGUE RESULTS:
SATURDAY 23 DECEMBER 1995

Coventry 2-1 Everton
Liverpool 3-1 Arsenal
Man City 0-1 Chelsea
Middlesbro 4-2 West Ham
Newcastle 3-1 Nott'm F
QPR 1-0 Aston Villa
Sheff Wed 2-2 Soton
Spurs 2-2 Bolton
Wimbledon 1-1 Blackburn

PREMIER LEAGUE TABLE ON CHRISTMAS DAY 1995

1	Newcastle United	19	14	3	2	40	16	45	24
2	Manchester United	19	10	5	4	36	22	35	14
3	Liverpool	19	10	4	5	34	16	34	18
4	Tottenham Hotspur	19	9	7	3	26	19	34	7
5	Middlesbrough	19	9	6	4	23	14	33	9
6	Aston Villa	19	9	5	5	25	15	32	10
7	Arsenal	19	8	7	4	24	15	31	9
8	Nottingham Forest	18	6	10	2	28	27	28	1
9	Leeds United	18	8	4	6	26	25	28	1
10	Chelsea	19	7	7	5	18	19	28	-1
11	Blackburn Rovers	19	7	4	8	29	25	25	4
12	Everton	19	6	5	8	23	22	23	1
13	West Ham United	19	6	5	8	21	28	23	-7
14	Sheffield Wednesday	19	5	7	7	28	29	22	-1
15	Southampton	19	4	6	9	19	30	18	-11
16	Queens Park Rangers	19	5	3	11	15	26	18	-11
17	Manchester City	19	4	4	11	10	28	16	-18
18	Wimbledon	19	3	6	10	24	39	15	-15
19	Coventry City	19	3	6	10	25	41	15	-16
20	Bolton Wanderers	19	2	4	13	18	36	10	-18

after the United game did not get much better. Ultimately, one can only truly count on the performance on your own team and whether or not it is right to openly question the competitiveness of others that one can appreciate the frustration. This was a situation for later in the season but it was clear to see where the later controversy originated.

After facing Liverpool and Leeds in consecutive games, the following game against Newcastle promised to provide United's toughest test of the season. A defeat would almost certainly see the visitors with one hand on the Premiership trophy.

"We extend a warm and admiring welcome to Newcastle United this evening," wrote Alex Ferguson in his programme notes, clearly speaking more about the personal touch rather than the climate, as those brave enough to form part of Old Trafford's largest crowd of the season (thanks to the partial opening of the North Stand) were forced to endure sub-zero temperatures. "There must be a passion and commitment this evening which, dare I say it, was shown by the Liverpool players when they crushed us at Anfield. I don't like saying that, but reality has to be faced and answered... I imagine I speak for the supporters who were at Anfield, as well as myself, when I say that Manchester United simply cannot accept such a lifeless performance when we all know what it meant... It spoiled my build-up to Christmas, as I am sure it did for a lot of other people. It wasn't the fact that we lost, it was how. Now we must set matters right with the kind of dominating display that it will take to beat Newcastle. There has got to be a real commitment because I cannot think of a more important game than this one. It is in the elite band of key games we have played over the last three or four years. It's a match that will involve our supporters too, because they have to make it clear that winning is important to them as well. The passion must come right through like never before because we need the accelerator down to the floorboards for the full 90 minutes."

GREY DAYS

27TH DECEMBER 1995 - FA CARLING PREMIERSHIP
OLD TRAFFORD, MANCHESTER. ATT. 42,024

UNITED 2-0 NEWCASTLE UNITED

Scorers: Cole 6, Keane 53
Team : Schmeichel, P.Neville, G.Neville, May (McClair 45), Irwin,
Beckham, Keane, Butt, Giggs, Cantona, Cole

Those were rallying words indeed and they were heeded by all; perhaps cajoled by the number of visiting supporters, and also by the difference made by Leeds fans to their own team's fortunes three days before (or maybe even just to keep warm), the United faithful were in fine voice from the off. An almost tentative opening exchange saw both sides probing, careful that the obvious strengths of both teams came in attack. Barely enough time had passed for there to be any analysis of how the game would pan out before Ryan Giggs received the ball following a challenge from Roy Keane in the sixth minute. The Welsh winger raced forward forty yards with the ball and kept his head up, looking for options. Cantona provided one, pulling Steve Howey wide left, to open up space behind Darren Peacock and John Beresford which Andy Cole was racing on to. It was no mean feat to execute the pass as it had to be done with perfection on the icy ground; Cole's finish, first time, was every bit as cold as the temperature, drilled into the corner to give United the lead.

This thrilling start set the game up perfectly; forcing Newcastle to come at their hosts (though one might argue they were never going to do anything but). Les Ferdinand was presented with a great opening but was denied by Peter Schmeichel's imposing frame.

Of course, a consequence of Newcastle's urgency was the opportunity to counter attack and in the opening seconds of the second half, as the Magpies launched straight into attack, they were almost caught with a sucker punch. Andy Cole was in menacing

73

mood but strangely didn't pounce on an opportunity that presented itself; instead returned the favour to Ryan Giggs, who was racing into the box from the left. The ball didn't present itself perfectly to the Welshman, who was forced to adjust his body and strike with his right foot and this had some effect on the quality of the finish, which skimmed the crossbar on the way over.

The home side didn't have too long to wait to double their advantage; after failing to make the most of a corner, Phil Neville (deputising at right back, with his brother Gary at centre half) lofted a ball into the box. Newcastle made a mess of their defensive line and Roy Keane suddenly found himself with plenty of time and space in the box. He was able to take a touch to compose himself and evade the oncoming opponent then, with his next touch, he toe-ended the ball past Pavel Srnicek.

Newcastle had no answer and found themselves hamstrung when both of their full backs were booked, limiting their capability to contribute with Giggs in full flow and Beckham as industrious as ever. United could have scored even more goals but nobody was complaining about a 2-0 result that was every bit as comprehensive as it seemed. "It was a top-class performance because we decided to attack and just went for their throats; they didn't know how to handle that," enthused Ferguson afterwards. When asked how the result changed the title race, Ferguson was literal. "Well first of all it pegs back Newcastle from ten to seven points which is vital in relation to the position in the league. We've had a bad December really but that hopefully will put us back on the right track again."

"Manchester United unfurled the full, glorious expanse of their football at Old Trafford last night to bite harder into Newcastle's spirit than the frost into the

OTHER LEAGUE RESULTS:

TUESDAY 26 DECEMBER 1995

Blackburn 2-0 Man City
Everton 4-0 Middlesbrough
Nott'm F 1-0 Sheff Wed
Arsenal 3-0 QPR
Chelsea 1-2 Wimbledon
Southampton 0-0 Spurs

WED 27 DECEMBER 1995

Bolton 0-2 Leeds

ground," the *Daily Mail*'s report read. And despite coming into the game on the back of two defeats, United's match day programme saw the funny side, featuring as this edition's 'Celebrity Red' none other than Father Christmas himself. The interview was conducted by the appropriately named 'S. Nowman'. "I think lots of people reckon I'm a United fan because I'm always dressed in red and white and I dare say that Rudolf's nose has probably got something to do with it. And to be fair I suppose I do have a soft spot for United," 'Santa' said.

It was all fun and games but United's defence had been no laughing matter in recent weeks. Paul Parker's injury problems had caught up with him so severely that his days of performing at this level seemed numbered. Gary Pallister's back problems were rendering him currently out of service, while Steve Bruce's decline had also been noted by the manager. It didn't yet seem clear whether or not David May, brought in as a right back, could be a senior defender for the first team at the highest level. And so, with numbers thin on the ground, Alex Ferguson swooped for a defender who could come straight in.

William Prunier, a Frenchman who was without a club after leaving Bordeaux, had a good amount of experience behind him with 221 league games at Auxerre (where he played with one Eric Cantona) and 35 games in a successful Marseille team. He was deemed a solid enough player to represent France in 1992. Alex Ferguson may have thought Prunier's spell at Manchester United was so insignificant that it didn't warrant a single mention in his 1999 autobiography but any record of this season would be incomplete without referencing the defender's short, but remarkable, time at Old Trafford.

Unsatisfied with how things were going at Bordeaux, it was reported that Prunier bought out the remainder of his contract and so was free to sign for any club and with David May picking up an injury in the Newcastle game, Ferguson was forced into a move so quickly that Prunier's name was nowhere to be found in the match programme on his debut. For the final game of 1995, United were forced to play Gary Neville and Prunier as their centre half pairing - thankfully, they had obliging opponents.

30TH DECEMBER 1995 - FA CARLING PREMIERSHIP
OLD TRAFFORD, MANCHESTER. ATT. 41,890

UNITED 2-1 QUEENS PARK RANGERS

Scorers: Cole 44, Giggs 52
Team : Schmeichel, Irwin, G.Neville, Prunier, P.Neville (Parker 55), Beckham, Butt, Keane, Giggs, Cantona, Cole

"William Prunier became an instant hero of the Old Trafford hordes on a debut when he was in the mood to storm the Bastille, never mind struggling Rangers," wrote Alan Nixon in *The Independent*. "Down Stretford way they like their Frenchmen mean and moody and this latest arrival looks as if he has come from Devil's Island FC, balding and so pale that he could do with a blood transfusion more than a contract. However, no sooner had the applause faded away than a Euro-sceptic voice was heard, and coming from the most important section of the stand, too. The manager, Alex Ferguson, was not yet ready to be swept away on a Gallic tide of emotion.

"Ferguson will reserve judgment and United cash before plunging in headlong. Tottenham today should be a more meaningful test before he gives his 'yes' vote. The United manager said: 'We will play William and what we will see is how he defends away from home. There is always that thing about European defenders and how quickly they can pick up the pace. It's a far quicker tempo here. People get into the box more than they do abroad. Most of their attacking ends with just one or two in the area. In our game you will see four or five at times.

"'I thought William improved as the game went on. He had the variety of facing Bradley Allen and then Daniele Dichio, who are both young. Teddy Sheringham is more experienced and we will have a better idea after seeing that.'

"Prunier's passing ability was superior to that of any other defender at United, but his addition to their squad might be of only short-term advantage. He played on the right, forcing Gary Neville to the left where he was uncomfortable in Rangers' bright opening. With Steve Bruce, Gary Pallister and David May all absent at this crucial stage of the Championship, Prunier would be a perfect asset for the moment. A contract until the summer would best suit United, but would it match the player's needs? That question was sadly left unanswered because Prunier has fallen under the wing of Eric Cantona. Getting sardines from the new trawler was equally unrewarding for the seagulls outside Old Trafford waiting for his thoughts."

High praise indeed from Nixon but it was probably appropriate – Prunier was not exactly outstanding but it was the ease with which he settled into an authoritative role that was so impressive (that said, Brian McClair revealed in his 'Choccy's Diary' column in the club's magazine that the training session the day before the game was "geared towards helping William Prunier understand a bit better how the team plays"). And it was he who helped provide the breakthrough here just before the half time interval. Giggs' corner was met by Prunier's distinctive head, forcing Juergen Sommer into an instinctive save. An in-form Andy Cole, in the kind of spell where everything fell to him, was there to gratefully convert for his third goal in as many games. United needed a second and some dogged persistence from Denis Irwin, playing at right back, eventually presented an opportunity for Ryan Giggs. Cool as you like, Giggs planted the ball comfortably past the goalkeeper to secure this result.

OTHER LEAGUE RESULTS:

SATURDAY 30 DECEMBER 1995

Arsenal 1-3 Wimbledon

Blackburn 2-1 Spurs

Bolton 1-2 Coventry

Chelsea 2-2 Liverpool

Everton 2-0 Leeds

Nott'm F 1-0 Middlesbro

Danny Dichio pulled a goal back to make it a close run thing after Schmeichel completely fluffed a clearance but United closed out 1995 with a deserved, if narrow, victory.

"We didn't play our normal passing game today, and I think that was mainly down to the fact that we couldn't water the pitch because of the conditions," explained Ferguson afterwards. "It is important we go on a run now. If people think that we reached the heights against Newcastle they are wrong. We can play better than that."

1ST JANUARY 1996 - FA CARLING PREMIERSHIP
WHITE HART LANE, LONDON. ATT. 32,852

TOTTENHAM HOTSPUR 4-1 UNITED

Scorers: Cole 36
Team : Schmeichel (Pilkington 45), Parker, G.Neville, Prunier, P.Neville (Sharpe 70), Beckham, Butt, Keane (McClair 70), Scholes, Cantona, Cole

Hopes that a better performance would follow at White Hart Lane were sadly misplaced. The bubble of optimism that followed back-to-back home wins was well and truly burst with a third successive defeat on the road. You could tell it was going to be a bad night straight from the kick off; Prunier received the ball and, bearing in mind the lofty praise about his supposedly superior passing ability, hit a cross-field pass towards no-one in particular. It set the tone for an error ridden display and United could ill-afford a crisis of confidence considering that Peter Schmeichel had suffered an injury in the warm up. However, with Denis Irwin joining Pallister and Bruce on the treatment table, Ferguson gambled to keep the experienced goalkeeper between the sticks behind a very inexperienced defence. Tottenham were not without their injuries too. Darren Anderton, Ruel Fox and David Howells were missing for the home team. "Tottenham have almost an entire midfield missing," commentator Peter Drury remarked, without really noting the fact that United had a list of absentees just as long, if not longer.

The home team were in charge long before they took the lead; Teddy Sheringham hit the post with a header and Chris Armstrong struck the bar with a long range effort. For the latter strike, Peter Schmeichel didn't even move, let alone dive, and he had his defenders taking the goal-kicks for him, such was his restricted movement. On a rare foray forward, United were generously awarded an indirect free kick when Ian Walker was judged to have handled a back pass. From the resulting set piece Cantona found himself in space but his effort was scrambled off the line. Cole and Giggs engineered a fine move which saw the latter have a shot saved but despite these signs of encouragement, United found themselves a goal behind moments later.

Gary Neville, playing at left centre-half to accommodate Prunier, was uncomfortable in possession and gave the ball away, Spurs were slick and Sheringham was found in space in the box. He had all the time he needed to finish comfortably past a stiff Schmeichel.

Within seconds of the restart United equalised; Butt and Phil Neville linked up in a fine move on the left, and the younger Neville's cross was met by Cole (after being missed by Beckham) dead centre of goal. The forward wasn't going to miss this opportunity to net for the fourth game in a row. The visitors were arguably the better team for the rest of the half but couldn't make their dominance pay but on the stroke of half-time United failed to clear a throw in and couldn't clear a Dean Austin cross, Sol Campbell arrived on the edge of the box to put Spurs back in front.

When United came back out for the second half, Schmeichel had been replaced by Pilkington and within two minutes, the young goalkeeper was picking the ball out of the net. Both Nevilles were caught ball-watching and Prunier was nowhere near Chris Armstrong, who stooped to head home. Within minutes, either side of half-time, the game had been turned on its head.

United pushed to get back into the game and thought they had started a comeback when Andy Cole scored a sensational overhead kick. Inexplicably it was ruled out for dangerous play, although whether it would have affected the outcome is a matter for debate, considering that Armstrong had already made it 4–1.

"The result is terribly disappointing. It looks as though the gods have conspired against us," said a dejected Ferguson afterwards.

"Frenchman William Prunier looked like a gendarme asked to do traffic duty at Piccadilly Circus," quipped the *Daily Mail*. And, before United would take to the field again, it had been announced that the defender had left the club.

"William Prunier's stay with Manchester United has ended after just two games following Alex Ferguson's offer of an extended trial and not a more permanent deal," reported *The Independent*. "The former Bordeaux centre-back, who has paid up his contract in France and is looking for full-time employment, met the United manager yesterday after call-ups against Queen's Park Rangers and Tottenham, which passed with varying degrees of success. United were prepared, indeed probably desperate, to have Prunier for Saturday's FA Cup third-round home tie with Sunderland when they would be without Steve Bruce, Gary Pallister and David May. However, the 28-year-old Prunier has decided to pack his bags and return to France where he has other offers."

"William Prunier, on trial for a couple of weeks, must have wondered what had hit him," Ferguson revealed in the

OTHER LEAGUE RESULTS:

MONDAY 1 JANUARY 1996

Middlesbro' 0-2 Aston Villa
Coventry 1-1 Southampton
Leeds 0-0 Blackburn
Liverpool 4-2 Nott'm Forest
Man City 2-1 West Ham
Sheff Wed 4-2 Bolton
Wimbledon 2-3 Everton

TUESDAY 2 JANUARY 1996

QPR 1-2 Chelsea
Newcastle 2-0 Arsenal

programme notes ahead of the FA Cup tie with Sunderland. "It was obviously a difficult game for him, but also for us because it made it hard to judge him. Indeed, I told him that I wanted to extend his trial period and look a bit closer before offering him a full long-term contract. Unfortunately, he and his agent wanted a quick decision because other clubs are interested in him and they weren't prepared to wait. So I'm afraid we couldn't reach agreement and William has gone. He is a good player though and we wish him well."

Certainly, the general opinion that has lasted ever since is not that Prunier was a good player, as he invariably features whenever an 'all time worst United XI' is selected. That may be a little harsh as, although he went to have a nomadic career, he finally settled at Toulouse where he was nominated in the Ligue 1 team of the season in 2002-03. There have been worse central defenders to have played for the club.

THE COMEBACK

6th January 1996 - FA Cup Third Round
Old Trafford, Manchester. Att. 41,563

UNITED 2-2 SUNDERLAND

Scorers: Butt 12, Cantona 80
Team : Pilkington, G.Neville (P.Neville 65), Bruce, Pallister, Irwin, Beckham (Sharpe 59), Butt, Keane, Giggs, Cantona, Cole

A STRONG UNITED TEAM took the lead early on when Nicky Butt took advantage of an Andy Cole assist to score in the 12th minute. It should have been enough to give the hosts control but instead the performance became flat and after half time Sunderland were encouraged to come out and attack. They were rewarded for their enterprise (Ferguson later admitted that United had been outplayed for most of the game) with two quick fire goals; substitute Steve Agnew equalised and three minutes later Craig Russell gave the visitors the lead after some incredibly slack defending presented him with plenty of space after which Gary Neville was immediately substituted for his brother. Sometimes however it takes such an event to wake a team up and the Old Trafford crowd finally roused themselves. Sunderland defended far better than their hosts and it took a moment of real quality; a floated ball from Lee Sharpe that was impossible to defend that was met by Cantona at the far post, to level things up with 10 minutes to go.

"I couldn't see us getting out of trouble," Ferguson admitted to the *Sunday Express*. It was a worrying confession to make and, when one considers the recent inconsistency of his team, one could reasonably assume that the manager was speaking as much about his team in general as about the individual result.

Kevin Pilkington had coped well enough with the pressure of deputising for the injured Peter Schmeichel and certainly hadn't let anybody down (on this occasion, horrendous defending in front of him had cost United the chance of victory). But there was a bigger picture to consider, although the defence that lined up in front of him for the Sunderland game was the strongest he could expect, it had not enjoyed a settled run together and whether through form or consistency, the manager would be justifiably have concerns. Peter Schmeichel had hardly been at his most reliable, his form hadn't been particularly poor since his return from surgery but United's rearguard had been vulnerable for sometime. Now, with the prospect of the Dane having a further period out of the side, Ferguson was forced into a corner. If there was any doubt regarding Schmeichel's ability to perform to the standard expected of him, it would be a dereliction of duty to not seek a senior reinforcement.

It was enough of a gamble that there was inexperience further up the pitch but it wasn't wise for United to field inexperience in goal. The injuries in December had proven such a hindrance to the title challenge and so for the first time this season (if the signing of Nick Culkin shortly after the York City game doesn't really count) the manager made a move into the market for a senior player. The £500,000 capture of Manchester City custodian Tony Coton is one of the most forgotten transfers in Manchester United history but is arguably one of the most important of the 90's, considering that it could be said to be a catalyst for a marked improvement in other players.

The consequences would be revealed later on but Coton, for some time sidelined by Eike Immel at Manchester City, came with the pedigree and experience that suggested he would bring a greater assurance to a back line unused to playing with each other. And, unlike Gary Walsh who had left in search of first team football, Coton was content to serve as deputy. "I've played over 500 league games and I'll be 35 soon so my circumstances are totally different to Gary Walsh's, who had to establish himself and get his career going," Tony explained to the club's official magazine, adding that he was 'ecstatic' when he heard of United's interest. Asked if it was true that his new manager had pointed out the example of Les Sealey to 'lure' him to Old Trafford, Coton replied, "He certainly did. If I can equal what Les achieved and be as lucky for the club as Les was, then that will be brilliant."

Predictably, as soon as he'd made a move to bolster the experience, the manager was forced to select a team without Gary Pallister for the visit of Aston Villa who, of course, had destroyed United on the opening day.

FA CUP THIRD ROUND

Watford 1-1 Wimbledon; Reading 3-1 Gillingham; Walsall 1-0 Wigan Athletic; Leicester City 0-0 Manchester City; Notts County 1-2 Middlesbrough; Aston Villa 3-0 Gravesend & Northfleet; Grimsby Town 7-1 Luton Town; Crewe Alexandra 4-3 West Bromwich Albion; Swindon Town 2-0 Woking; Ipswich Town 0-0 Blackburn Rovers; Tranmere Rovers 0-2 Queens Park Rangers; Fulham 1-1 Shrewsbury Town; Barnsley 0-0 Oldham Athletic; West Ham United 2-0 Southend United; Norwich City 1-2 Brentford; Plymouth Argyle 1-3 Coventry City; Bradford City 0-3 Bolton Wanderers; Millwall 3-3 Oxford United; Crystal Palace 0-0 Port Vale; Huddersfield Town 2-1 Blackpool; Charlton Athletic 2-0 Sheffield Wednesday; Arsenal 1-1 Sheffield United; Hereford United 1-1 Tottenham Hotspur; Stoke City 1-1 Nottingham Forest; Peterborough United 1-0 Wrexham; Birmingham City 1-1 Wolverhampton Wanderers; Liverpool 7-0 Rochdale;

SUNDAY 7TH JANUARY 1996: Southampton 3-0 Portsmouth; Derby County 2-4 Leeds United; Everton 2-2 Stockport County; Chelsea 1-1 Newcastle United

WEDNESDAY 10TH JANUARY 1996: League Cup Quarter-finals - Arsenal 2-0 Newcastle United; Aston Villa 1-0 Wolverhampton Wanderers; Leeds United 2-1 Reading; Norwich City 1-1 Birmingham City

13TH JANUARY 1996 - FA CARLING PREMIERSHIP
OLD TRAFFORD, MANCHESTER. ATT. 42,667

UNITED 0-0 ASTON VILLA

Team : Schmeichel, Irwin, Bruce, G.Neville, P.Neville,
Sharpe (Scholes 78), Keane, Butt, Giggs, Cantona, Cole

The manager was well aware of the task that faced his side, describing Villa as a 'very tough team' under Brian Little. And for all of United's title aspirations, it is worth pointing out that Villa were just six points behind them with two games in hand. A win for the away team would give them a realistic opportunity of overhauling their opponents, although Newcastle also had two games in hand and a seven point lead. Anything less than a win for United at Old Trafford felt as if it would mean that the title race was as good as over.

But Villa came as spoilers, content for a point with a three man central defence of Ehiogu, McGrath and Southgate. The crowd did their best to inspire the home team and it was the Reds who had the best of the chances (led by the freshly shorn Eric Cantona, who was described as having a 'menacing, convict-style look' by the *Daily Mirror*) but it was as nailed on a 0-0 as there was ever likely to be in a league fixture.

The *Daily Express* suggested that was as much down to United's inability to click as Villa's impressive rearguard display. "Cantona's co-ordination with Andy Cole is not what he enjoyed with Mark Hughes," they wrote. In addition to the comment made about Cole's inability to match his movement in co-operation which United's passing moves, there was now a strong theory that suggested the forward may simply not be compatible. After all, with Cantona guaranteed of selection and with the style of football played by the young players breaking through bordering on telepathic, Cole was faced with the task of getting himself in sync with this or face the consequences. And, although Ferguson was a fan of the striker, he was first and foremost faithful to success.

A third draw in five home league games had, alongside those three away defeats, contributed towards a serious deficit in the league. Newcastle, with two games in hand, could stretch their advantage to twelve points before United next kicked a ball in the league at Upton Park the following Monday. They did just that, defeating Coventry City and then Bolton Wanderers by single goals. These narrow victories suggested that Newcastle

OTHER LEAGUE RESULTS:

SATURDAY 13 JANUARY 1996

Bolton 1-0 Wimbledon
Everton 1-1 Chelsea
Leeds 2-0 West Ham
Middlesbro' 2-3 Arsenal
Nott'm Forest 1-0 Soton
QPR 0-1 Blackburn
Sheff Wed 1-1 Liverpool
Spurs 1-0 Man City

SUNDAY 14 JANUARY 1996

Coventry 0-1 Newcastle

were resolute enough to cope with the run-in, although, even after seeing his team secure that twelve point lead, Magpies manager Kevin Keegan was a little cautious. "We're in a great position but we've got to go to some tough places and some tough opposition is still to come here," he insisted. "Man United have got to come here yet and they really turned us over at Old Trafford. I don't mind everyone else singing our praises as long as myself, Terry Mac, Arthur Cox and the lads realise what situation we're in and how much work we've got to do to win it."

Before Bolton went up to Newcastle to be defeated, United travelled to the North East themselves, for the FA Cup replay against Sunderland.

16TH JANUARY 1996
ROKER PARK, SUNDERLAND. ATT. 21,378

SUNDERLAND 1-2 UNITED

Scorers: Scholes 69, Cole 89
Team : Schmeichel, Parker (Sharpe 46), Bruce, G.Neville, Irwin,
P.Neville, Butt (Scholes 62), Keane, Giggs, Cantona, Cole

Flying high in the division below, with every expectation that they would be promoted to the Premier League at the end of the year (an expectation that was fulfilled) Sunderland were full of confidence. United, struggling with their central defensive pairing of an out of position Gary Neville and out of form Steve Bruce, had an extra man in there for this game, Paul Parker. The idea was that three would be better than two (although a variation of this formation had been tried for a period in that disastrous game at Spurs) and as the manager said, "I played an extra man at the back because I didn't want them to score in the first half." That plan lasted for 24 minutes. United were punished for their poor play in that area when Phil Gray (who appeared to be offside) popped up to slot past Peter Schmeichel. Parker was hauled off at half-time for Sharpe and United switched to a more attacking formation to chase the game.

With nothing forthcoming after the break and the 'Roker Roar' in full cry, joyously revelling in the schadenfreude of former Newcastle hero Andy Cole's supposed lack of fortune, Ferguson made a decisive switch, bringing on Paul Scholes for Nicky Butt in the 62nd minute. It paid instant dividends; Scholes manipulated some space at the edge of the area just six minutes after coming on and powered the ball past the previously excellent Alec Chamberlain.

Having put so much effort into the tie, Sunderland's players began to tire, and it was United on the front foot as the game looked destined to head to extra time. As the game headed for injury time, Lee Sharpe whipped in a fabulous cross into a packed penalty area and who else but Cole was waiting at the far post. His header was nonetheless excellent, flying into the opposite corner, giving Chamberlain absolutely no chance. If seasons can be defined by moments, this could certainly be seen as a turning point in retrospect.

"They're not lucky. They've got quality players who come up with the goods when they need it," said a sporting Peter Reid afterwards. United's reward for this victory was another First Division opponent, Reading at Elm Park in the Fourth Round. Before that, there was a trip to West Ham United, a team who had made it a point to enjoy the misery of the Red Devils in recent years.

OTHER RESULTS:

FA CUP THIRD ROUND REPLAYS

Blackburn Rovers 0–1 Ipswich Town Shrewsbury Town 2–1 Fulham Sunderland 1–2 Manchester United Oxford United 1–0 Millwall Port Vale 4–3 Crystal Palace

WEDNESDAY 17TH JANUARY 1996

Wimbledon 1–0 Watford; Manchester City 5–0 Leicester City; Stockport County 2–3 Everton; Newcastle United 2–2 Chelsea (2-4 on pens); Sheffield United 1–0 Arsenal; Tottenham Hotspur 5–1 Hereford United; Nottingham Forest 2–0 Stoke City; Wolverhampton Wanderers 2–1 Birmingham City; Oldham Athletic 2–1 Barnsley

THE COMEBACK

22ND JANUARY 1996 - FA CARLING PREMIERSHIP
UPTON PARK, LONDON. ATT. 24,197

WEST HAM 0-1 UNITED

Scorer: Cantona 8

Team : Schmeichel, P.Neville, G.Neville, Bruce, Irwin, Giggs, Butt, Keane, Sharpe, Cantona, Cole (Beckham 77)

If it was commonly agreed that Eric Cantona and Ryan Giggs had been the star men in United's season to this point, then it should also be observed that rarely had the two combined with each other to any great extent this campaign. A goal against Southampton; Giggs winning the penalty against Liverpool – these were brief moments that proved the exception to the rule. This was corrected as early as the eighth minute here when Giggs' outrageous piece of skill on the half way line caught out the physical menace of Julian Dicks. Giggs was quick enough to speed on to a back-heeled flick which spun around the former Liverpool defender, and then carry the ball forward towards the penalty area. Dicks came back at him but he was beaten again, then Giggs played a one-two with Cole, and drilled a right footed cross with accuracy across the face of goal. Lee Sharpe, playing on the left wing, missed it but Cantona was lurking on the line of the six yard box close to the byline. It was not an easy finish, but the Frenchman took it on first time with his left foot and it went high into the goal.

It seemed that United had a point to prove to a club that had derived such pleasure from their failures in recent years and it was their combativeness which gave this game an edge. They were physical and dominant, clearly deserving to be in front but at times they were guilty of stepping over the line. Bruce, Neville, Sharpe, Cole and Butt were all booked, with the latter seeing red for a second bookable offence. That was the only way it seemed West Ham would get back into the game and they fought back at that point, bringing out the best in Gary Neville and Peter Schmeichel in goal. United held on to grind out a win that was made more uncertain than it needed to be but the manager was nonetheless impressed with the performance. "We should have been three or four up, some of the football was marvellous, but we got careless with possession after half time," he said.

"We have the quality, there's no question about that," he told Sky Sports after the win. "It really depends on how Newcastle handle it. They've some tough away fixtures–we've had a lot of tough away fixtures all out of the road. But I think once it comes to March, it doesn't matter which game you're playing when you're going for the title every one's really hard, each one's difficult, it doesn't matter who it is; we've experienced that over the years and who knows?"

One extra point of note was that at various points when tempers threatened to flare, Eric Cantona stepped in to diffuse the situation–between Julian Dicks and Roy Keane. "In the middle of the flying boots and fury of Upton Park, Cantona turned into Daddy Cool. He even acted as peacemaker at one stage," said the *Mail on Sunday*. It was a good time to display this new found tranquil side–next up for United in the league was a return to Selhurst Park.

LEAGUE CUP QUARTER-FINAL REPLAY - Birmingham City 2–1 Norwich City

OTHER LEAGUE RESULTS:
SATURDAY 20 JANUARY 1996
Arsenal 1-2 Everton
Blackburn 3-0 Sheff Wed
Chelsea 1-0 Nott'm Forest
Liverpool 5-0 Leeds
Man City 1-1 Coventry
Newcastle 2-1 Bolton
Soton 2-1 Middlesbro
Wimbledon 2-1 QPR
SUNDAY 21 JANUARY 1996
Aston Villa 2-1 Spurs

THE COMEBACK

27TH JANUARY 1996 - FA CUP FOURTH ROUND
ELM PARK, READING. ATT. 14,780

READING 0-3 UNITED

Scorers: Giggs 36, Parker 56, Cantona 89
Team : Schmeichel, P.Neville (Parker 53), G.Neville, Bruce, Irwin,
Giggs, Butt, Keane, Sharpe, Cantona, Cole

Before then, however, it was down to Reading for an FA Cup game. "This was FA Cup heaven," gushed the *Telegraph*, referring to the conditions at Reading's small Elm Park; the wooden stands and a dreadful pitch that looked as if it had been read the last rites after a long winter. The sort of pitch commentators are fond of describing as a leveller. "It was the story of the banana skin that wasn't," said the *Daily Mail*, after United had cantered to a comfortable 3-0 victory. "Manchester United's sure-footed progress into the fifth round was conspicuous, not only for Eric Cantona's polite return of the half-eaten banana some ignoramus threw at him in the second half."

Cantona had the final say in this tie, scoring in the last minute to round off the 3-0 scoreline. Ryan Giggs had given the Reds the lead with a simple goal in the 36th minute and then Paul Parker, only just on as a substitute, scored with a mis-hit cross which flew wildly past Nicky Hammond 10 minutes after half time.

It was a disciplined and controlled performance from United and the manager was particularly impressed by how his young stars played. "I am relieved to come away with a win," he said. "I told them to be sensible and keep it simple. Reading are one of the best footballing sides in the First Division. I thought that Neville and Bruce were magnificent. They are both good organisers, which in Neville's case is amazing for a 20 year old. He is performing like an experienced player."

Impressive though it was, it was as routine a victory as should be expected but United's next game would be decidedly more tense, particularly as Newcastle sought to maintain their nine point lead with a straightforward home game against Sheffield Wednesday.

FA CUP FOURTH ROUND - Everton 2–2 Port Vale; Tottenham Hotspur 1–1 Wolverhampton Wanderers

SUNDAY 28TH JANUARY 1996 - Sheffield United 0–1 Aston Villa

MONDAY 29TH JANUARY 1996 - Queens Park Rangers 1–2 Chelsea

PREMIER LEAGUE AS AT 1ST FEBRUARY 1996									
1	Newcastle United	23	17	3	3	45	19	54	26
2	Manchester United	24	13	6	5	42	27	45	15
3	Liverpool	23	12	6	5	46	21	42	25
4	Tottenham Hotspur	24	11	8	5	33	24	41	9
5	Aston Villa	22	11	6	5	29	16	39	13
6	Blackburn Rovers	24	11	5	8	37	26	38	11
7	Arsenal	24	10	7	7	32	24	37	8
8	Nottingham Forest	23	9	10	4	33	32	37	1
9	Everton	24	10	6	8	35	26	36	9
10	Chelsea	24	9	9	6	25	25	36	0
11	Leeds United	23	10	5	8	30	32	35	-2
12	Middlesbrough	24	9	6	9	26	26	33	0
13	Sheffield Wednesday	23	6	8	9	33	36	26	-3
14	Wimbledon	24	6	6	12	33	46	24	-13
15	Southampton	23	5	8	10	22	33	23	-11
16	West Ham United	22	6	5	11	22	33	23	-11
17	Coventry City	23	4	8	11	29	45	20	-16
18	Manchester City	23	5	5	13	13	33	20	-20
19	Queens Park Rangers	24	5	3	16	18	36	18	-18
20	Bolton Wanderers	24	3	4	17	23	46	13	-23

THE COMEBACK

WIMBLEDON 2-4 UNITED

Scorers: Cole 41, Perry og. 45, Cantona 71(pen),81
Team : Schmeichel, P.Neville, G.Neville, Bruce (Beckham 15), Irwin,
Giggs, Butt, Keane, Sharpe, Cantona, Cole

Though an injury forced Ferguson into an early reshuffle, he was left thoroughly satisfied by his side's response. "When Steve Bruce was stretchered off, we were left with an extremely young team. But I think they coped remarkably well, particularly in the first half," said the boss. He was right to give such praise. By half time, United had settled down so admirably that they had cruised into a two goal lead through an Andy Cole header and a Chris Perry own goal. Marcus Gayle pulled one back for the Dons early in the second half before Cantona converted a spot-kick three minutes later. Within minutes however Jason Euell had put the game back in the balance to make it 3-2.

David Beckham, on the periphery of the first team in recent weeks, had been brought on for Bruce and seized his opportunity, particularly impressing in the second half. It was from his 81st minute chipped cross that Cantona scored his second goal and United's fourth to sew up the points.

"Few experts have given United the praise they deserve for sticking to home-grown players and largely ignoring foreign imports," reported the perceptive *Daily Mail*. "Lads like Gary Neville, who saved his side with a couple of outstanding tackles, have the loyalty and camaraderie that good teams need to foster to become great teams."

Suddenly, United had four away wins on the spin under their belts. Newcastle had won their game against Sheffield Wednesday to keep their nine point lead and they still had a game in hand, too, so it wasn't necessarily a case of chasing Newcastle rather than keeping faith and developing the kids.

In truth, there were mature performances from all of the young heads on the Selhurst Park pitch. Phil Neville, in an extended run at right back, was beginning to impress so much that Gary Neville's deputising at centre half was to come at a cost as Gary Pallister and David May were back in contention for the following game at home to Blackburn Rovers.

Rovers had recovered some form on the back of strong home form, following a harrowing start to the season that had seen their title defence crumble before it had began and an embarassing first foray into the Champions League end in disarray. Yet Rovers' away form was almost as dreadful as Leeds United's had been in their own title defence of 1992/93. Now in sixth place, nineteen points behind Newcastle, their ambitions were scaled back to qualifying for the UEFA Cup.

OTHER LEAGUE RESULTS:

WEDNESDAY 31 JANUARY 1996

Aston Villa 0-2 Liverpool
Nott'm Forest 2-1 Leeds
West Ham 3-2 Coventry
Southampton 1-1 Man City

SATURDAY 3 FEBRUARY 1996

Arsenal 1-1 Coventry
Aston Villa 3-0 Leeds
Blackburn 3-1 Bolton
Liverpool 0-0 Spurs
Man City 2-0 QPR
Newcastle 2-0 Sheff Wed
Southampton 2-2 Everton
West Ham 1-0 Nott'm F

SUNDAY 4 FEBRUARY 1996

Chelsea 5-0 Middlesbrough

★

In early February, Kevin Keegan completed the protracted signing of the controversial Colombian striker Faustino Asprilla. Only the Newcastle manager can explain what particular qualities he had hoped Asprilla would bring to his team, although it seems logical to suggest that he wanted the 'Cantona' effect on his own team. to find that missing piece that plugged everything together and, perhaps, added an extra attacking spark to what was already a pretty effective unit.

Like Cantona, Asprilla brought bags of talent and unpredictability to Tyneside but thoughts turned to another controversial showman signed at the height of a title race; Rodney Marsh signed for table-topping Manchester City in 1972 and later admitted he cost the Blues the league. His play, like Asprilla's, was laden with tricks and flicks but at the expense of a well established team dynamic.

If Keegan wished for the same kind of talisman Ferguson had discovered in Cantona he was let down in two crucial elements. Firstly, the prospect of signing his man out of the blue, and secondly, the fact that Asprilla was rarely first choice at Parma. The Newcastle manager perhaps hoped that the lack of football would make the signing happen swiftly but Parma chairman Giorgio Pedraneschi wasn't playing ball. It transpired that the Magpies claimed that they had concerns over a knee injury allegedly suffered by the forward (after the clubs had agreed a fee and Asprilla had already undergone a medical) and were seeking to reduce the price for him. Pedraneschi was so outraged by the allegation that he threatened to go to FIFA to seek arbitration.

Their insistence that coach Nevio Scala simply didn't fancy playing him didn't necessarily portray Asprilla as the box-office star they had hoped to unleash on Tyneside but when the move was finally concluded, it didn't stop the reports of the signing suggesting such. The time it took to resolve the signing did not impress the new man. "I'm still tempted by Newcastle's offer but, seeing how things have gone, I'm quite happy to stay at Parma," he had said on February 4th, just days before arriving at Newcastle.

After this saga, it is probably little surprise that despite enjoying cult status in the North East, the signing didn't quite have the desired impact, even if Asprilla made an immediate impression in the Tyne-Tees derby on February 10th.

With Newcastle trailing to Middlesbrough, he came off the bench to immediately create an equaliser for Steve Watson. When Les Ferdinand shot from the edge of the area and ex-United stopper Walsh felt it squirm under his body and into the 'Boro net, commentator Martin Tyler excitedly prematurely exclaimed, "When things like that happen, you must believe that you're gonna win the Championship!"

FA CUP FOURTH ROUND - Shrewsbury Town 0-4 Liverpool; Huddersfield Town 2-0 Peterborough United

WEDNESDAY 7TH FEBRUARY 1996 - Southampton 1-1 Crewe Alexandra; Nottingham Forest 1-1 Oxford United; Middlesbrough 0-0 Wimbledon; Coventry City 2-2 Manchester City; West Ham United 1-1 Grimsby Town; Charlton Athletic 3-2 Brentford - REPLAY: Wolverhampton Wanderers 0-2 Tottenham Hotspur

10TH FEBRUARY 1996 - FA CARLING PREMIERSHIP
OLD TRAFFORD, MANCHESTER. ATT. 42,681

UNITED 1-0 BLACKBURN ROVERS

Scorer: Sharpe 14
Team : Schmeichel, P.Neville, Pallister, May, Irwin, Beckham, Keane, Giggs, Sharpe, Cantona, Cole

If United had been aware of events at the Riverside Stadium, it may have made this occasion more nerve-wracking but this low key encounter was decided very early on when Lee Sharpe's instinctive response after Andy Cole's shot had hit the post on 15 minutes was crucial. Sharpe was arguably the game's outstanding player, having been given a short run in the team after a poor outing at Leeds. "Sharpe was a revelation on the left flank," said the *Sunday Mirror*. "Sharpe has feared his days at Old Trafford were numbered as he failed to find his best form. But there was proof enough here that he's back to the player the fans had worshipped when he was a talented teenager."

The point was never to do with Sharpe's talent, more, his application of it. Whilst not possessing the same pace or perhaps mesmerising dribbling ability of Giggs, he did seem more assured and clinical in front of goal and also had the kind of direct penetration that was of wonderful value. In the absence of Kanchelskis, it was vital that he was kept around, only, of course, while he was applying himself in the proper manner. Perhaps Sharpe's eventual departure from United is a matter for a record other than this but it is worth noting that when he applied himself, he was capable of great things.

His goal spread confidence in the team so that they were able to display the maturity required to register their first home league win since the turn of the year, a time when William Prunier was deemed the answer to United's defensive woes. A lot had happened in those five weeks but at least now the Red Devils were on the right track and it seemed that Alex Ferguson may even have stumbled upon a winning combination in the centre of defence with May and Pallister coping with the threat of Alan Shearer, the division's outstanding striker, with so much ease that the Blackburn number nine ended up being booked for a lunge on Schmeichel in frustration. Perhaps that annoyance was more to do with Blackburn's season in general but it said much about what the neutral thought of the scale of this fixture that it wasn't even selected for television. A fall from grace indeed for the two teams who had finished as champions and runners-up in each of the last two seasons.

OTHER LEAGUE RESULTS:

SATURDAY 10 FEBRUARY 1996

Bolton 0-2 Aston Villa
Coventry 1-0 Chelsea
Everton 2-0 Man City
Middlesbro' 1-2 Newcastle
Nott'm Forest 0-1 Arsenal
Sheff Wed 2-1 Wimbledon

SUNDAY 11 FEBRUARY 1996

QPR 1-2 Liverpool

MONDAY 12 FEBRUARY 1996

Spurs 0-1 West Ham

★

There was nothing low key about United's next game. With the North Stand nearing completion, Manchester City supporters were allowed in to Old Trafford for the second derby of the season, and it made a far better occasion than the October clash.

Before that, however, on Valentine's Day, Merseyside was shocked by the passing of Bob Paisley, a manager considered by many to be Liverpool's greatest ever. Paisley won six league titles and three European Cups duiring his nine year reign – a period that will be remembered as the most successful in the club's history. Having been handed the task of succeeding Bill Shankly, it was no mean feat, especially as many doubted that Shanks' achievements could ever be matched, never mind bettered. Manchester United's own problems in finding successors for their successful managers is an indication of the scale of Paisley's achievements in maintaining Liverpool's position at the top of the tree for so long,

Now, with Manchester United still nine points behind Newcastle (who still had that game in hand), despite their recent improvement in form and performances, few suggested that Alex Ferguson would be claiming his third title in fourth years; let alone that he would ultimately go on to surpass Paisley's impressive haul of seven titles in nine seasons.

LEAGUE CUP SEMI-FINAL FIRST LEG - Birmingham City 1–2 Leeds United

FA CUP FOURTH ROUND - Swindon Town 1–0 Oldham Athletic

TUESDAY 13TH FEBRUARY 1996

FA CUP FOURTH ROUND - Ipswich Town 1–0 Walsall

REPLAYS - Crewe Alexandra 2–3 Southampton; Oxford United 0–3 Nottingham Forest; Wimbledon 1–0 Middlesbrough

WEDNESDAY 14TH FEBRUARY 1996

FA CUP FOURTH ROUND- Bolton Wanderers 0–1 Leeds United

FA CUP FOURTH ROUND REPLAY - Port Vale 2–1 Everton; Manchester City 2–1 Coventry City; Grimsby Town 3–0 West Ham United

LEAGUE CUP SEMI-FINAL FIRST LEG - Arsenal 2–2 Aston Villa

THE COMEBACK

18TH FEBRUARY 1996 - FA CUP FIFTH ROUND
OLD TRAFFORD, MANCHESTER. ATT. 42,692

UNITED 2-1 MANCHESTER CITY

Scorers: Cantona 38, Sharpe 77
Team : Schmeichel, P.Neville, Bruce, Pallister, Irwin,
Sharpe, Keane, Butt, Giggs, Cantona, Cole

The presence of away fans helped the derby atmosphere immensly and the players appeared more up for this derby from the off compared to the earlier league game between the two clubs which had been a moribund affair. Immediately Cantona was involved in a tussle on the right hand side and Roy Keane found himself yellow-carded as early as the third minute. Ferguson's team set out to match any physicality and Keane may even have found himself sent off after reacting furiously to Michael Brown, who had to leap out of the way of a reckless Nicky Butt tackle. Butt's challenge was the type that could have easily earned a red card in the modern era, but Brown's reaction, stamping on Butt, was enough to rile Keane, with some justification. It may have been the manager's intention to send his team out riled up but it appeared as if the physical battle had distracted them from their game and City took advantage. Their main playmaker, Georgi Kinkladze, played a painfully simple through ball to Uwe Rosler and the likeable German ran into space before chipping the ball over an advancing Schmeichel to the delight of the City fans housed in K Stand.

United's response was anxious but they came close when Roy Keane headed a Ryan Giggs corner towards goal, Eike Immel in the City goal had to extend at full stretch to deny him an equaliser. Yet the game turned at the resulting corner. Michael Frontzeck and Cantona jumped for the ball and the whistle blew. Roy Keane is seen remonstrating with the referee Alan Wilkie before it dawns on him that he has given a penalty. Then it is the City players' turn to remonstrate. Replays suggest that although there was a contact the ball flew 10 feet over the penalty area. Nevertheless Cantona, as cool as ever, sent Immel the wrong way to restore parity and City's sense of being aggrieved only served to further intensify the atmosphere. Ironically, it was Alan Wilkie who had dismissed Cantona at Selhurst Park back in January 1995 so he clearly attracted controversy.

While the half-time break came at the right time to calm some tempers, the torrential downpour of rain and sleet that followed the referee's whistle meant that there was little chance of diffusing that typical cup tie atmosphere. City were deflated, perhaps feeling that their opportunity had passed them by, and fuelled by the anger of the penalty and the thought they should be facing a team with just 10 men. United were able to keep their composure and their patience finally paid off when Phil Neville raced on to a Ryan Giggs through ball and clipped the ball back into the area. Lee Sharpe met it on the half volley, and the shot was too powerful (or too slippery) for Immel to deal with. City's response was timid and the game petered out with nothing of the intensity it had started with. Not that it mattered to United, who recorded their fifth consecutive win to march in to the quarter finals, with the hope that consistency was finally starting to develop.

OTHER RESULTS - SATURDAY 17TH FEBRUARY 1996

FA CUP FIFTH ROUND: Grimsby Town 0–0 Chelsea; Liverpool 2–1 Charlton Athletic; Swindon Town 1–1 Southampton; Ipswich Town 1–3 Aston Villa; Huddersfield Town 2–2 Wimbledon

THE COMEBACK

WEDNESDAY 21ST FEBRUARY 1996
FA CARLING PREMIERSHIP
OLD TRAFFORD, MANCHESTER. ATT. 42,459

UNITED 2-0 EVERTON

Scorers: Keane 30, Giggs 81
Team : Schmeichel, P.Neville, Bruce, Pallister, Irwin,
Sharpe (Beckham 83), Keane, Butt, Giggs, Cantona, Cole

Andrei Kanchelskis was able to last the full ninety minutes on his return to the club where he had made his reputation, though it was hardly any more enjoyable than his first experience of playing against his former team. "At Old Trafford the experience was surreal!" he now admits. "The fans were understandably hostile and brimming with the emotion that I was so familiar with. But at that time it was not to my benefit... To be honest I didn't feel an awful lot at first. I was too busy concentrating on my game. Then after ten or fifteen minutes the nerves kicked in. Seeing all the familiar faces play against me, rather than with me, was an interesting feeling that I have never really experienced in that kind of environment."

What would have been familiar was the cold; freezing temperatures and snowfall made for a bitter experience for all in attendance in this evening fixture. "We are going to try our utmost for the championship, let there be no doubt about it,'"declared a positive Ferguson in his programme notes.

Everton were game, starting brightly and having plenty of the ball. Then United warmed up themselves and managed to get a crucial goal during a period of dominance. Nicky Butt and Roy Keane linked up on the half hour, the latter scoring the goal to give the hosts the lead. Though decisive, Everton refused to lie down and accept defeat; midfielder John Ebbrell forcing Schmeichel into an outstanding second half save to deny the Toffees an equaliser. United were finally able to relax nine minutes from time after they scored a truly exceptional goal; Cole and Giggs countered at top speed, with the number 17 providing a wonderful cross for the man who normally provided goals. Giggs was as clinical as he had been to settle the reverse fixture, lobbing the bouncing

OTHER LEAGUE RESULTS:

Chelsea 1-2 West Ham
Middlesbrough 1-4 Bolton
Sheff Wed 1-3 QPR
West Ham 2-0 Newcastle

ball over his experienced compatriot Neville Southall. It was a goal of the highest quality which sealed a seventh consecutive win and sent a message to Tyneside about United's true title credentials.

"Just as the pressure mounted and almost destroyed Blackburn last season, United are once again staging an ominous onslaught," reported the *Daily Star*.

Meanwhile in London, the pressure seemed to be felt by the league leaders, who succumbed to defeat at Upton Park. West Ham, with goals eight minutes from the start and end, inflicted Newcastle's fourth league defeat of the season and by the time Alex Ferguson's team were back in action, Newcastle had dropped another two points at relegation strugglers Manchester City. It was an epic, topsy-turvy 3-3 draw that saw the Magpies come from behind on three separate occasions, giving some indication of their fighting spirit but the concession of three goals to a struggling team highlighted a defensive frailty ahead of their next league game, at home to Manchester United.

OTHER RESULTS:

FA CUP FIFTH ROUND : Leeds United 0-0 Port Vale

LEAGUE CUP SEMI-FINAL SECOND LEG: Aston Villa 0-0 Arsenal (agg 2-2 – Villa won on away goals)

25TH FEBRUARY 1996 - FA CARLING PREMIERSHIP
BURNDEN PARK, BOLTON. ATT. 21,481

BOLTON WANDERERS 0-6 UNITED

Scorers: Beckham 3, Bruce 15, Cole 70, Scholes 75,78, Butt 89

Team : Schmeichel, P.Neville, Bruce, Pallister, Irwin, Beckham, Keane, Butt, Giggs (McClair 57), Cantona (Scholes 73), Cole

And so the Reds made the short trip to Burnden Park knowing that a win would reduce the lead at the top to four points. Bolton were rooted to the bottom, nine points from safety, and seemed like sitting ducks with United developing their vibrancy. The growing sense of optimism and momentum was in their favour; ironically, their opener here came about as the Trotters attempted to seize the early initiative. Bolton fatally decided their best way of getting a result was to push up and see if they could force an early goal; it was a tremendous gamble which didn't seem to appreciate the pace in United's side.

And sure enough, it took less than five minutes for this plan to be exploited; Cantona and Cole exchanged passes to deal with a clearance up the pitch from Bruce and Giggs was released on the left hand side. Giggs' recent form had been irresistible and he was clearly in the kind of mood to torment his opponent, Jimmy Phillips the unlucky victim on this occasion. The winger showed wonderful manipulation of the ball on a poor pitch to flick the ball over Phillips' head and then attempt what seemed like a ridiculous volley, just inside the box. The ball defeated veteran Keith Branagan but not the crossbar; it then bounced down against the inside of the post but to save any debate about whether

OTHER LEAGUE RESULTS:

SATURDAY 24 FEBRUARY 1996

Blackburn 2-3 Liverpool
Coventry 0-0 Middlesbro'
Everton 3-0 Nott'm Forest
Man City 3-3 Newcastle
Southampton 2-3 Chelsea
Spurs 1-0 Sheff Wed
West Ham 0-1 Arsenal
Wimbledon 3-3 Aston Villa

the ball had crossed the line, David Beckham was first to react to power home a header from close range.

The game was effectively over after just fifteen minutes. Beckham turned provider from a corner and Bruce was there to thunder in a trademark header of his own. Bolton were defeated and their heads went down; United conserved their energy and toyed with their opponents. That was until the 70th minute when Andy Cole rocketed in an effort following cute build up work from Nicky Butt and Brian McClair. The forward's shot smashed in via the crossbar with all the relief you might expect of a player struggling for form and confidence, not to mention a place in the side.

One player who was apparently immune to such struggles was Cantona; but with the Reds three goals to the good, the manager saw fit to give him a rest and give Paul Scholes a run out. If Bolton thought that was time to relax, they were horribly mistaken. Cole, free from the burden of trying to find a goal, now became the provider, finding Scholes in the box, and his shot took a nick before flying in. The youngster had been on the pitch for 100 seconds. And, in another 100 seconds, he found the net again; McClair's effort was dragged wide, so much so that it turned into the perfect pass for Scholes who was given a criminal amount of time and space in the box to instinctively convert, amid protestations of offside.

Bolton continued to search for some consolation and thought they had it when Nathan Blake converted a rebound but the goal was disallowed for a foul on the goalkeeper. And the woes of the hosts were compounded further in injury time when Cole put Butt through to score the sixth. It was a goal fully deserved for the midfielder, arguably the game's star performer, and it was also a goal which earned United their biggest away victory for almost 36 years (almost to the very day, a 6-0 win at Blackpool on 27th February, 1960).

"United took just 15 minutes at Burnden Park to prise open the Championship race with a victory that was like nipping next door and taking away your neighbour's furniture, although to be honest there is not a lot worth taking from Bolton," reported the *Daily Express*. Not true! Three valuable points were worth an awful lot and, considering the circumstances, perhaps more than their actual value.

OTHER RESULTS:

SUNDAY 25 FEBRUARY 1996

LEAGUE CUP SEMI-FINAL SECOND LEG: Leeds United 3–0 Birmingham City (agg 5-1)

TUESDAY 27TH FEBRUARY 1996

FA CUP FIFTH ROUND REPLAY: Port Vale 1–2 Leeds United

WEDNESDAY 28TH FEBRUARY 1996

FA CUP FIFTH ROUND:

Nottingham Forest 2–2 Tottenham Hotspur

FA CUP FIFTH ROUND REPLAY:

Chelsea 4–1 Grimsby Town;
Southampton 2–0 Swindon Town;
Wimbledon 3–1 Huddersfield Town

PREMIER LEAGUE AS AT 1ST MARCH								
1	Newcastle United	27	19	4	4	52	25	61	27
2	Manchester United	28	17	6	5	55	29	57	26
3	Liverpool	27	15	7	5	53	24	52	29
4	Aston Villa	26	13	7	6	37	21	46	16
5	Tottenham Hotspur	27	12	9	6	34	25	45	9
6	Arsenal	27	12	8	7	35	25	44	10
7	Everton	28	12	7	9	42	30	43	12
8	Chelsea	28	11	9	8	34	30	42	4
9	Blackburn Rovers	27	12	5	10	42	31	41	11
10	Nottingham Forest	27	10	10	7	35	38	40	-3
11	West Ham United	28	11	5	12	31	37	38	-6
12	Leeds United	25	10	5	10	31	37	35	-6
13	Middlesbrough	28	9	7	12	28	37	34	-9
14	Sheffield Wednesday	27	7	8	12	36	43	29	-7
15	Southampton	26	5	10	11	27	39	25	-12
16	Wimbledon	27	6	7	14	39	55	25	-16
17	Coventry City	27	5	10	12	33	49	25	-16
18	Manchester City	27	6	7	14	19	39	25	-20
19	Queens Park Rangers	27	6	3	18	22	41	21	-19
20	Bolton Wanderers	28	4	4	20	28	58	16	-30

ON THE MARCH

4TH MARCH 1996 - FA CARLING PREMIERSHIP
ST. JAMES' PARK. ATT. 36,854

NEWCASTLE UNITED 0-1 UNITED

Scorers: Cantona 51
Team: Schmeichel, Irwin, Bruce, G.Neville, P.Neville, Giggs, Keane, Butt, Sharpe, Cantona, Cole

THE WIN AT BOLTON had set up the long anticipated game of the season. The day before, Liverpool took Aston Villa apart to remain two points behind United and six behind Newcastle. The Koppites were determined that if there was to be more than one horse in this race, there would at least be three. But the likelihood was that if Newcastle won this game, they would restore their seven point advantage over Manchester United and, with a game still in hand, it would theoretically give them a ten point advantage with ten games to go. If the game was truly be a title decider, a home win was necessary, anything else would leave it wide open.

"Nothing, of course, will be decided tonight, whatever the score, but if we win I will feel the title is there for the taking," admitted Kevin Keegan in his pre-match programme notes about what he described as 'a mega game'.

And the 'Toon Army' were boosted by two disciplinary issues; David Ginola was available after suspension and Faustino Asprilla would also be able to play amid talk of an FA charge for misconduct following an altercation with Keith Curle in the game against City.

Additionally, Newcastle were giving a debut to David Batty, the fearless midfielder and title-winning star of the Leeds United side of 1992 and, of course, Blackburn of 1995. It was hoped that his experience would prove the difference. As Keegan put it himself, it was "the strongest squad of players this club has ever had".

It could certainly not be reported to be the same at Old Trafford, although the kids coming through would rapidly become the backbone of United's best ever squad. This task was a true test of their resolve and there were few better placed to comment on the fixture than David McCreery, who had starred for both clubs. "Anyone brought up in the youth set-up at Manchester United has the best possible start in life," he said in the programme.

Back at St. James' Park after wobbling in their last two games, Newcastle were looking to add to their perfect home record of thirteen consecutive wins in the 1995/96 season (fourteen if you included their last day victory in the 1994/95 season). With Manchester United on the back of eight consecutive wins of their own, this was the perfect footballing cliché - the immovable object against the irresistible force.

The home side were fired up from the off; twice in the opening five minutes, Les Ferdinand found space at the side of Steve Bruce. The first time, an on-rushing Peter Schmeichel managed to smother the ball before the England international was able to muster a shot, but the second time, the keeper was forced into a more orthodox save. Philippe Albert rattled the crossbar from a free kick and Ferdinand spurned the rebound, lashing it high and out of play.

Yet the abiding memory of the game being all Newcastle is somewhat selective; the visitors settled into their rhythm and could have scored themselves in the first half but Ryan Giggs' goal-bound effort was blocked by a home defender before it could trouble the goalkeeper. It was probably against the balance of the game but not against the run of it when the Reds took the lead

Eric delivers the coup de grâce

early in the second half. As stated, Batty was making his debut and it was clearly hoped that his credentials would add the composure to the Magpies' midfield but the symbolism on this day belonged to Roy Keane, whose part in the only goal of this game is often forgotten. Batty and Keane were contesting a loose ball which had been cleared out of the Newcastle defence but Keane won the battle easily and spread the ball left to Phil Neville, who exchanged passes with Andy Cole before lofting a left footed cross into the area. At the back post, arriving perfectly on cue, was Eric Cantona, striking his volley into the ground. The bounce made it awkward, impossible even, for Pavel Srnicek to deal with, and the ball went across him into the goal.

Sensing the importance of the goal, the forward's team-mates rushed towards him to join in the celebrations – the energy and adrenaline Cantona must have been feeling was clear for all to see when they caught up with him. Unable to struggle free from the grasp of Keane, Nicky Butt and Denis Irwin, Cantona released a primal scream. It became an iconic and enduring moment.

"We have hit a vein of form," Ferguson said later, "you've seen tonight the determination and team spirit we've got. That will carry us a long, long way, it gives us a chance, and a few weeks ago, the chance wasn't great."

When people speak of title deciders, there are few games in the Premier League era as defining as this one, fewer that lived up to the billing as this one did. In some senses, maybe it has gone too far the other way – maybe time has been kind to elements of Peter Schmeichel's performance. That is not to say it wasn't exceptional, but not in the way people tend to remember.

Talk of that game now and people will automatically refer to it as the best game of Schmeichel's career, the most prominent example of why he was rated by many as the best goalkeeper in the world. But were his saves that remarkable? Was he tested to the maximum? There are a plethora of more remarkable, gravity defying moments that hallmarked Schmeichel as a master of the art of goalkeeping. Denying Don Hutchison in front of Liverpool's Kop, that Gordon Banks style save in Vienna and the indelible memory of that huge frame suspended in the air at White Hart Lane, or, the star jump to deny Ivan Zamorano of Inter Milan in 1999. Even the 1997/1998 St. James' Park fixture between these two teams where Schmeichel pulled off a save probably more outstanding than any made in March 1996, flying through the air to deny John Barnes. All were examples more spectacular than any particular save he made in the game that has come to define his career.

Yet his performance could still be described as important for other reasons. Make no mistake, the saves had to be made. Someone not of Schmeichel's frame or instinct or big-game temperament may have struggled with Ferdinand's early efforts. Someone of lesser experience may have let the emotion of the occasion get to them after impressing so early on. And if one of those shots had found their way into the goal, then what impact would it have had on the rest of the season? Say Newcastle won, then what would that have done for their confidence?

It was Schmeichel's solidity and assurance that was exceptional. It was the arrogance to make those saves look easy, an Apollo Creed-esque routine of showboating to say 'you can't beat me', that saw the confidence slowly drain from the hosts as the visitors, weathered the early storm and the younger players grew accustomed to the occasion. Gary Neville took a while to get into it having been recalled to the team to replace Gary Pallister late on. However daunting the fixture seemed at kick-off, how much harder woiuld it have been had United conceeded early on?

United had struggled in the big games thus far that season. It is no coincidence that from this moment on the 'Fledglings' coped with the high pressure situations thrown at them. We can talk about obvious turning points in the title race but perhaps 4th March, 1996 was a turning point in the careers of the likes of the Nevilles, Nicky Butt and even Roy Keane, who was now becoming the boss of these big games.

Despite it not being perhaps his greatest showing, Schmeichel's performance was good for the reasons described for it dictated the pattern of the game and influenced the path of a title race still in the balance. Most importantly it helped men grow out of boys – how many goalkeeping performances have been as influential as that?

It is intriguing how that game is perceived as time has gone on. Ahead of Manchester United's visit to Newcastle in January 2016, *The Times* revisited the game with some quotes from the players. It's perhaps most appropriate to start with Schmeichel. "With players like Eric in the team it gave you the confidence to carry on, never give in, and think, 'We are going to win this'... I'm not trying to be arrogant, but you have to be like that every game. If you don't, you can't play for Manchester United. That's where the manager excelled; he infused that mentality in you."

Schmeichel's more contemporary recollection corroborates the account of Ferguson's himself in his 1999 autobiography.

"They say managers earn their wages in the ten or fifteen minutes they spend with their man at half-time," he wrote. "It is a wild over-simplification but there was some truth in it on this occasion. Motivation is never merely a matter of gung-ho ranting. Naturally, footballers cannot all be stirred by the same means. Some are self-motivated but sometimes even they have to be reminded of their own standards. That was the case in this match and so my words carried a general message for everyone in the room. In essence, I was asking if we could be happy with our standards in the first half and could we claim, on the basis of how we had performed in those forty-five minutes, that we wanted to win the title as much as Newcastle did? We were transformed after the interval and at least began to express ourselves effectively."

It wasn't just the away dressing room that seemed to present a telling mentality. "The tide was turning slightly and we were being chased, but Kevin Keegan, our manager, just said to us, 'This is where we put a marker down, this is where we win the league'. I remember Les (Ferdinand) coming in at half time and apologising, but it wasn't that he'd missed chances, it was just that Schmeichel was phenomenal," John Beresford told *The Times*. "Most of the time when you lose a game, you can understand it. That is the only defeat of my entire career that doesn't make any sense. That was the turning point." Steve Howey revealed that the mood after the game was difficult for the home team. "The dressing-room was deathly quiet afterwards. We were all looking at each other and thinking, 'How the fuck have we lost that?' It was complete pain."

In reality, the highlights of the game reveal a different story. Schmeichel made several good saves early on, Albert hit the bar from a free-kick and Les Ferdinand should have had two or three by half-time but after Cantona's goal, he was hardly troubled. Like Newcastle's title challenge, it fizzled out at the slightest set-back.

It could be said that this game marked the start of the 'mind games' era. The myth of United's invincibility is said to have lasted from here all the way up to Ferguson's retirement in 2013, barring a few seasons after the arrival of Jose Mourinho. Ferguson's role in proceedings here was given an unearthly quality. Schmeichel and Cantona may have been the heroes who did his bidding but few were in any doubt that it was the manager's input that had the greater impact. In stark contrast to his opposite number…

That one game, taken by itself, provides a compelling insight into Newcastle's fragile mentality and the importance of mind over matter in professional sports. It cannot be doubted that Newcastle had as much talent in their ranks as the Blackburn team that had won the title the previous season. They didn't have Alan Shearer (yet) and there's little doubt that Shearer would have buried at least on of the chances Ferdinand spurned, but they weren't lacking goals. Their front line had compensated for a perceived lack of defensive dominance all season and, of course, their defenders all seemed to have attacking prowess themselves. They were not dubbed "the Entertainers" with good cause, but the more that Newcastle's title challenge is studied, the more it always seemed destined to fail. Not so much because of the quality of their players but their mental attitude seemed lacking.

Any amateur psychologist could deduce that using phrases such as 'even if we don't win it' at the turn of the year at a time when they appeared in command, as a sentiment lacking authority and confidence. Newcastle had blown most teams away but it was beginning to feel as if their own manager was their biggest obstacle. The signing of Asprilla seemed reasonable in terms of what it was hoped he would provide, likewise Batty, but another message it sent

OTHER LEAGUE RESULTS:

WED 28 FEBRUARY 1996

Aston Villa 2-0 Blackburn

SATURDAY 2 MARCH 1996

Coventry 2-2 West Ham
Leeds 0-1 Bolton
Man City 1-1 Blackburn
Middlesbrough 0-2 Everton
QPR 1-1 Arsenal
Sheff Wed 1-3 Nott'm Forest
Spurs 1-0 Southampton
Wimbledon 1-1 Chelsea

SUNDAY 3 MARCH 1996

Liverpool 3-0 Aston Villa

to his own team was that he felt those two players were needed to get them over the line. That perhaps they, as a group, weren't good enough, even with such a huge lead. Of course, this theory is perfectly summarised by the sequence of events on match-day. It had gone from the manager declaring they could win the title here, to half time apologies, and full time heartache and within a few short weeks a realisation and even an acceptance of the inevitable. At the very least, there was a significant and tangible self-doubt present in the Newcastle team, and this was something that could be taken advantage of.

OTHER RESULTS:

UEFA CUP QUARTER-FINAL FIRST LEG - Bayern Munich 2–1 Nottingham Forest

11TH MARCH 1996 - FA CUP SIXTH ROUND
OLD TRAFFORD, MANCHESTER. ATT. 45,446

UNITED 2-0 SOUTHAMPTON

Scorers: Cantona 49, Sharpe 90
Team : Schmeichel, P.Neville, Bruce, G.Neville, Irwin,
Sharpe, Keane, Butt, Giggs, Cantona, Cole

There was a tremendous sense of deja-vu as, almost a week to the very minute since he had scored at St. James' Park, Eric Cantona maintained his record of scoring in every round in this season's FA Cup, thanks to an assist from Ryan Giggs. Southampton gave everything in an enterprising Cup tie, meaning Peter Schmeichel had to once more be on top form. The visitors had six efforts on target, meaning the goalkeeper was just about as over-worked as he had been the previous week. Once more, he could claim to be the game's best player, with Cantona the decider before he set up Lee Sharpe to score a second in injury time. The Old Trafford crowd, the largest of the season following the tiered opening of the North Stand, went home happy that their club had qualified for their third successive FA Cup semi-final.

"I thought it was a really tremendous cup tie tonight," said Alex Ferguson afterwards, although it's easy to be generous in victory; particularly one as straightforward as this eventually was.

"The Frenchman with a fuse as notoriously short as his shaven hair would not be everyone's obvious choice for the calm head in a storm," reported the *Daily Express* of the newly-shorn Cantona, "but on a night when United were forced to navigate through choppy waters to reach the FA Cup semi finals, King Eric proved his side's leader of men."

OTHER LEAGUE RESULTS:

TUESDAY 5 MARCH 1996

Arsenal 3-1 Man City

WEDNESDAY 6 MARCH 1996

Aston Villa 3-2 Sheff Wed

QPR 1-2 Leeds

SATURDAY 9 MARCH 1996

Aston Villa 4-2 QPR

Everton 2-2 Coventry

West Ham 2-0 Middlesbro'

ON THE MARCH

SATURDAY 9TH MARCH 1996

FA CUP FIFTH ROUND REPLAY: Tottenham Hotspur 1-1 Nottingham Forest
(Forest won 3-1 on penalties)

FA CUP SIXTH ROUND: Chelsea 2-2 Wimbledon

SUNDAY 10TH MARCH 1996: Leeds United 0-0 Liverpool

WEDNESDAY 13TH MARCH 1996: Nottingham Forest 0-1 Aston Villa

16TH MARCH 1996 - FA CARLING PREMIERSHIP
LOFTUS ROAD, LONDON. ATT. 18,817

QUEENS PARK RANGERS 1-1 UNITED

Scorer: Cantona 90
Team : Schmeichel, G.Neville, Bruce, May (Butt 74), Irwin, Beckham (Sharpe 74), Keane, McClair (Scholes 59), Giggs, Cantona, Cole

With Newcastle not due to play until Monday evening, Alex Ferguson had the perfect opportunity to test all of those theories about mentality and get his team to the top of the Premiership for the first time this season. And what better place to do it as their third consecutive away league game was at Queen's Park Rangers, who were 19th in the league. United started the game confidently, playing the sort of bright football which had seen them destroy Bolton (Ferguson later claimed he felt his team could have scored 'four or five' goals before half time); however Rangers, despite their problems, were still an established top division side, and so had the quality and promising young stars to suggest that they would be up for the challenge. In Danny Dichio, Kevin Gallen and Trevor Sinclair, the hosts boasted a collection of youngsters as highly rated as those at Old Trafford; and after 64 minutes of an evenly fought battle, Danny Dichio looked as if he might have made a crucial contribution to the both the title race and the relegation scrap. His effort from the edge of the area was deflected goalwards off Schmeichel and Denis Irwin couldn't get enough on to it to clear

115

the bar.

Now with a precious and unexpected lead, the hosts seemed hesitant and unsure. Their manager, ex-United midfielder Ray Wilkins, had set his team up in the right way, but as they closed in on a crucial victory, they started to make the kind of mistakes associated with a team struggling at the wrong end of the table. Firstly, they did what all teams do in that situation – waste time as much as possible. With minutes remaining, Wilkins substituted his young forwards for the experienced striker Mark Hateley and young defender Karl Ready. By this time, Ferguson had made every gamble he could, throwing on Sharpe, Butt and Scholes. With all six substitutes made, and the wasted time, there was a significant amount of injury time awarded by League Cup Final referee Robbie Hart.

OTHER LEAGUE RESULTS:

TUESDAY 12 MARCH 1996
Chelsea 1-1 Man City

WEDNESDAY 13 MARCH 1996
Blackburn 1-0 Leeds
Liverpool 2-2 Wimbledon

SATURDAY 16 MARCH 1996
Coventry 0-2 Bolton
Liverpool 2-0 Chelsea
Man City 2-1 Southampton
Middlesbro' 1-1 Nott'm F
Sheff Wed 2-0 Aston Villa
Spurs 2-3 Blackburn
Wimbledon 0-3 Arsenal

SUNDAY 17 MARCH 1996
Leeds 2-2 Everton

MONDAY 18 MARCH 1996
Newcastle 3-0 West Ham

It seemed that Rangers were becoming victims of their own indecision and they were made to pay in the cruellest way when a Ryan Giggs cross finally broke their resistance. And who else but Eric Cantona was there at the far post to head home a dramatic equaliser with just seconds remaining. United had avoided defeat and went top, albeit by the narrowest of margins, their superiority by a solitary goal on goal difference, although Newcastle's Monday night win against West Ham restored their three point advantage and they still had a game in hand.

"It wasn't a good result for us, but you may look upon it in a few weeks as a very good outcome," remarked Ferguson afterwards.

March, as ever, was the proving ground in the title race; the time when even the most innocuous of decisions can turn out to be crucial. The recall of Lee Sharpe could be said to have been a wise choice by the manager; that Sharpe was in that first choice selection for the trip to Newcastle spoke volumes over whether he still had the trust of the manager. Sharpe's uncertain status at the club provoked a number of letters to the club's official magazine; one notable submission came from Alan Dixon of Bristol and is revealing in how different the club's official communications where then compared to today.

"We've all seen the stories printed about Lee Sharpe in the gutter press recently. I hope all the people who doubted his ability, including some United fans, are now feeling totally gutted," Alan wrote. The editor replied, "You may have noticed that the press cynically waited for Lee to hit top form again before they printed more scandal. And it's not as if he's the only one this season. Les Ferdinand, Stan Collymore, Keith Gillespie and Gary Speed, among others, have appeared in more or less lurid stories in the papers. Lee needs the fans to back him, not turn on him."

20TH MARCH 1996 - FA CARLING PREMIERSHIP
OLD TRAFFORD, MANCHESTER. ATT. 50,028

UNITED 1-0 ARSENAL

Scorer: Cantona 66
Team : Schmeichel, G.Neville, May, Bruce, P.Neville, Sharpe, Keane, Butt, Giggs, Cantona, Cole (Scholes 59)

Sharpe was in the team again for the crucial visit of Arsenal. Newcastle's return to form had wiped out much of the advantage of United's win at St James's Park a few weeks ago and if they were to falter here, it would negate all the good work done recently in hauling in the run-away leaders.

This was a solid performance all over the pitch, but particularly up front, giving supporters plenty to cheer. Chance after chance fell to the home side, they created a staggering 27 in all, and these did not include the half a dozen balls put into promising areas that Andy Cole just couldn't get to in time.

But just to prove the toughness of the opposition, once again, Peter Schmeichel was required to make a string of saves of his own

Another day, another winner...

validating, as if it were required, Paddy Crerand's statement to the club magazine that "Schmeichel's form has been remarkable since Tony (Coton) arrived!" As the Dane kept the goals out at one end, it was once more left to Eric Cantona to put them in at the other; on the kind of evening when it was always going to take a mistake or a moment of magic to provide a breakthrough, United benefitted from a little bit of both.

With three quarters of the game gone, Phil Neville's floated cross was headed away by an Arsenal defender but David Seaman

OTHER LEAGUE RESULTS:

TUESDAY 19 MARCH 1996
Aston Villa 0-0 Middlesbro
WEDNESDAY 20 MARCH 1996
Bolton 2-3 Spurs
Soton 0-1 Sheff Wed

had made a rare error by coming out to try and punch the ball. The headed clearance went a reasonable distance, but as it dropped to Cantona, ever the opportunist, he chested and half-volleyed it towards goal. The dipping drive would have beaten Seaman even if the experienced stopper had been closer to his line, given that it clipped the crossbar on its way in. It was an outstanding goal and an outstanding moment; United were heading back level at the top, albeit behind on goal difference.

"We played some of our best football of the season," purred a delighted Ferguson afterwards. In his programme notes for the next game, he elaborated. "I thought our first-half performance against Arsenal was quite breathtaking," he wrote, before going on to extend lengthy praise to the supporters who had turned out for the biggest gate of the season. That record would broken again against Spurs.

The buoyancy in mood after the Arsenal game, restoring complete positivity after momentum had stalled with the QPR result, was undermined slightly by concerns over profligacy in front of goal. To create over thirty chances and only convert one, even against a side as good as Arsenal, highlighted both a flaw in this United team. When the momentum is good, though, this is when the flaws tend to be few and far between.

OTHER RESULTS: UEFA CUP QUARTER-FINAL SECOND LEG

Nottingham Forest 1–5 Bayern Munich (agg 2-7)

FA CUP SIXTH ROUND REPLAY

Wimbledon 1–3 Chelsea; Liverpool 3–0 Leeds United

24TH MARCH 1996 - FA CARLING PREMIERSHIP
OLD TRAFFORD, MANCHESTER. ATT. 50,157

UNITED 1-0 TOTTENHAM HOTSPUR

Scorer: Cantona 51

Team : Schmeichel, G.Neville, May, Bruce, P.Neville (Beckham 63), Sharpe, Keane, Butt, Giggs, Cantona, Cole (McClair 72)

'It will be another tough game,' admitted Ferguson in his pre-match notes for a fixture that was probably won by that momentum more than anything else. Anything after an at times exhilarating display against Arsenal was likely to feel flat, yet almost without realising it, United had closed the gap completely on Newcastle once more. And the flatness was in spite of the fact that Newcastle had, the day before United faced Spurs, been to Arsenal and been defeated.

This now presented Ferguson with a genuine opportunity to gain an advantage and United were looking forward, but the tide had well and truly been turned. It would take a while longer until it could be said that the twelve point gap had been mathematically chased down, but the chase had been so fierce that it had hardly been noticeable that we had entered what the manager would later famously describe as the 'squeaky bum' phase of the season.

It was a genuine test of the mettle of the youngsters. Both Nevilles and Butt were in the starting line up, as well as May trying to solidify his own position against opponents that had thrashed them earlier in the season. Phil Neville, in particular, was running on empty and plans to give him a rest after the Southampton Cup tie had been shelved following an injury to Denis Irwin. He was eventually substituted midway through the second half, by which time the points had been decided.

There could be no debating that the circumstances which led to the game's only goal were controversial. Referee Gerald Ashby neglected to award a corner for Spurs, to the chagrin of the away support and Spurs boss Gerry Francis. It would be too simplistic to blame that decision for the events which transpired as to do so is to suggest that Spurs were especially vulnerable from opposition goal kicks, an insult to the intelligence of any reasonable football fan. However it is still entirely true that when one bad decision leads to the concession of a goal, or the difference between losing and drawing, that no matter how tenuous, that decision will be remembered. This is not to say Eric Cantona found himself with a free run at goal in the 51st minute after collecting a ball from Roy Keane (the goal kick had been contested and won by the veteran Gary Mabbutt, who was struggling with an injury and imminently due to be replaced). Cantona still had the attentions of three Spurs midfielders, but he evaded the challenges of Jason Dozzell and David Howells more easily than the visiting manager would have liked. Approaching the box and the formidable frame of Sol Campbell, Cantona moved to the left. It was a clever, decisive move. Campbell hesitated, not knowing whether he should vacate his left-sided central position, but knowing no-one else was close enough. It bought Cantona the space and time to measure an effort with his weaker foot from just outside the box. It was a beautiful example of how to use your body and space; the kind of work which should be on instruction videos for young aspiring players. Spurs were helpless and Ian Walker, at full stretch, could get nowhere near the most accurate of finishes.

Ryan Giggs continued to provide a goal threat with a number of attempts on the visitors' goal, but a further strike wasn't necessary. It's fair to say that it wasn't the most controversial moment in the history of the sport (and far from even being the most controversial moment from this particular Premier League fixture) although perhaps it is natural that the memory of the contentious decision to not give a corner is what remains with the visitors.

"Funnily enough, the corner that wasn't given and United scoring 30 seconds later is the one thing I remember from that game," recalls ex-Spurs star Darren Anderton, who watched the game from the bench. "There wasn't much between the teams on the day and it was one moment of magic from Eric Cantona that proved the difference. Cantona was the main man for me and was my player of the year for sure."

"Compared with the speed and flair against Arsenal on Wednesday, this was a lean footed Cantona with his fifth goal in five games; goals that have earned United 10 points from a possible 12-rescued them with his strike five minutes into the second half,' reported *The Guardian*. *The Times*, meanwhile, seemed to have their finger on the pulse. "Day by day, piece by piece, the picture is becoming clearer. When the Championship jigsaw is complete, it will surely reveal a central image. Eric Cantona of course, for this brilliant Frenchman seems determined to bring the trophy back to Old Trafford on his own."

The Frenchman may have been standing out to all (and is quite rightly identified as a major reason for the team's success) but nobody could ignore the way that United's young stars were beginning to blossom in these high pressure situations. "I wasn't surprised to see how the boys from United who I played with for England went on to have such great careers; Becks, Gary and Phil Neville, Nicky Butt and the best of them all Scholesy... Great players with great attitudes," admits Anderton now.

In addition, David May had probably been the best player on the pitch, marshalling the defence with an authority more commonly associated with his partner on the day, Steve Bruce. May would perhaps be derided a little unfairly later in his Old Trafford career, but there was no doubt that the form he was, at this point, at the start of a purple patch; an 18 month period which should have seen him earn international recognition.

OTHER LEAGUE RESULTS:

SATURDAY 23 MARCH 1996

Arsenal 2-0 Newcastle
Bolton 2-1 Sheff Wed
Chelsea 1-1 QPR
Everton 2-4 Wimbledon
Nott'm Forest 1-0 Liverpool
West Ham 4-2 Man City

MONDAY 25 MARCH 1996

Southampton 1-0 Coventry

Ferguson later confessed that the result was better than the performance. "I thought a few of our players suffered from nerves today, and a few look tired as well," he said.

Thankfully there was a full week for the team to recover ahead of what would turn out to be an epic FA Cup semi final against Chelsea.

OTHER RESULT:

SUNDAY 24TH MARCH 1996:

LEAGUE CUP FINAL (WEMBLEY)

Aston Villa 3-0 Leeds United

PREMIER LEAGUE AS AT 24TH MARCH 1996									
1	Manchester United	32	20	7	5	59	30	67	29
2	Newcastle United	30	20	4	6	55	28	64	27
3	Liverpool	31	17	8	6	60	27	59	33
4	Aston Villa	32	16	8	8	46	30	56	16
5	Arsenal	32	15	9	8	44	28	54	16
6	Tottenham Hotspur	31	14	9	8	40	31	51	9
7	Everton	32	13	9	10	50	38	48	12
8	Blackburn Rovers	31	14	6	11	47	36	48	11
9	Nottingham Forest	30	12	11	7	40	40	47	0
10	Chelsea	32	11	12	9	37	35	45	2
11	West Ham United	32	13	6	13	39	44	45	-5
12	Leeds United	29	11	6	12	35	42	39	-7
13	Middlesbrough	32	9	9	14	29	42	36	-13
14	Sheffield Wednesday	32	9	8	15	43	51	35	-8
15	Wimbledon	31	7	9	15	46	63	30	-17
16	Manchester City	32	7	9	16	26	49	30	-23
17	Coventry City	30	5	12	13	37	55	27	-18
18	Southampton	29	5	10	14	28	43	25	-15
19	Bolton Wanderers	32	7	4	21	35	62	25	-27
20	Queens Park Rangers	32	6	6	20	28	50	24	-22

31st March 1996 - FA Cup Semi Final
Villa Park, Birmingham. Att. 38,421

CHELSEA 1-2 UNITED

Scorers: Cole 55, Beckham 59
Team : Schmeichel, P.Neville, G.Neville, May, Sharpe, Beckham,
Keane, Butt, Giggs, Cantona, Cole

"This was the best semi-final in my time here," enthused Ferguson after a pulsating tie. That was quite a statement, considering the epics with Oldham Athletic and the entertaining if controversial ties with Crystal Palace at the same venue in 1995. But it was clear what the manager meant; the quality was much higher because the standard of opponent was that much greater. Chelsea were in the very early stages of their foreign transformation. Ruud Gullit had been convinced to go to Stamford Bridge, a trailblazer for a number of stars to follow from Serie A.

But tough games were nothing new to this young Manchester United team, who had proven themselves up for the fight and capable of matching any team in the land. In an exciting start, United took the game to the Blues and were almost rewarded early on for their invention when David Beckham met Ryan Giggs' drilled cross with a powerful drive inside a crowded area, the ball cannoned off a post. Giggs himself came close with a header, though it was comfortably handled by Kevin Hitchcock.

It was then Chelsea's turn to have some forays forward; defender Michael Duberry advanced with the ball and hit a speculative left foot effort from thirty yards. It may have even been a cross but it almost went in, striking the crossbar and bouncing back into play before Phil Neville cleared it.

Cole and Cantona combined to create an opportunity for Giggs but although it sat up favourably on the Welshman's stronger side, he sliced his finish. United were already regretting these missed chances, and they were made to do so more bitterly ten minutes before half time. Mark Hughes was too strong for Beckham and too quick on the ball for Phil Neville, clipping a left foot cross over the head of Gary Neville to Gullit, who was unmarked in the six yard box and made no mistake. *Daily Express* reporter Matt Dickinson later said of the elder Neville's performance "he showed yet again that he can be the outstanding centre-half of his generation" and while it is true that his recovery in this game was fine (and provides an interesting footnote that around fifteen years later, Dickinson would ghost Neville's autobiography 'Red'), Gullit's goal demonstrated why the youngster would not quite live up to that lofty expectation; his height and his momentary positional lapse, two contributory factors. The latter could be fixed with experience and it would be extremely harsh to categorise this goal as a mistake but it was the type of goal you would find difficult to imagine United conceding with Bruce and Pallister at the back, or indeed if Neville and May were in reverse positions. It could be contested in Neville's defence that he wasn't particularly helped by Lee Sharpe in the first half, who was not enjoying playing at left full back.

Gary would of course go on to become arguably the greatest right back in United's history and perhaps even the greatest Englishman to play the position going by sheer weight of achievement but in 1996 he was perhaps the most vulnerable of the back four once everyone was fit. Irwin and Pallister, once back, would obviously walk in to the team, and May was doing enough to keep out Steve Bruce. It was, then, a straight up fight for the right back position and Gary found himself in the unusual position of competing with his brother. Phil was in fine form once more at Villa Park and while his efforts were more unsung, the very obvious contributions of Eric Cantona continued. He struck an inventive volley from long range which hit Hitchcock's other post, and, in the second half, was even so far back that he cleared an effort off the line.

The much maligned Andy Cole with a vital toe-poke

By then, the game had changed. Terry Phelan had pulled up with a calf injury trying to chase a ball, and it seemed nonsensical that he would continue but manager Glenn Hoddle kept him on. United saw an opportunity and began to concentrate on the right hand side knowing that Phelan's movement would be limited. Phil Neville got to the byline, skillfully getting past John Spencer, and crossed to Cantona. Erland Johnsen could only help it on its way to the Frenchman, Cantona headed across goal and Cole threw an outstretched leg out to poke it in. It wasn't crystal clear whether or not the ball was on its way in anyway but Cole's insurance got his name on the scoresheet.

Chelsea went back on the offensive but when Craig Burley received the ball with his back to his own goal, he made a careless and catastrophic error, hooking a woefully directed back pass across his back four. It was so poor that it was difficult to understand what his intention had been. Crucially for the destiny of this game, the ball rolled into the path of David Beckham and Terry Phelan. Phelan had no chance and Beckham was able to take all the time he needed to guide the ball past Hitchcock. Hoddle then removed

Phelan but it was like shutting the stable door after the horse had bolted.

Chelsea responded swiftly but Cantona's intervention, stopping Spencer's shot after Schmeichel had unsuccessfully attempted to clear Ruud Gullit's attempt, rescued United. The Reds finished the game strongly, with Beckham, Cantona and Cole all going close. A third goal

OTHER LEAGUE RESULTS:

SATURDAY 30 MARCH 1996

Blackburn 0-3 Everton
Bolton 1-1 Man City
Leeds 0-1 Middlesbrough
QPR 3-0 Southampton
Spurs 3-1 Coventry
Wimbledon 1-0 Nott'm F

looked more likely for Ferguson's team but it wasn't necessary. The manager was delighted with the performance of his team, particularly the match–winner.

"Beckham was one of the best players today, and it's very difficult to keep him out of the team. He's straight out of the top drawer. Within two years, he'll be a very good player indeed. We had heroes everywhere. Ruud Gullit gave us some problems in the first half but apart from that I didn't think we were in danger. David May was outstanding, Gary Neville had a fine game and Eric Cantona was just magnificent."

It was the first game in this FA Cup run that Cantona had failed to score but nobody could miss his influence on this fixture; it seemed that as long as United could field the Frenchman, they couldn't fail. The thought was backed up by fact he hadn't yet been on a losing Manchester United team in the FA Cup. Fate and destiny may have felt as if they played a part but there was nothing fortunate about the club's advancement to a remarkable third consecutive FA Cup Final. "...the real passing football was played by Alex Ferguson's young side: short, measured, chess–like moves in little groups of three and four," reported journalist Steve Curry. "When patience was needed they showed it. The Neville brothers, Beckham, Nicky Butt and Ryan Giggs, all applied executive brains to apprentice experiences."

United would play Liverpool in the final on 11th May. Robbie

Fowler had scored his 32nd and 33rd goals of a fantastic season in the other semi-final against Aston Villa at Old Trafford. The celebrations were dampened somewhat by growing selection headaches for the manager. The day after the semi-final, he told the *Manchester Evening News*, "It never rains but it pours. I wouldn't think Steve (Bruce) will make the derby. He was struggling yesterday and the game is only six days away. We'll just see how it goes this week. But realistically I'll be thinking about having him back for the game at Southampton a week later." Gary Pallister was, apparently, a little further away from a return. "Gary could be training in a couple of weeks. He wants to play in the (European) Championships but it depends on how he does in the next few weeks."

OTHER RESULT: FA CUP SEMI-FINAL (OLD TRAFFORD) - Liverpool 3-0 Aston Villa

★

On the Tuesday before the derby, it was revealed that Martin Edwards had sold 785,000 shares at 270p apiece, while his wife also sold shares, raising £3m collectively. A club spokesman said that the decision was taken for 'tax and financial planning purposes'. It was a move that, at any other time, would probably have tipped supporters over the edge after what they perceived to be significant underinvestment in the squad, particularly after seeing the purse strings tightened due to the North Stand construction. But as it stood, United were ticking along very nicely against all odds; nobody was quite sure yet if it was accident or design, and nobody was certain that this group of young players had actually learned from their misfortune of the previous year, or if, in fact, they were destined to be also-rans.

That their Cup Final opponents would be Liverpool only made for a more intriguing spectacle and only with the benefit of twenty years of hindsight can we truly appreciate the cultural significance of this time. 1996 saw Britpop at its height, there seemed to be a new found confidence in just about every aspect of British life – from art and fashion to politics and football. The forthcoming European Championships in England would prove to be a turning point in the game's place in popular culture, for good or ill.

It is an interesting contrast to the modern day campaign to re-introduce safe standing in British football but it cannot be reasonably challenged that all-seater stadiums played a significant part in cleaning up the sport's image following the numerous disasters of the 1980s. For consecutive seasons during the 1980s football attendances had fallen. Some believed the game was dying out, others that it was slowly being euthanised by a Conservative government unable to stem the weekly tit-for-tat terrace violence.

The death of 96 Liverpool supporters at Hillsborough forced the authorities to switch tactics. Clearly, football could still rouse passions and attract big crowds but the grounds in which they were housed were antiquated and deadly. The Taylor Report paved the way for the introduction of all-seater stadia and one by one the iconic terraces of the First Division disappeared.

The next development was the monetisation of football, principally through increased ticket prices and a huge hike in the price of football rights. The two-year contract for rights to televise the Football League in 1983 had cost just £5.2m yet the four-year contract exclusively landed by ITV in 1988 cost £44m. BSkyB's rights cost £191.5m in 1992 and would cost £670m in 1997.

The money pumped into the game went increasingly to players and owners and it was during this period that the introduction of foreign players became possible. The ability to compete with the Italian and Spanish leagues for the best players helped and the arrival of sexy foreign footballers to the game's coverage increased the interest of women, a demographic previously thought impervious to the charms of the game. Quickly the tabloid press began to peer into the private lives of the new stars and they were soon transformed into celebrities in a way not seen since George Best was in his pomp.

David Beckham would become the focus for the tabloids. The good looking boy next door with the pop star girlfriend (later wife) was a gift to the 90s tabloids. Later, it would go too much the other way as some would dismiss his talent as style over substance. But in the wake of deciding the FA Cup semi-final, and the comment from the manager that he was practically undroppable, Beckham found himself in the spotlight for the first time in April 1996.

"I didn't even know I was playing until an-hour-and-a-half before kick off," he told the *Manchester Evening News*, "I've actually played more than 30 games this season and I didn't have time to get nervous about the semi-final. But I still find it difficult to take in that I'm training every day and playing for the club I always idolised. To get the winner in a semi-final was unbelievable - a dream come true-but I've got to be realistic about the final. It is another ambition to cherish because I've never played at Wembley, but the manager will have players like Steve Bruce, Gary Pallister and Denis Irwin all coming back from injuries and I would expect them to be chosen ahead of me. I've got plenty of time, though. Just achieving what I've done so far is great. It's been wonderful to come through with such a terrific set of lads from the youth team like the Nevilles, Paul Scholes, Nicky Butt. We've all helped each other and we always got great encouragement from the older players like Brucie and Paul Ince, who is from the same neck of the words as me. Eric Cantona's a marvellous help, too. He doesn't say much but he has this presence and he'll just wink at you as if to say 'come on-you can do it'."

Attentions turned back to the league and the derby at Maine Road. With City in dire relegation danger, the temptation to compare it to the infamous 1974 clash between the sides was too much to resist for the *Evening News*, who interviewed Sammy McIlroy, the legendary midfielder who had played for both clubs, although, of course, he was far more renowned as a United star.

"After so many years at Old Trafford I still look for their result first and I want them to win the Premiership title," McIlroy, then manager of Macclesfield, said. "However, I'd also love City to stay in the division. I like the way Alan Ball wants his side to play football and I want him to escape for that reason as well. They were unlucky in the Cup match at Old Trafford when I thought they played very well for half an hour or more. It's whether they can sustain it for the full 90 minutes that's the key. Ominously, though, United just seem to keep rolling on. They are magnificent."

6TH APRIL 1996 - FA CARLING PREMIERSHIP
MAINE ROAD, MANCHESTER. ATT. 29,688

MANCHESTER CITY 2-3 UNITED

Scorer: Cantona 7(pen), Cole 41, Giggs 77
Team : Schmeichel, P.Neville, G.Neville, Bruce (May 75), Irwin,
Beckham, Keane, Butt, Giggs, Cantona, Cole (Sharpe 75)

United were boosted by the unexpected recovery of Steve Bruce but came into the game having not only achieved the very unlikely accomplishment of eliminating Newcastle's points advantage, but also having done it with a month of the season left to play.

Newcastle had played Liverpool in midweek and lost a seven goal thriller that would go down as one of the all-time top tier games. The sight of Kevin Keegan with his head down and arms dejectedly draped across the advertising hoardings spoke a thousand words. From the twelve point lead that had been established on the 20th January, it had taken Ferguson's team just 74 days to achieve parity; Liverpool's victory kept United three points in front, and although Newcastle still had a game in hand, United also had a three goal superiority on goal difference.

They played simultaneously on Saturday, with United due to play earlier on Easter Monday just 48 hours later. Ferguson may have been hoping, then, for a drab low energy affair like the first derby back in October but, with their local rivals fighting for their futures in the division as well as their pride, it was unlikely to be dull.

Alex Ferguson later declared "in the first half we were the better side" and that might have been true but it wasn't necessarily reflective of the quality on show. Roy Keane was due to miss the Coventry game through suspension (in these days, suspensions for accumulated yellows or red cards would begin from 14 days after the offence) but made a contribution here as early as the sixth minute; his clever reverse pass found Irwin, who was chopped down by the hapless Nicky Summerbee inside the area. Eric Cantona coolly sent Eike Immel the wrong way from the spot, to celebrate his well-earned Player of the Month award for his perfect March performances.

Andy Cole might well have added a second, but under pressure from Summerbee could only manage a tame poke that was straight into the arms of the goalkeeper. United then became scrappy and embroiled in the type of game which suited City; the Blues benefitted in the 40th minute when a cross was headed down by Niall Quinn into the path of debutant Mikhail Kavelashvili. After the success of Georgi Kinkladze, Ball was clearly hoping lightning would strike twice with Georgian imports, and it certainly did the trick here when the new striker equalised.

It was indicative of the game and City's own predicament that they couldn't even hold on to a level score for a minute, let alone until half time. Indeed, the goal was probably a good thing for United, reminding them that there was a game to win. Butt carried the ball forward into City's defensive third and threaded the ball to Cole. Cole swapped passes with Cantona, showing the kind of instinct he had been accused of lacking so often this season before latching on to the return pass to score United's second. His finish was hardly the most convincing, a scuffed effort with his left foot, but his twelfth goal of the season was enough to give United a half time lead.

City changed their shape at half time, perhaps sensing the hesitancy in the United team, and it made for a dramatic second period. It may not have been clear to those on the pitch, the action was non-stop, but it did not escape the attention of those in the terraces that Queen's Park Rangers had taken an early second half lead up at Newcastle. As things stood, that was a telling scoreline for both teams; Rangers would be a point behind City in the race to avoid relegation, and United were looking at a potential six point lead at 5pm.

In order to do that, they had to see out this game, and City looked a different team after the break, as they bombarded the United goal. Kavelashvili forced Schmeichel into one of his outstanding trademark saves with his huge frame, before Kinkladze embarrassed Bruce with a trick, only for Keane to rescue United with a last-gasp challenge. It was clear that the Gary Neville/Bruce partnership was struggling; Bruce was clearly unfit and United paid

Eric gets the ball rolling at Maine Road

the price in the 71st minute when Uwe Rosler picked the ball up in a wide left position. Bruce tracked him but couldn't commit and so kept a reasonable distance away. Rosler continued his run into the box and unleashed an unstoppable drive beyond the reach of Schmeichel to the delight of the home supporters. The Germans celebration was telling as he raced toward the City bench to make a point to manager Alan Ball who had dropped him recently.

The goal prompted Ferguson to haul off Bruce for David May; the veteran would play for the club again, but if there was ever a moment which suggested

OTHER LEAGUE RESULTS:

WEDNESDAY 3 APRIL 1996
  Liverpool 4-3 Newcastle
  Leeds 1-0 Southampton
FRIDAY 5 APRIL 1996
  Middlesbro' 3-1 Sheff Wed
SATURDAY 6 APRIL 1996
  Arsenal 2-1 Leeds
  Chelsea 1-2 Aston Villa
  Coventry 1-0 Liverpool
  Everton 3-0 Bolton
  Newcastle 2-1 QPR
  Nott'm Forest 2-1 Spurs
  Soton 1-0 Blackburn
  West Ham 1-1 Wimbledon

the manager knew his once-reliable defender's time was up, it was arguably this one. The end was nigh for Steve Bruce but the replacement of Cole by Lee Sharpe was staggering and sent a clear message; it did not appear as if, when the going got tough, the manager trusted Cole to deliver.

It is said that substitutions change games and that of course is true; however, on this occasion, it was the players who were already on the pitch who perhaps had their concentration sharpened by how ruthless the manager could be. Within two minutes of Rosler's goal United were back in front with a lead they wouldn't throw away. Keane won the ball and played it to Cantona; the Frenchman measured his options before picking out Giggs, who was racing forward with Keith Curle for company. Curle pointed, or gestured, with his right hand; it is unclear whether he was goading Giggs into shooting from an improbable angle, or, he was unaware of the position of his team-mates as he was a good five yards behind anyone else in a blue shirt. Giggs ignored the gesticulations and advanced towards goal, his shot was hit with such venom that it flew past Immel and into the near top corner. At first it seemed like a trick of the light; he couldn't have scored from there, could he? Yes, in fact, he could and had. The improbable nature of the goal contributed to Giggs' obvious delight.

"Manchester United may have bagged the points but if there can ever truly be glory in defeat, it went to Manchester City," was the *Manchester Evening News* diplomatic take on the game. It cannot be disputed that City deserved a share of the spoils on the balance of play; United had scored from three of only four efforts on target (most publications even dismissed the validity of Cole's weak effort after his goal) while City tested Schmeichel eight times in addition to the two that beat him. But their approach was hardly a victory for football, more a case of United not really knowing whether or not they had control of a game when they appeared to. Just as in the Tottenham game, there was an uncertainty about whether they could kill a game off when it seemed that it was there for the taking.

At precisely the same moment as Giggs was putting his laces through the ball to earn United all the points, Peter Beardsley was staging a one-man rescue act up at St. James' Park. A five minute double for the one-time Red turned the game around and maintained parity. Newcastle were hanging in and would have felt relieved after their victory but one newspaper, at least, felt that they'd seen enough.

'IT'S OVER!' stated Lee Clayton for the *Daily Star*. 'A Two-Horse race? Nah, surely only one team can win it now. Just one look at the remaining matches tells you everything about the battle for the championship. Yes, it's all but over. Finished. Won. Decided."

YOU CAN'T WIN ANYTHING WITH KIDS

8TH APRIL 1996 - FA CARLING PREMIERSHIP
OLD TRAFFORD, MANCHESTER. ATT. 50,332

UNITED 1-0 COVENTRY

Scorer: Cantona 47
Team: Schmeichel, Irwin, Sharpe, May, Neville G., Beckham, Butt,
McClair, Cole, Cantona, Giggs

"IT'S NOT OVER!" declared the *Manchester Evening News* after
United eased to a win over strugglers Coventry. It was 'Flag Day'
at Old Trafford, though the Evening News seemed to believe that
Newcastle wouldn't be waving their own white flag just yet.

This game, of course, was not remembered for the result. Nor
was it remembered for Cantona's cool decider; the sixth consecutive
league game he'd scored in. It has, instead, been remembered for the
horrific injury suffered by Sky Blues defender David Busst in the
second minute. Coventry were on the front foot and from a corner
forward Noel Whelan forced Schmeichel into a save and Busst flew
in for the rebound. Schmeichel was able to hold on to the ball.
The Coventry man appeared to have been hurt in a collision with
Denis Irwin, though no blame could be put on the left back. Busst's
leg was stuck in the ground and horrifically twisted; Schmeichel
jumped up immediately and raced to the edge of the box, throwing
the ball out to the touchline and putting his head into his gloves.
He simply could not bear to look. The game was delayed for nine
minutes while the physiotherapists and paramedics came on with
a stretcher and air.

"That's definitely the only time I've ever been shaken in a
game," Ryan Giggs later told news presenter and celebrity red
Eamonn Holmes in an interview for the club's official magazine.
"I couldn't believe what I saw. I started walking over and I caught
sight of his leg: I just couldn't go any closer."

This was not a day for recriminations; with most in attendance now distracted and hopeful of good news about Busst, a below-par game of football unfolded which seemed to be of secondary importance. Of course, Cantona's goal was celebrated, and the intensity of the occasion was brought home in two late Kevin Richardson opportunities, but this was not exactly the cut and thrust affair we'd seen on Saturday.

United could have had this game in the bag before the tense finale; Cole was again wasteful with four opportunities, but the Old Trafford crowd were generous and encouraging of his efforts.

"Far from marching to victory, Manchester United were often too inclined to stroll around in the manner of men assuming that the points were theirs for the taking," reported *The Guardian*, somewhat unfairly.

Cantona was once more the decider but that only told half of the story, as Schmeichel and May impressed again keeping their opponents at bay. "Hopefully, I am in the right place at the right time this time," said May. "I was at Blackburn when United pipped us two years ago and I had moved here when Rovers won the title last season."

May was speaking ahead of his former club's game with Newcastle on Easter Monday evening. When David Batty scored on his return to Ewood Park to give Keegan's men the lead in the 76th minute, it seemed as if they had recovered from the considerable hiccup of losing four out of the last seven league games. Blackburn had the Geordies' favourite son, Alan Shearer, leading their line, but it was another North East lad, and another self confessed Newcastle fan, that turned the game. First, Shearer's shot from the edge of the area was turned in by Graham Fenton in the 86th minute and then the two combined with one minute remaining for the latter to pounce.

For the first time, Manchester United had a definitive lead in the title race, their six point advantage meaning that Newcastle's game in hand could only reduce it to three. If Newcastle supporters were now left looking to their manager for signs of hope, none was forthcoming in the immediate aftermath of the defeat at Ewood Park. "If it's not meant to be, it's not meant to be... I'd like for us to finish runners' up if we can't win it," said a dejected Keegan.

Compare that to Ferguson's proud enthusiasm of his youngsters. "We have gone into every game knowing we have to win it. It has been part of the character-building at this club over the last five years that we can go into games like Monday's

OTHER LEAGUE RESULTS:
MONDAY 8 APRIL 1996
Blackburn 2-1 Newcastle
Aston Villa 3-0 Soton
Bolton 2-1 Chelsea
Leeds 1-3 Nott'm Forest;
Liverpool 2-0 West Ham
Man Utd 1-0 Coventry
QPR 3-1 Everton
Sheff Wed 1-0 Arsenal
Spurs 1-1 Middlesbrough
Wimbledon 3-0 Man City

Coventry fixture and hold our nerve. The kids have four games left to make themselves successful. They are handling it superbly and I know they'll cope.'

In between the City and Coventry games, it had been reported by the *Mail on Sunday* that Alex Ferguson was set to complete the signing of Edgar Davids. As already revealed earlier in this book, the Ajax midfielder was keen to take advantage of the new Bosman ruling and did eventually move, but to AC Milan. Journalist Bob Cass, a known confidante of United boss Ferguson, went as far as to claim that a wage package of £1m a year had already been agreed. Greek winger

1	Manchester United	34	22	7	5	63	32	73	31
2	Newcastle United	33	21	4	8	61	35	67	26
3	Liverpool	34	19	8	7	66	31	65	35
4	Aston Villa	34	18	8	8	51	31	62	20
5	Arsenal	34	16	9	9	46	30	57	16
6	Tottenham Hotspur	34	15	10	9	45	35	55	10
7	Everton	35	15	9	11	57	41	54	16
8	Nottingham Forest	33	14	11	8	45	43	53	2
9	Blackburn Rovers	34	15	6	13	49	41	51	8
10	West Ham United	34	13	7	14	40	47	46	-7
11	Chelsea	34	11	12	11	39	39	45	0
12	Middlesbrough	35	11	10	14	34	44	43	-10
13	Leeds United	33	12	6	15	38	48	42	-10
14	Sheffield Wednesday	34	10	8	16	45	54	38	-9
15	Wimbledon	34	9	10	15	51	64	37	-13
16	Southampton	34	7	10	17	30	50	31	-20
17	Manchester City	35	7	10	18	29	56	31	-27
18	Queens Park Rangers	35	8	6	21	35	53	30	-18
19	Coventry City	34	6	12	16	39	60	30	-21
20	Bolton Wanderers	35	8	5	22	38	67	29	-29

George Donis was also being linked to the club but his current team Panathinaikos said "If United are interested, they should put their money where their mouth is."

The Reds had another opportunity to extend their advantage at the top when they travelled to Southampton the day before Newcastle entertained Aston Villa. Four of United's last five away games had been against the bottom five teams of the division and the other had been against title rivals Newcastle, all teams with something to play for. In the days before multiple Champions League places, it perhaps stood to reason that the toughest opposition would be those teams fighting to avoid the drop.

13TH APRIL 1996 - FA CARLING PREMIERSHIP
THE DELL, SOUTHAMPTON. ATT. 15,262

SOUTHAMPTON 3-1 UNITED

Scorer: Giggs 89
Team : Schmeichel, Irwin, G.Neville, Bruce, Sharpe (May 55), Beckham, Butt (Scholes 45), Keane, Giggs, Cantona, Cole

The Guardian's post-Coventry suggestion that perhaps United, having already overhauled Newcastle's advantage, were becoming complacent, was given credence here. The most obvious conclusion to draw is that, having reached the top, the youngsters were there to be shot at; and it must be said that following ninety minutes at Southampton's notoriously difficult home ground, there appeared to be some weight to the theory.

When United conceded a 10th minute free kick, Ken Monkou was not only afforded the space to leap and power a header at Schmeichel, he was also inexplicably the quickest to react to convert after the Dane had done all that could be expected with a wonderful stop. Jason Dodd fluffed a further opportunity for the Saints before Matthew Le Tissier struck a post; the visitors were at sixes and sevens. United were equally slow to react to stop Alan Neilson getting to the by-line and swinging a cross back to Neil Shipperley at the near post 12 minutes later. A quarter of the game gone and United were 2-0 down. It was three before they got to half time, Shipperley floated in a cross and Schmeichel was at fault this time, getting a hand to it but dropping it at the feet of Le Tissier. The Saints' enigmatic forward was more renowned for scoring thirty-yard screamers but was unerring in straight forward situations such as this.

Then came the controversy; United emerged for the second half wearing their blue and white away strip, having worn the grey shirt and white shorts and socks in the first half. They tried in vain to get back into the game and when they finally scored in the last minute via a Ryan Giggs close range effort, it was the first time the Reds (or greys/blues) had registered a shot on target.

"When you defend as badly as that, you are going to lose games, there is no doubt about that," fumed Ferguson afterwards. "We weren't reacting to second balls. As for first and third balls, when Schmeichel saved, nobody reacted to his saves. It was a poor performance from us in the first half." On the kit change, Ferguson revealed, "The players prefer the blue, so we changed, that's it. It is a difficult subject to talk about. It is something that is out of my hands and I can't do anything about it, but enough's enough... seeing is the main problem. But I have no more to say about it."

The media lapped it up... "Grey? Blue? Whatever the colour, Manchester United looked anything but the championship elect we expected them to be," taunted Des Kelly in the *Express*. "Maybe it was plain old superstition. Maybe they really could not see each other against the backdrop of the crowd, but they still decided to emerge in a more fetching blue number after the break. No United team should be draped in grey, especially not such a youthful, talented bunch of players. And whoever chose the colour scheme should be made to wear it forever as a mark of shame...

the real United simply failed to turn up and outfits of flourescent pink with lemon yellow trim and sequined tassles would have made no difference. They were poor, especially in defence."

"It was nevertheless United's attitude, rather than their apparel, which raised eyebrows here and pointed them towards their first defeat in 19 matches," reported Patrick Barclay for the *Sunday Telegraph*.

And even Southampton manager Dave Merrington was keen to twist the knife. "Did they tell us about their kit change at half time? Well, let's just say... nothing. United's players earn a lot of money and sometimes they're touchy and

OTHER LEAGUE RESULTS:

SATURDAY 13 APRIL 1996

Chelsea 4-1 Leeds
Coventry 1-0 QPR
Man City 1-0 Sheff Wed
Middlesbro' 1-2 Wimbledon
Nott'm F 1-5 Blackburn
West Ham 1-0 Bolton

SUNDAY 14 APRIL 1996

Newcastle 1-0 Aston Villa

MONDAY 15 APRIL 1996

Arsenal 0-0 Spurs

TUESDAY 16 APRIL 1996

Everton 1-1 Liverpool

prima donnas, but when players work as hard as they do then they get their reward." Merrington had a vested interest, the childhood Newcastle supporter admitted that "there will be a few drinks in celebration going down in Tyneside tonight, that's for sure". He added "Their fans had better not get too carried away because we have to go up to St. James' and play them on Wednesday night."

The Saints hardly provided the same kind of resistance to Newcastle as they had showed at the Dell. They conceded an early goal to Rob Lee and succumbed to a routine 1-0 defeat, Newcastle's second victory by that scoreline in a week, having overcome Aston Villa with a Les Ferdinand goal on the Sunday.

Before those midweek fixtures, United were still caught in the controversy over the grey shirt and both the manager and chairman made further public statements. "The players have not liked the grey kit since we first got it," Ferguson admitted in a *Daily Express* story headlined 'Manchester United could be stuck with their notorious grey strip for another 18 months'. "The

A barely visible Nicky Butt eludes Southampton's Francis Benali

players say they find it difficult picking out team-mates against the background of the crowd, especially from one wing to the other," the boss continued. "We have a very good working relationship with Umbro and I don't want to upset them but enough is enough. We will have to look at our agreement with them, but obviously we would prefer not to wear it again."

"If the manager doesn't want to wear it anymore, we won't wear it," United chairman Martin Edwards confirmed. *The Express* reported, "Manchester-based Umbro will be deeply disappointed by United's decision to dump the grey number. It has proved highly popular with the fans, helping to persuade the company to bring in grey for the new England change outfit. Umbro believe fans like the grey shirts because they are complemented by jeans. But sales are sure to dip if United refuse to wear it in the future. Leeds abandoned their green and blue striped shirts this season because they said they could not pick out their black players in night games. They now play in a bright yellow strip."

The club and strip manufacturer came to an agreement and hosted a press conference to announce a new white strip to replace it the following season, that would be sold at a £10 discount. The grey shirts were sold with discounts of up to £23.

17TH APRIL 1996 - FA CARLING PREMIERSHIP
OLD TRAFFORD, MANCHESTER. ATT. 48,362

UNITED 1-0 LEEDS UNITED

Scorer: Keane 72
Team : Schmeichel, P.Neville, Bruce (May 17), Pallister, Irwin,
Beckham, McClair (Scholes 45), Keane, Giggs, Cantona,
Cole (Sharpe 71)

Finally (and just in time for the European Championships) the third tier of the North Stand was opened for the first time. Supporters with heart problems were warned about climbing to the top and were also told 'don't look down!' Of course, they had to, to see the action, and at least those brave enough to scale the heights would be able to pick out the players; United in red, Leeds in their traditional white. Still, the new capacity of 53,000 was not utilised fully, with assistant secretary Ken Ramsden explaining that the nature of the fixture meant that it was inappropriate to put tickets on general sale.

This game kicked off at 8pm, while Newcastle's game against Southampton started at 7.45pm. The teams may have taken to the field knowing that the Magpies had already scored and, considering their perfect home record following the blip against the Reds, it was presumed that this was not an advantage they would throw away.

This game was just over a quarter of an hour old when both sides had to make major changes. David May coming on for the injured Bruce, who had once more damaged his hamstring, while Leeds were forced into a greater reshuffle when Andy Cole chased down a ball and goalkeeper Mark Beeney raced out to meet him. Beeney misjudged his own position and handled outside of the area and referee Kevin Cooper deemed this a red card offence. Suddenly, not only were United looking at victory, but they could also perhaps address the goal difference damaged by the heavy defeat at the Dell. After all, with just three substitutes able to be named and used, it was not always the case that goalkeepers were chosen. On this occasion, neither boss had done that, so Wilkinson opted to bring on Lucas Radebe, the South African defender, as goalkeeper.

Any thought that Leeds would shut up shop and defend was wide of the mark, they were more competitive than the recent defeats to Nottingham Forest and Chelsea (3-1 and 4-1 respectively) suggested and youngster Andy Gray called Schmeichel into action with a couple of smart long range efforts. The tigerish and tireless efforts of the opposition meant that not only did United fail to register a goal in the first half, it seemed as if they may not get one at all; it was an exercise in patience and perseverance for both players and supporters. The efforts were appreciated and Leeds' own commitment made for a fantastic atmosphere as the game ticked into the final quarter.

Ferguson withdrew Cole for Scholes in the 71st minute, and the ginger-haired midfielder was right in the thick of the action straight away. Cantona played him the ball and he was immediately challenged by two flying Leeds tackles. One of them won the ball, only for it to roll to Giggs at the edge of the area. Giggs was calm, playing the ball to Roy Keane. Keane had Sharpe advancing on his left and it was this run which made all the difference. Gary Kelly and David Wetherall had a moment's hesitation, and that was enough time for Keane to steady himself and shift the ball onto his right foot. It enabled him to skip past Wetherall's desperate lunge and time a shot into Radebe's bottom right corner. Old Trafford erupted, recognising the significance of the moment and, also, the timing. It came just as news was filtering through that Newcastle had won 1-0.

"It was a fraught night. I thought after their keeper was sent off it was a marvellous opportunity not only to win but score goals. But Radebe was magnificent," observed Ferguson after seeing his team ease out the victory, before shining the spotlight on his opponents. "I just cannot understand Leeds. Howard does not deserve his players to play like that tonight with the position he has been in after the last few weeks. If they played like that every week they would be in the top six. It is pathetic, because it seemed like it

OTHER LEAGUE RESULTS:

WEDNESDAY 17 APRIL 1996

Aston Villa 1-1 West Ham
Blackburn 3-2 Wimbledon
Newcastle 1-0 Soton
Nott'm Forest 0-0 Coventry
Sheff Wed 0-0 Chelsea

was only against Manchester United. No wonder managers get the sack. Howard has done a lot for that club and deserves better. Leeds play Newcastle in their next game and I would like to see the video of that one. We have watched Leeds in our last three games and I could not identify them tonight."

These comments were similar to the ones made on television when he said "Why are they not in the top six? I just don't understand it. They've got good players and if they produced the effort like that, they would be top six. But of course you think for some of them it's more important to get a result against Manchester United to stop them winning the league than anything else, which to me… they're cheating their manager, that's all it is.

"Of course, when it comes to Newcastle, you wait and see the difference. You know? It's sad to say that but I'm very disappointed in Leeds."

Wilkinson didn't respond, but it was clear that the comments frustrated some of the Leeds players. "Old Trafford was a daunting place to go at that time with Roy Keane in the centre of the park, and Paul Ince before," recalls Brian Deane. "A lot of teams were beaten before they went on to the pitch and in no time at all they might be one or two down. But we played well in that particular game even when we lost the goalkeeper. Afterwards, Alex Ferguson made remarks about us letting the manager down… obviously there was some kidology in there but at the end of the day I felt it was wrong for him to criticise us as players. It's easy to come out with statements like that but as a professional you always give one hundred percent. We were a little bit low on confidence and perhaps not playing as well as we could but you couldn't criticise our effort. It was probably aimed more at getting under Kevin Keegan's skin than at us and I don't suppose it will bother Man United fans too much, but I thought it was harsh and unprofessional."

More from Deane later, but it is revealing that Ferguson claims in his 1999 autobiography that Leeds "appeared to draw a new determination from the opportunity to reduce Manchester United's chances of gaining more glory" and also insisted that "My remarks on 17 April were never meant to have anything to do with Kevin Keegan; they were aimed entirely at Howard Wilkinson's players."

Ferguson was clearly in garrulous mood on psychological matters after the game and closed with a ringing endorsement of his own players. "Newcastle have got three games to win. But we can handle the pressure all right. Five years of this kind of run-in will ensure that. It brings certain kind of experiences and ways of coping in these situations."

1	Manchester United	36	23	7	6	65	35	76	30
2	Newcastle United	35	23	4	8	63	35	73	28
3	Liverpool	35	19	9	7	67	32	66	35
4	Aston Villa	36	18	9	9	52	33	63	19
5	Arsenal	35	16	10	9	46	30	58	16
6	Blackburn Rovers	36	17	6	13	57	44	57	13
7	Tottenham Hotspur	35	15	11	9	45	35	56	10
8	Everton	36	15	10	11	58	42	55	16
9	Nottingham Forest	35	14	12	9	46	48	54	-2
10	West Ham United	36	14	8	14	42	48	50	-6
11	Chelsea	36	12	13	11	43	40	49	3
12	Middlesbrough	36	11	10	15	35	46	43	-11
13	Leeds United	35	12	6	17	39	53	42	-14
14	Wimbledon	36	10	10	16	55	68	40	-13
15	Sheffield Wednesday	36	10	9	17	45	55	39	-10
16	Southampton	36	8	10	18	33	52	34	-19
17	Coventry City	36	7	13	16	40	60	34	-20
18	Manchester City	36	8	10	18	30	56	34	-26
19	Queens Park Rangers	36	8	6	22	35	54	30	-19
20	Bolton Wanderers	36	8	5	23	38	68	29	-30

GLORY DAYS

O	N THE MORNING OF United's penultimate game of the season, their final home game against Nottingham Forest, it was revealed in the press that Eric Cantona was to be named the Football Writer's Player of the Year that evening for his exceptional season following his return from suspension. And so, despite the pressing matters of a Premiership title on the horizon, some attention was turned to the Frenchman, with the Sunday morning features commenting on the remarkable turnaround of Cantona's career.

Alex Ferguson was quoted by Joe Melling of the *Daily Mail* as explaining "What encouraged me about Eric was that I knew he was a good guy. I see the other side of him and it is all good. Believe me, this is an honest and straight fellow. There is no hidden agenda with him. A lot of players come to me and ask if I can sort out their problems but not Eric. He has sorted things out for himself. He knew what he had to do. The end result tells you everything about his moral fibre. This is a man who possesses unbelievable guts and determination. His training programme when he was out of the game never changed. The players at United love him. His preparation for games is impeccable; better than anyone else I have ever known. His entire schedule is programmed to going out on the pitch to perform as a top player. A lot of managers can never experience the pleasure of having such a wonderful player. I was not going to kick him out. I was determined to see it through. If he had left us we would probably have got £2m or £3m for him. That cannot buy a decent full back in today's market and here we are talking about a great player."

Jurgen Klinsmann, the German striker who had won the award when he played for Tottenham before rejoining Bayern Munich, felt that Cantona was worthy of the accolade. "Eric is a deserved winner, no doubt about that... he has been under the most enormous pressure because the eyes of everyone have been on him and huge expectations demanded of him."

Even David Ginola, a title rival no less, concurred. "I'm full of admiration for him, who wouldn't be? Eric revived the title race single-handedly," Ginola told the *Express*.

One person not quite so satisfied was Liverpool legend Emlyn Hughes, who told *The Sun*, "There is no way Cantona should have been named Footballer of the Year. The fact he has picked up the award is an indictment to all the past winners." Lest we forget that, upon Cantona's arrival at Old Trafford in the first place, Hughes had described the signing as "a panic buy", the "latest big gamble of Alex Ferguson" and dismissed Cantona as a "flashy foreigner".

★

There was a sense of occasion in the air as the month of April closed out. United's players were given a couple of welcome distractions ahead of the Forest game by attending Cecil Gee's in St. Ann's Square for their Cup Final suit fitting. They also marked the event by releasing a music single–another tradition. United had released 'Come On You Reds' in 1994 with Status Quo and staggeringly it had reached #1 in the charts; memorable, of course, for its team-sheet refrain of 'Schmeichel, Parker, Pallister / Irwin, Bruce, Sharpe, and Ince / Hughes, McClair, Keane and Cantona / Robson, Kanchelskis and Giggs!'

Their 1996 offering 'Move Move Move (The Red Tribe)' didn't do quite so well but still made it to number 6. Liverpool's 'Pass and Move (It's the Liverpool Groove)' earned the Spice Boys musical bragging rights, peaking at number 4.

The lyrics to United's offering read:

'When we come like a hurricane, blowin' everyone away,
there's nowhere you can run and hide
So stylish, so skilful, with an iron will too, eleven devils side by side
We've got all the right moves, so defence is no use,
nothing's gonna get in our way
We're strong, we're united, there's no way to fight it, y
ou're never gonna keep us at bay...

No-one can move, move, move, like the Red Tribe do,
there's no man that can stand in our way
No-one can move, move, move, like the Red Tribe do,
they just can't take the heat when we play

When we rise like a tidal wave, sweeping everyone away,
you'll know that we are truly the best
'Cos unity is power, and we're gonna tower high up above the rest
We've got heart, we've got pride too, respect is overdue,
we'll earn it but someone must pay
No-one can keep us held down so pass the robe and crown,
we're going all the way'.

The track came complete with a cheesy music video and feature in the official club magazine. "At the Manchester recording venue, Tony Coton revealed a great singing voice during rehearsals, and the video shows David May is a natural performer with great rhythm," reads the column. "So who knows, perhaps Pete Waterman will make him the next Rick Astley?"

Meanwhile Liverpool's song, with the bridge 'Go Robbie, go Robbie, go', gave some indication of the person they were hoping would dictate the final in a fortnight's time.

★

Silverware was on everyone's minds. They say that defeat can be a good thing and that was almost certainly the case with United's hiccup at Southampton. It hadn't been too costly and heading into the game against Forest, the Reds were three points ahead of Newcastle who would have two games in hand; their trip to Leeds and then a game at the City Ground against Forest. United's goal difference now was just two better than Newcastle's, with an almost identical for and against column. There was some talk about a special play-off in the event that the teams finished on the same points, goals and goal difference (apparently, United's two victories over Newcastle would count for nothing) but Kevin Keegan seemed in laid back mood about the suggestion. "I won't be around for that, I'll be away with Alex Ferguson in Marbella by then. Maybe we can have a game of golf to decide it all, I hear he's a bit of a hacker!" the Newcastle boss quipped. Indeed, so prepared were the Premier League for the play-off that tickets were printed and dates and a venue arranged. The game would take place on either Thursday 16th May or Tuesday 21st May (dependent on the FA Cup Final ging to a replay) at Wembley.

The league leaders were a lot more serious about their chances in the run-in. Steve Bruce would miss the Forest game and faced a race to be fit for the Cup Final but spoke to the *Manchester Evening News* in his capacity as club captain. "It is fantastic that we are in this nail-biting finale yet again. It's a terrific achievement by everyone at the club to have got to this point again... for a club to be battling it out for a possible double for a third successive season is tremendous in the modern game. Now we face Forest and they are capable of causing you almighty problems. They defend deep and hit you on the counter attack... they'll make it difficult for us, there is no doubt about that."

The captain was also interviewed by the club's official magazine about his future. "I'll see how I go next year. There's gonna be a time when I'm not good enough, but I'll know that myself. For the meanwhile I'm gonna have a nice summer and relax on a beach somewhere with a beer. It's easier to relax when you've won something."

"So you're not about to announce your retirement then?" the interviewer asked.

"No, no, no! I've got my testimonial next year. I'm not that stupid."

Bruce's replacement was David May, and he too was in conversational mood. "Nobody even thinks about the title until an hour before kick-off," he insisted. "That's when we get really focused. We have got the experience but it counts for nothing if you don't win games. It's important that we keep clean sheets in the final two matches and stick a few chances away."

Before the Forest game, Alex Ferguson dropped a bombshell by naming Andy Cole as a substitute and playing Paul Scholes up front with Eric Cantona. Scholes had scored thirteen times from sixteen starts and twelve substitute appearances but the timing of the decision was headline news.

"The folk of Manchester now take Andy Cole's wanton shooting as they regarded Eddie the Eagle on the ski jumps," Steve Curry of the *Daily Express* had quipped after the Leeds game. It was harsh without question but highlighted a separate point; Cole seemed too anxious to please for an instinctive goalscorer. Clearly, Scholes' record of converting the chances which fell to him had led to his selection.

YOU CAN'T WIN ANYTHING WITH KIDS

28TH APRIL 1996 - FA CARLING PREMIERSHIP
OLD TRAFFORD, MANCHESTER. ATT. 53,926

UNITED 5-0 NOTTINGHAM FOREST

Scorers: Scholes 41, Beckham 44,54, Giggs 69, Cantona 90
Team : Schmeichel, P.Neville (G.Neville 81), May, Pallister, Irwin,
Beckham, Keane, Giggs, Sharpe, Cantona, Scholes

Before the game, the Reserve and 'A' teams were presented with their own Championship trophies, demonstrating the strength in depth at a club that started the season looking as if its playing squad was threadbare.

Over the previous ten seasons, United had won eight and drawn two of their last home games, with one of those draws coming against Coventry City in 1994, when the club had already won the league. The signs were promising, although Nottingham Forest did have the distinction of being the only club in the last two seasons to have taken all three points away from Old Trafford.

"I don't know about you, but the season seems to have gone very quickly," said Alex Ferguson in his final programme notes of the campaign. "Life rushes past, and though I occasionally wish there was more time to savour the great moments, I suppose I wouldn't really have it any other way because it means we are being successful... There were doubts in the early days following the departure of three experienced players but I always knew our youngsters would deliver. I didn't know exactly how they would come with the big games but they had to be given their chance and I am delighted to say that they have shown themselves to be equipped with that final, important factor of temperament... I am sure nerve-ends will be twitching both on and off the field as we commit ourselves to maintaining the form it takes to win the League. We know what we have to do and I know our players won't let us down. They have come too far to contemplate losing out now."

The scoreline told one story but not the whole one; for forty minutes this was a cagey and tense affair. United didn't even look as if they would create a chance, let alone be wasteful with them. With half time on the horizon, the excellent Giggs tested Alf-Inge Haaland (he of future Roy Keane-related infamy) and took him to the byline. Giggs had started centrally in the absence of Nicky Butt but was switched to the left to see what penetration he could provide. Haaland offered no challenge and Giggs' pullback was met by Scholes whose headed finish was the first attempt on target, and fully justified the manager's decision. Seconds before half time, having broken Forest's resistance, United pounced again. From a corner, Cantona's volley looked to be heading wildly wide of the mark, but David Beckham bravely stuck his head in and diverted it towards goal. Peter Schmeichel, in front of the Stretford End, fell to his knees and raised his hands high up in the air.

It was a bizarre assist - unintended, unquestionably, but Cantona's actual deliberate influence on the game had been a major reason for United's advantage going into the break. "The Footballer of the Year showed why he deserved those votes from his biggest critics with another gem of a display," said the *Daily Mirror*, while the *Express* went further still. "As United struggled for the breakthrough, he repeatedly made the space which eased the desperate pressure on passing outlets from midfield."

Stuart Pearce, the veteran left back, would have a memorable swan-song with England in the European Championships but he was having an afternoon to forget here as Beckham repeatedly gave him the run-around.

"I knew the day I met him, there was no-one like him playing," says Pearce. "He was a top footballer and the best to come out of England." Forest were struggling and United. now freed from pressure, went for the jugular and it was no surprise when Beckham scored again. Scholes clever movement created space for his team-mate in the box and the number 24's low measured shot went across the goal and into the corner.

The growing confidence resulted in two further goals; one from Ryan Giggs, which he could only cheekily claim he intended. He hit a low, left footed ball across the box, which Scholes avoided. Forest stopper Mark Crossley may have anticipated the touch, but was beaten despite the slow roll of the ball anyway.

In injury time, Cantona attempted to play a through ball, only for Steve Chettle to intercept; however, Colin Cooper didn't react quickly enough, so Cantona raced around him, chested the ball down and half-volleyed it past an advancing Crossley. The goal was celebrated on the bench as if it were the first and in the stands supporters were keenly aware of just how crucial the goals could be and just how emphatic a message Cantona's final act had sent to Kevin Keegan's Newcastle.

"When Beckham got the second goal it lifted the pressure off the players, and they were able to enjoy the rest of the match," said Ferguson afterwards. "In the second half we saw the real United with fluent passing and movement. Beckham played brilliantly and he fully deserves his man of the match award. But the back four played well too. They did nothing wrong at the back today. I'm fully prepared for the title to go to the last day.'"

The praise for Beckham was echoed by the *Manchester Evening News*. "The young Londoner's campaign has been haunted by the spectre of Andrei Kanchelskis. He's had to live with the constant demoralising argument that his Ukranian predecessor's defection was the loss from last summer's exodus to really hurt United. But, having scored the goal that took United to Wembley in the FA Cup semi-final, he turned in a match of the match display yesterday with two goals to boot."

The tone was perhaps a little unnecessarily critical, Beckham's form had never really dipped, it was more a case of the manager trying to figure out the best blend of a midfield packed with talent. In the post–Christmas months, that meant finding space for

Paul Scholes and Lee Sharpe and invariably, someone had to miss out. Indeed, Beckham was dreadfully unlucky to miss the cut for England's European Championship squad. Then again, on the same day as Beckham was cutting Forest down, Paul Gascoigne was enjoying his finest hour for Glasgow Rangers with a wonderful hat-trick against Aberdeen to seal the club's eighth straight title in Scotland.

Beckham had said he was taking things one step at a time just a couple of weeks prior to the game and was understandably thrilled with his contribution, but remained level-headed. "I think that getting the points in the bag was what we wanted. The goals are a bonus. Now, we'll train every day as normal and wait on Newcastle's results."

"United's performance was as savage as it was clinical," reported Paul Walker for the *Daily Star*. One thing was certain; Newcastle knew that United were going to Middlesbrough with the intent of winning and winning big. So in order for Newcastle to feel as if they held an advantage on the final day, they would have to win at Leeds and Forest (an altogether different proposition on home soil, as United themselves had discovered) by a combined goal tally of seven.

Newcastle played at Leeds the following day and gave a performance of merit of their own which indicated that they might yet have the fortitude to take the title all the way. Keith Gillespie's 18th minute header felt as if it had come too early in the game as Leeds put Newcastle under sufficient pressure to allay any fears Ferguson may have had about their commitment. Their efforts were still not enough and so the Magpies were able to hold on and see the game out. Part one of their job done, then, and if they could match United's five goal haul against Forest, they would go into the last game just a goal worse off.

However, as we all know now, the biggest story coming out of Elland Road on Monday, April 29th 1996 wasn't Newcastle's well-earned victory. It was Kevin Keegan's post-match interview with presenters Richard Keys and Andy Gray for Sky Sports.

"We just wanna keep our hopes alive," Keegan began, "a lot of things have been said over these last few days. Some of it almost slanderous. We've never commented. We've just got on working, trying to pass the ball like we do in training."

Keys interjected. "What do you mean by that? That people have been having a go at you and your team?"

"No, no I think things have been said about... I think you've got to send Alex Ferguson a tape of this game haven't you? Isn't that what he asked for?"

Andy Gray in the Sky Studio, "Well I'm sure if he was watching it tonight Kev, he can have no arguments about the way that Leeds went about their job, they really tested your team..."

"And we're playing Notts Forest on Thursday, and he objected to that!" Keegan responds. "Now that was fixed up four months ago. We were supposed to play Notts Forest. Now that sort of stuff, we're bett... we're bigger than that. "

OTHER LEAGUE RESULTS:

SATURDAY 27 APRIL 1996

Aston Villa 0-1 Man City
Blackburn 1-1 Arsenal
Bolton 0-1 Southampton
Liverpool 1-0 Middlesbro'
QPR 3-0 West Ham
Sheff Wed 2-5 Everton
Spurs 1-1 Chelsea
Wimbledon 0-2 Coventry

MONDAY 29 APRIL 1996

Leeds 0-1 Newcastle

THURSDAY 2 MAY 1996

Leeds 1-3 Spurs
Nott'm F 1-1 Newcastle

PREMIER LEAGUE AS AT 28TH APRIL								
1	Manchester United	37	24	7	6	70	35	79	35
2	Newcastle United	35	23	4	8	63	35	73	28
3	Liverpool	36	20	9	7	68	32	69	36
4	Aston Villa	37	18	9	10	52	34	63	18
5	Arsenal	36	16	11	9	47	31	59	16
6	Everton	37	16	10	11	63	44	58	19
7	Blackburn Rovers	37	17	7	13	58	45	58	13
8	Tottenham Hotspur	36	15	12	9	46	36	57	10
9	Nottingham Forest	36	14	12	10	46	53	54	-7
10	Chelsea	37	12	14	11	44	41	50	3
11	West Ham United	37	14	8	15	42	51	50	-9
12	Middlesbrough	37	11	10	16	35	47	43	-12
13	Leeds United	35	12	6	17	39	53	42	-14
14	Wimbledon	37	10	10	17	55	70	40	-15
15	Sheffield Wednesday	37	10	9	18	47	60	39	-13
16	Coventry City	37	8	13	16	42	60	37	-18
17	Southampton	37	9	10	18	34	52	37	-18
18	Manchester City	37	9	10	18	31	56	37	-25
19	Queens Park Rangers	37	9	6	22	38	54	33	-16
20	Bolton Wanderers	37	8	5	24	38	69	29	-31

Kevin Keegan delivers the most famous
post-match interview in football history

"But that's part and parcel of the psychological battle, Kevin..."
Keys attempted to say. Andy Gray disagreed, but not as vocally or
passionately as Keegan.

"No! When you do that with footballers like he said about
Leeds, and when you do things like that about a man like Stuart
Pearce... I've kept really quiet but I'll tell you something, he went
down in my estimation when he said that. We have not resorted
to that. But I'll tell you, you can tell him now, he'll be watching it,
we're still fighting for this title and he's got to go to Middlesbrough
and get something. And I'll tell you, honestly, I will love it if we
beat them. Love it. But it really has got to me. I've voiced it live,
not in front of the press or anywhere. I'm not even going to the
press conference. But the battle's still on and Man United have not
won this yet."

The outburst was box office; it hasn't been replayed time and
time again without good cause. Keegan, who had seemingly been
struggling under the weight of the pressure since Christmas, had
arguably done the worst thing possible with two games left to play.
Had he remained quiet on the matter (he wasn't asked a leading

question about Ferguson's comments) he could have let his team's impressive performance speak for itself. But there was enough evidence to suggest that the manager's words and actions were beginning to affect the mood of the Newcastle players.

"After the game you're concentrating on your own performance," Brian Deane says now, explaining that he didn't witness the interview live but quickly became aware of it as the news of it spread around Elland Road. "He was showing how passionate he was. The reputation of Newcastle fans goes without saying and I think they had the right man representing them. I overheard a conversation between two Newcastle players who I won't name, but they seemed really surprised by what he had said. Bemused. But, like I said, after losing, I was reflecting more on my own performance and feeling bad about not scoring."

Keegan's comments were perceived as evidence that the pressure had got to him. Deane feels that is probably a little unfair. "I just thought Kevin was letting off steam. Looking back, I think it's brilliant. We go on about a lack of characters and a lack of soul in the game... what that did was give the supporters an insight into the desire he had. I think he should be commended for saying it because it's the kind of thing fans want to hear."

Without doubt it was a rallying cry for the Toon Army but the public reaction wasn't kind. Ferguson's reaction in his first autobiography seems a little disingenuous; for someone who had made it his business to ensure he took every conceivable advantage, it seems not entirely straightforward that he would not have understood that his comments after the Leeds game would have annoyed Keegan. "After the final whistle I... was stopped dead in my tracks by Kevin's outburst. God, I felt for him. Looking at replays later, I was better able to digest what he had said and at first it made me feel a bit guilty... Although I was a little disappointed when he attacked me, I just put it down to pressure."

Interestingly, Steve Howey told the *Daily Telegraph* in March

2016, "The funny thing about that interview was, Kevin had started to get worried about the players speaking to the media. We used to speak to the press all the time, but Kevin was more guarded than he had been because the media twist people's words sometimes and he was fed up with it.

"After that game, we were sitting on the team bus and we had Sky Sports on. I don't think we were shocked. We knew what Kevin was like. When he spoke like that, that was one of the reasons we loved playing for him. We had seen this sort of thing loads of times before. Even after it had finished and they'd gone back to the studio, we were silent. Then someone piped up, 'He doesn't want us to speak to the media in case we say something daft'. Everyone burst out laughing."

Newcastle's win had ensured that the title race would go down to the final day, this was perfect for Sky, whose manipulation of the fixture list had worked wonderfully for the dramatic requirements of the viewing public. And so, it should be said, there ought to have been a little less pressure on Keegan's side heading into that game with Forest on Thursday 2nd May. Peter Beardsley's solo effort in the first half gave Newcastle an advantage which they held for most of the game but as the second half wore on Forest began to get more and more into it, and Newcastle seemed to get increasingly rattled. The equaliser, fifteen minutes from the end, was delivered with from the dynamite left boot of Ian Woan. Woan had developed a reputation for scoring long range screamers and this 25-yard stunner was as good as any other. They held on for a point and the draw may as well have been a defeat as far as Manchester United supporters were concerned. Their superior goal difference of six meant that so long as United avoided defeat they would win the title, as it was unlikely that Newcastle would beat Spurs by six goals.

Asked if he and his team-mates saw a vulnerability in Newcastle that they felt they could exploit after the 'love it' interview, Pearce speaks with the diplomacy which you would expect of someone who not only went on to play for Newcastle but also worked with Keegan at Manchester City (and was even recalled to the England team under Keegan at the age of 37!). "Newcastle under Kevin were a top team-they just missed out on that top one (the title)," he says.

★

So, for a second year in succession, the Premier League title race went down to the last day. With it already understood that the fledglings had done remarkably, it is worth now reflecting back twelve months from this point, to the game at Upton Park. The 1-1 draw, and the loss of the Premier League title by the narrowest of margins was seen in the cynical world of football as a failure. It didn't matter that in that team-that was, let us not forget, a team with many injuries itself-the kids did themselves proud. The perception was one of failure. And the reason for that is because, on the final day, when the trophy was handed out, it went to Blackburn Rovers and not them.

There has been sympathetic revisionism – such as that from Pearce – in the theory that Newcastle should have won the league in 1995/96. They are still affectionately remembered as the entertainers by supporters up and down the land. Yet the fact remains that Manchester United scored more goals (indeed they scored nine more goals away from home) and lost fewer games. And, importantly, Newcastle's implosion didn't happen right at the death; Ferguson's side had an advantage as early as March, and had closed the gap completely by early April. It was United's to lose, even with the Southampton defeat and Newcastle's draw at Forest gave them a points advantage on the last day.

And yet, with United having earned this advantage, there were now rumbles of conspiracy in the air. Middlesbrough were United's final day opponents and were managed by Reds legend Bryan Robson. Robson vehemently contested this in his programme notes. "I've got a message for anyone who believes Middlesbrough will lay down and allow Manchester United to clinch the Premiership trophy today – Boro are going all out to win. There have been suggestions over the past couple of weeks that Boro, because of the links between myself and some of the coaching and playing staff with Old Trafford, will simply hand United the title. This is not the case... This game is our chance not only to play a part in deciding the championship but to end the season on a high note. The lads are professionals and no footballers like to lose games. All the players want to win this one and Alex knows that."

5TH MAY 1996 - FA CARLING PREMIERSHIP
RIVERSIDE STADIUM, MIDDLESBROUGH. ATT. 29,921

MIDDLESBROUGH 0-3 UNITED

Scorers: May 13, Cole 54, Giggs 80
Team : Schmeichel, P.Neville, May, Pallister, Irwin, Beckham, Keane,
Butt, Giggs, Cantona, Scholes (Cole 53)

Robson felt that the best chance of success for his team would be
to capitalise on any nervousness in United's players who were yet
to taste success; Ferguson had boldly stuck with the side that took
Forest apart, meaning Phil Neville, Nicky Butt, David Beckham and
Paul Scholes (over Andy Cole) were all started. To an outsider this
may have seemed like a little bit of a gamble, with Cole, McClair,
Sharpe and even Gary Neville representing more experienced
options. But at this point the manager had such conviction that this
was his strongest team, and, crucially, a team with the momentum,
confidence and form which made them less vulnerable to anxiety.

And still, for ten minutes, the edginess of the occasion remained;
as is often the case in showpiece matches like this, both teams take
a little while to become accustomed to the atmosphere and pace.
What was clear was that Middlesbrough were most definitely up
for spoiling the day but United's confidence and ability found a way
through as early as the 13th minute. Ryan Giggs' corner was met
at the back post by David May, who headed it back across goal and
down into the ground. The effort beat former Reds' stopper Gary
Walsh, and, on the bounce, it also evaded the Brazilian defender
Branco, who was only able to get a head to it after it crossed the
line. On the day when all was to be decided, it was fitting that May,
a player who had tasted title disappointment for two years running,
would score the opener. His relief told its own story.

News undoubtedly filtered through to the Newcastle game,
and the hosts became flustered with their efforts to break down

Spurs; after a draining season, the prospect that no matter what they did, it might not be enough, seemed sufficient to rattle a few of the Magpies' stars.

They would have headed into the second half remembering the events of the final day in 1995; how everything changed and the late drama. However it became clear they were contending with two forces –rying to beat an opponent on the pitch whilst anxiously waiting for a reaction from the terraces which would give them an indication of events at the Riverside Stadium.

United, meanwhile, were composed and in control. They won a corner early in the second half, and 'Boro knocked it out for another. Ferguson then made the decision to substitute Scholes for Cole, perhaps feeling that now the real edge was out of the situation, he may settle into the game more. His decision brought instant reward; Giggs whipped in another corner and it was flicked by Cantona to Cole, the forward had his back to goal in the six-yard box and was tightly marked by a red shirt. With nothing else on, the club record signing flicked an instinctive right foot effort over his shoulder and it flew into the top, unguarded corner, of Gary Walsh's goal. Cole seemed overwhelmed by delight and all of his outfield team-mates, realising the significance of the moment, rushed to celebrate with him.

Seconds later, Spurs midfielder Jason Dozell cleverly found space in a very restless Newcastle box and struck the ball into the net, past the despairing dives of both goalkeeper and a defender.

The title was on its way to Manchester, and with half an hour left to indulge in celebrations, all of the Riverside Stadium joined in with choruses of 'Cheer up Kevin Keegan', a chant to the tune of 'Daydream Believer.' Perhaps freed by the pressure for the first time in months, Newcastle actually grew into their game and netted an equaliser fifteen minutes later when Asprilla pulled back from the byline for Ferdinand to score from close range.

But any hopes of an unlikely comeback by their neighbours were abruptly ended ten minutes from time. Nicky Butt fought for a ball with the brilliant Brazil maestro Juninho and came out on top – he played it inside for Ryan Giggs, who was able to float into the centre and pick it up. The home midfield were immediately off guard because of his marauding and, initially, no-one picked him up. So Giggs seized the initiative and ran towards the goal; but, just as with Roy Keane's goal against Leeds, his initial movement had created all the havoc that was necessary to achieve the space and time he needed before striking a smart left footed effort from fully twenty yards. It flew past Walsh. "A fitting way to crown the new champions," remarked Sky Sports commentator Andy Gray.

On a day when his intervention wasn't required for once, Cantona received the ball and was about to turn to launch another attack when the final whistle went. He bent down and held the ball aloft; an enduring moment for a man who controlled so much of the destiny of this title race.

"It's been a great year, great for our younger players and older players too," Sir Bobby Charlton told Sky Sports later.

"It's always great to win the league title. It's the hardest league in the world," said a notably relieved and relaxed Ferguson. "I thought that March was an important month, March and possibly April. We had to start winning games and fortunately once we got our defenders back, from the West Ham game, we had a marvellous run really. Tremendous run. It's credit to them, 16 wins out of 17 games put us right in the frame again."

"Our congratulations go to Man United and the supporters," said a downbeat but ultimately gracious Keegan. "It was a tremendous thing to catch us. You know, everybody talks about our collapse, but they don't do credit to Man United who, with all the young players in their side and three or four old heads, have turned around what looked like an impossible situation. We're good losers up here as well, and they'll be great representatives of this league in Europe."

The man who scored the goal that effectively decided the destiny of the title, David May, reflects on an extraordinary year. "Blackburn had just won the league so I was just determined to win the league back," he says now. "To lose the league to the team I had just come from, I was gutted, absolutely gutted. Then to lose the FA Cup Final… if we'd have beaten West Ham in that last league game I'm sure we would have gone on to win the final, I'm sure of that. But these things happen, people move on, you get new faces in, you become stronger and you become more determined. Even though it was the last game of the season (in 1996), it was still quite easy, Newcastle were 12 or 13 points in front of us at one point. I never thought for a minute we'd lose that game at Middlesbrough."

May's own contribution to the cause was understated at the time but deserves a mention; with Bruce struggling for form and fitness and Pallister struggling for fitness but struggling nonetheless, it was left to the then 25 year-old May to be the senior head in a crucial position on the pitch. His performances, particularly in the home games against Arsenal, Spurs and Leeds, and obviously against

FINAL LEAGUE TABLE 1995/96									
1	Manchester United	38	25	7	6	73	35	82	38
2	Newcastle United	38	24	6	8	66	37	78	29
3	Liverpool	38	20	11	7	70	34	71	36
4	Aston Villa	38	18	9	11	52	35	63	17
5	Arsenal	38	17	12	9	49	32	63	17
6	Everton	38	17	10	11	64	44	61	20
7	Blackburn Rovers	38	18	7	13	61	47	61	14
8	Tottenham Hotspur	38	16	13	9	50	38	61	12
9	Nottingham Forest	38	15	13	10	50	54	58	-4
10	West Ham United	38	14	9	15	43	52	51	-9
11	Chelsea	38	12	14	12	46	44	50	2
12	Middlesbrough	38	11	10	17	35	50	43	-15
13	Leeds United	38	12	7	19	40	57	43	-17
14	Wimbledon	38	10	11	17	55	70	41	-15
15	Sheffield Wednesday	38	10	10	18	48	61	40	-13
16	Coventry City	38	8	14	16	42	60	38	-18
17	Southampton	38	9	11	18	34	52	38	-18
18	Manchester City	38	9	11	18	33	58	38	-25
19	Queens Park Rangers	38	9	6	23	38	57	33	-19
20	Bolton Wanderers	38	8	5	25	39	71	29	-32

Middlesbrough, were so good that there was no question he had played himself into a definite starting position in the Cup Final.

Still in 'head over heart' mode, as far as sentimentality was concerned, in crunch matches that meant that Bruce facing a race against fitness that would see him miss out at Wembley. May recalls that Bruce wished him the best. "He was exactly as I was in 1999 for the Champions League Final – he patted me on the back, wished me well, just said make sure I do the business and fair play to him," May says now. "It's a team game. He's an absolute gentleman."

At the other end of the table Manchester City joined QPR and Bolton in the relegation zone after a typically cathartic afternoon at Maine Road. City, needing to better the results of fellow strugglers Southampton and Coventry because of their poor goal difference, recovered from a two-goal deficit against a Liverpool team with one eye on the FA Cup Final thanks to Uwe Rosler's penalty and Kit Symons converting from a corner. Yet in the dying minutes incorrect information filtered through to the players that a draw was enough to keep them up, despite their rivals both drawing 0-0. At the final whistle the reality of the situation set in and City were down - they would take another five years to return to top flight football.

★

So to the FA Cup Final. Still, as recently as 1996, the biggest day in the English football calendar. There was no inflated media expectation of their clubs qualifying for the Champions League Final every year and it's probably best to sweep Blackburn Rovers' campaign in that competition under the carpet. The fascination of continental football was more or less confined to Saturday morning coffee shop accounts of the Italian league brought to us by Channel 4.

Maybe Liverpool had been enamoured by exotic tastes; maybe in direct competition to Manchester United, they saw an opportunity to live up their effectively unflattering nickname. The Liverpool squad arrived at Wembley in cream Armani suits.

"Yeah, erm, nice day, so we thought, why not?" Steve McManaman said with a grin to BBC's Ray Stubbs on the Wembley pitch before kick off. "Be better if it was really sunny, wouldn't it? We'll need our glasses then we'll be in business," said Robbie Fowler. Jason McAteer and Jamie Redknapp exchanged pleasantries about their 'nice suits'.

"People still remind me about the white suits all the time," Fowler said in 2008. "It's one of those things - if we had won the game nobody would have mentioned it but we lost and it has become infamous."

Liverpool, at the time, were clearly made up with their designer clobber; their opponents felt they had already struck an important chord in their quest for glory. "I said to Brian Kidd '1-0'. Because of that," Ferguson said in the BBC documentary 'Sir Alex Ferguson: Secrets of Success'. "I think that's, what would you call it? Arrogance or over-confidence. It was ridiculous. Absolutely ridiculous. Blue shirt, red and white tie and white suit. And a blue flower. Who designed that? They say it was Armani. I bet his sales went down. I mean Jamie Redknapp's got sunglasses on, but you know the most telling part of it is Roy Evans and Ronnie Moran had black suits on. I think they were embarrassed."

"Liverpool had arrived at Wembley in their cream-coloured Giorgio Armani suits which made them look more like a Dixieland jazz group than rough and tumble athletes," quipped Joe Melling of the *Mail*.

As entertaining as it was, the cream suits were merely a subplot for the main event, and the star of the show, the man everyone wanted to talk to in Cup Final week - Eric Cantona.

"I wanted to win the Premiership title for Alex Ferguson and it's exactly the same with the FA Cup," Cantona told the *Daily Express*. "I have tried to pay back everyone at Manchester United, particularly the manager and my team-mates. As long as I am in England, I hope to win the title every year... there were a lot of critics, especially from France, who thought I deserved everything I got. I thought it was too much. But I'm not naive. I know that there will be a lot of praise now and that, too, will probably be too much. Talking is not important. What matters is winning on the pitch."

However, Cantona wasn't quite done with his public engagements. As part of BBC's Cup Final day coverage, Des Lynam sat down with the striker to talk about his journey over the last eighteen months. "The first one (Premier League title) with Manchester was great, this one was very important for the club after last season, and very important for myself, because I had a lot of things to prove after... well, everybody knows, last year," Cantona told Lynam. The experienced BBC presenter interjected, suggesting that although the 'incident' (the kick on Simmons at Crystal Palace) was a negative thing, some good had come out of it. "I always try to put things in that way," Cantona said. "I think we learn from everything, and a bad thing can be turned (into a) good thing. It's very difficult at the moment but in the future, we look to put the future under the sun."

Lynam asked how much persuasion was required on the part of Alex Ferguson to keep Cantona at Old Trafford. "He just asked me if I wanted to leave English football because he knew it was a difficult time for me, but I just said no. But he didn't try to persuade me," the Frenchman insisted. "I wanted to stay."

"How close were you to not wanting to stay?" asked Lynam.

"Just... I was close to signing somewhere else because I wasn't sure if Manchester United wanted me to stay, at that moment, because I receive a lot of critics, and them too. I just wanted to stay... When I arrived here I felt 'now I am in a big club, a great club' all of the players around me were good... great... I knew I had a lot to prove but I wasn't afraid about it. I'm very confident, always, I've been like that. I'm sorry, but... I'm not arrogant, like people say, I'm just confident by myself."

Questioned if winning the league meant he would play with more freedom in the Cup Final, Cantona replied, "Yeah, I think so. I think so. I think, last season we lost in the Final because we didn't win the league the week before..."

"Mind you, you weren't playing," Lynam interrupts.

"Yeah, but... it was my team-mates, it was me. It's like a big family."

Lynam then asks how United's star man felt about the departure of other big names the previous year. "I'm a true optimist," he responded. "I think I can win a game if I play only on my own against eleven players, so I'm not worried about nothing. But I respect them, though, because we had a lot of great times together but life is like that. Before us, it was a life, afterwards, it will be another one... the most important season for them (the young players) is the next one."

The subject of captaincy is brought up, and Lynam asks why it seems to be that Cantona has remained as 'an island' (in the reporters words) with the armband whilst others seem very vocal. "Or is that a misconception on my part?" Lynam asks.

"No, you may be right! Maybe sometimes I wanted to say something, but I couldn't find the word, I need time to find the word... in football you need to think very quickly."

Almost every word from Cantona's lips was becoming a prophecy; Lynam discussed the European Championships, and Eric was relaxed about whether he would be selected for France (it was becoming increasingly obvious that he wouldn't). Instead, he talked about the following season, returning fit and fresh and going for the Champions League. "It is important for us and for English football," Cantona said, "or nobody will remember us."

"And what about after that?"

"When we win I want to stay in football, when I lose, I want to quit!" Cantona joked. "But... I don't know. Maybe a manager, or maybe something else."

Finally, Lynam asked about his relationship with the United fans. "They absolutely idolise you. How do you feel about them?"

"Oh," Cantona sighs, "It's... what can I say? I respect them very much. I love them. They never stopped singing... even... (clicks fingers) fifteen seconds in a game, they thought about it. I'll never forget it. Ever. I will try to give them the pleasure they need to receive, every time."

"For the next two years?"

"For the next two years. Or maybe longer... or maybe shorter. We never know in life. But I am very, very, very happy."

★

There had been speculation raging about the team news for United. In particular, the potential selections of David May, Steve Bruce, Gary Neville, Phil Neville, Paul Scholes and Andy Cole were all up for discussion, with the manager appreciating he would have some tough decisions to make. "It's a horrible job but it has to be done," he admitted to the *Manchester Evening News*. "You have to be practical and give yourself the proper protection with the right variety on the bench."

Ferguson was given an unwelcome headache on the Thursday before the Cup Final when Tony Coton picked up an injury. United had gone without a substitute goalkeeper for many matches that season but, with no decision yet made for the final, Kevin Pilkington was called into the squad and quickly measured for his suit then put on a train. "Before the game, we arrived at the stadium and got into the changing rooms. I took my blazer and tie off, before I got a tap on the shoulder from the gaffer saying, 'sorry son, but I'm not having a goalkeeper on the bench today'," Pilkington recalls. "It was really hot and he'd decided to put an extra outfield player on the bench. To console myself I thought that I could at least be able to sample the atmosphere and warm up on the pitch before the game but Peter told me 'TC's going to warm me up.' Tony's injury was just to his wrist, so he could help with the other training. I didn't even get to do that, and was gutted to miss out on a medal."

Ferguson ultimately opted to make one change for the final - recalling Andy Cole for Paul Scholes. That meant Scholes had to settle for a place alongside Gary Neville and Lee Sharpe on the bench against opponents that had proven too difficult to beat in the league in the past season.

United had proven themselves to be the best side in the country but the Final presented a new challenge and Liverpool, with their own young stars, were seen as equals. The 1996 FA Cup Final was as much an indicator for the future of English football as it was a showpiece occasion for the season just gone – and what could be better than the victors beating their closest rivals, particularly when one of their opponent's most famous sons had written them off on the first day. "There was an element of we'll show him," Pilkington admits. "I'm sure plenty of the other lads were thinking it too. Especially him being an ex-Liverpool player."

And so, then, to the end of what Cantona had described as a 'long but beautiful year'. Manchester United were aiming to become the first ever team to win the League and FA Cup Double on two occasions; Liverpool were aiming to do what United had done to them in 1977, when a 2-1 victory dashed the Scousers' hopes of a treble.

11TH MAY 1996 - FA CUP FINAL
WEMBLEY, LONDON. ATT. 79,007

UNITED 1-0 LIVERPOOL

Scorer: Cantona 85
Team : Schmeichel, P.Neville, May, Pallister, Irwin,
Beckham (G.Neville 89), Keane, Butt, Giggs, Cantona,
Cole (Scholes 65)

Despite the hype and pre-match expectations of a classic, the showpiece event turned into a tactical battle. It wasn't a case of two sides cancelling each other out, as so often tends to happen in these big games. There could be no doubt that Manchester United were the superior team in the first half; Roy Keane, by far the most impressive player on the pitch, was bossing proceedings and providing, with Nicky Butt, a stranglehold on the possession and supply line to Liverpool's most creative players. Their own central midfielders, Jamie Redknapp and Jason McAteer, were simply unable to compete on the same level. Yet Liverpool kept their defensive discipline and turned it into a cagey affair and United's best opportunities in the first half came from distance; Ryan Giggs teed up David Beckham, whose twenty yard effort in the first five minutes was acrobatically tipped over the bar by David James. In a similar position at the other end, Redknapp could only blaze his effort wildly over the bar.

In the second half, both teams were attacking the end of the stadium where their own fans were situated; though the hope that that would translate into genuine excitement did not bear fruit; United made early advances with Cantona improvising a near post volley that forced James into action, before Cole could react. But it settled down once more into the kind of game dictated by the grafters rather than the artists. That was certainly the case with Cole; the pragmatism of both sides meant service for the strikers was in short supply, and United's record signing was kept on the periphery, just as Collymore and Fowler were for Liverpool. So Ferguson decided to replace Cole with Scholes to provide a link to Cantona. Liverpool countered by doing nothing at first; yes, United were theoretically tightening up, but any change to this evenly contested battle was likely to have a significant repercussion somewhere. With quarter of an hour left, Roy Evans brought off Collymore for Ian Rush; the Liverpool legend was leaving Anfield on a free transfer but Rush was the leading scorer in the competition's history and Evans made a change in the hope that destiny would smile on his side.

Earlier in the week Ferguson had been quoted in the *Daily Mail* as saying that he felt this final could be as memorable as the 'Matthews final' between Blackpool and Bolton Wanderers in 1953. In the end the only similarity with that 4–3 thriller of 42 years earlier was the lateness of the winner and the totemic identity of the scorer. For Stan Mortensen read Eric Cantona.

By the 85th minute Liverpool looked spent as United chased a late winner; David Beckham hit an outswinging corner with Gary Pallister and Eric Cantona lurking in the box. Beckham would become synonymous with his excellent crossing, though this was far from one of his best. Still, it invoked such uncertainty in David James that despite having seven Liverpool men around him, he felt compelled to come out for the ball. James got there ahead of David May, who had made a late run, and got a solid fist to the ball; Pallister had remained statuesque, while Cantona had tracked the ball and movement of his team–mates and, perhaps anticipating there was likely to be a collision in front of him, took two or three steps backwards. As James connected, the ball bounced, and Cantona was still moving his body backwards. He twisted his body to arch his right foot fully around the ball and connected sweetly with a half-volley which somehow found its way cleanly through three Liverpool shirts and into the goal. James, on his knees, was helpless. Among those in the (mostly) joyous Wembley crowd

The perfect finish

was the man of the match in that 1977 Cup Final, the late Brian Greenhoff, who celebrated with such vigour he later said he fell forward a number of rows.

Liverpool's reaction was not quite as energetic; instead of throwing the kitchen sink as they wanted to, they were deflated, defeated and despondent. When referee Dermot Gallagher blew for full time, the United team and bench, to a man, made a beeline for the enigmatic star who had once more been the difference.

"It was Cantona, of course. It had to be Cantona," reported the *Mail on Sunday*'s Patrick Collins. In the on-pitch celebrations, commentator Clive Tyldsley asked Cantona if this was the best moment of his United career. "It was important after we done the double two years ago... now I can go on holiday."

"What a contrast with twelve months ago," Tyldsley said.

Cantona simply shrugged and said, "That's life. Up and down."

Ferguson was delighted with his man's contribution. "I can't believe it has happened. Sometimes I have to pinch myself to believe it is all real... It was a quite magnificent goal; Eric showed great composure and such accuracy with the shot, it couldn't have come at a better time," he said, while looking to the future. "We've conquered England and now we must go and conquer Europe. Next season we have got to have a good go at the European Cup we've been in it twice before and disappointed. We intend to make England proud of us again and make the country a force in Europe again."

Amidst the celebration, Ferguson made a note to pay tribute to those who missed out on a medal. "It's a horrible job, management- there are disappointments," he confessed. "Steve Bruce wasn't even a sub but he was brilliant, different class. It's ridiculous that we can't have five substitutes. I just couldn't risk him and there was no game to try him out in before today. To me, he represents one of the most courageous players this club has had, but I felt I could not take any chances. I would have liked him to be captain to pick up this trophy... I had to tell Steve in stages that he wasn't playing. Yesterday, I told him he was not starting in the team but how terrific it could be on the subs' bench, to break it to him gently. Then, today, I told him he wasn't even a sub."

The manager may have been enthusiastic about Bruce's contribution but the truth is that captains are supposed to be the irreplacable players, the voice of the manager on the pitch. As fine a servant as he had been, and as solid a player as he still was, Bruce was no longer the indispensable force he had been for many years in this Manchester United side. Ferguson had generously explained his absence with the injury but this gentle way of letting Bruce down had a greater message; this was a new time, a time of regeneration, and it was time for Bruce to move on. Cantona revealed that he had talked with the man he had shared the armband with in recent weeks. "I wanted him to pick up the Cup but he said to me, 'I have done it before, now it is your turn.' It was a tremendous honour."

Roy Evans was as gracious as Kevin Keegan had been after

seeing United lift. "You have to give United credit," he admitted. "Any team that does what they have done this season is absolutely fantastic."

That Merseyside sportsmanship was not shared by supporters; as United went to pick up the trophy, one Liverpool fan spat on Cantona, while another swung a punch at Ferguson. "It's totally unacceptable," blasted FA Chief Executive Graham Kelly, who announced he would launch an inquiry into it with the country keen to show that they could host a European Championships free of controversy. Even this sour note could not dampen the mood amongst the Old Trafford contingent; from the outstanding leaders Schmeichel and Cantona, to the generals in midfield Butt and Keane, to those like David May (who had improved immeasurably to shrug off his 'Trojan Horse' tag in the United support) to the rest of the Fledglings, Manchester United were not only the team of tomorrow, they were the team of today.

YOU CAN WIN ANYTHING WITH KIDS

S O WITH THE BENEFIT of 20 years hindsight, was Alan Hansen's comment really unreasonable? Was it the clanger that history has judged it? Speaking after a summer in which United had sold their best players and had taken the risk of trusting in youth, it must have seemed, to an experienced pro, that the manner of the team's defeat against Aston Villa instantly ruled them out of the running for title. In Hansen's defence, such a young unproven team hadn't won the title since the 1950s.

That said, I hope we have proved that it wasn't completely unexpected that Manchester United might succeed in this remarkable season and, in having a lighthearted laugh about the misjudgement of one August 1995 quote, it's probably fair to balance it with the excellent foresight in the Vol 8, Issue 2 editorial of the United fanzine *Red Issue*. "[United's second half performance against Aston Villa] was in many respects reminiscent of the display last December against Galatasaray, the teamwork and knowledge of each other has to be one of the main reasons why Fergie has apparently shown so much faith in their potential. Indeed, in Fergie's continued defence it might not be too ridiculous a comparison to make to compare United now with the Ajax side of three or four years ago. Working on the theory that players who grow up playing the same system week in week out for years will ultimately be more effective than a team of cobbled together stars, Fergie might well have taken the decision that although in the short term this might leave us on the edge of contention for major domestic honours, in the long term it could lead to a period of success that we can only dream of."

It really is the perfect description of what actually did unfold; United continued to benefit through what seemed, at times, to be a telepathic bond amongst its breakthrough stars. Who is ever to know: if the team had suffered a blip against Middlesbrough and Newcastle had done their own job, and then, Liverpool proved too tough at Wembley – would the 'Fledglings' have had the confidence to go on and enjoy the success they ultimately did. That success can be defined by the fortunes of one or two days against the pure talent of an entire career seems unfair; it's almost illogical to argue against the theory that, even with the transition from the 1994 to 1996 'Double' teams taken into account, even eventually when Eric Cantona retired, that Manchester United were the best team in the country from 1993 to 2003.

The first Arsenal team under Arsene Wenger, which benefitted from a mix of his imports and the existing defensive structure put in place by George Graham, raised the competitive bar on a domestic level and inspired the Manchester United team to a relentless consistency that has rarely been seen in English football; certainly not since the Liverpool team of the early 80s. United lost just nine league games over three seasons winning championships from 1999-2001 (and three of these were lost after the the league was won in 2001). To put that achievement in perspective, the Liverpool team which won a hat-trick of titles between 1982 and 1984 lost 21 games: albeit from a dozen more games.

By 2000, the fluency and vibrancy in the teamwork that existed amongst the youth players was hard-wired into the team: a team that could score six goals against their closest rivals in 2001, a team against whom you could be leading by two or three goals and still not be entirely sure of victory; a team that could still win even if they were losing in the last minute; a team that did all of the above so often that these characteristics came to define an era. Indeed, it was often said (with some degree of accuracy) that the team resembled the character of its manager and that is true but it also resembled the character of the players within it. The desire to win was overwhelming and it had been bred in the players from the moment that the majority of them signed for United as schoolboys.

Is it a surprise that, with the final day of 1995 hanging over them, United achieved so many late victories over the coming years? This desire was no doubt increased by the tremendous criticism that was levelled at the injury-ravaged United team that threw away a large points advantage to Arsenal in 1998 – it is little wonder then that the club became adept at winning the league by Easter.

The mental strength and capability of the younger players can be attributed to the discipline that surrounded them as well as the disappointments they had endured; the bark of Ferguson, the heat of Schmeichel's angry voice on the back of their neck, the wrath of Eric Harrison, and, of course, that quest for footballing perfection instilled by the likes of Eric Cantona. That fifteen minutes or half an hour every day when he would keep back some of the young players to continue to train had a profound effect on them: if it was good enough for Cantona, it was good enough for them. And so, in turn, it set a great example for the next generation, watching the likes of Neville and Beckham staying behind to practice and improve, as observed by Danny Higginbotham. It's easy to say that the club had a bonanza in 1992 and has failed to match it ever since but the truth is that, from then up until around 2003, its youth system was prolific: not just in terms of players breaking through to the first team (it's hard to be the 'next class of 92' when the first ones aren't at their peak) but also in providing young players with the best education before a career in league football.

Higginbotham played only a handful of games for United before having a very good career at Derby and, most notably, Stoke. David Healy was another of the very many names who couldn't quite break past the superstars at United but, had such an excellent career that he became Northern Ireland's record goalscorer by a considerable distance. These players, and plenty like them, were unquestionably helped by the competitive environment in which they grew up but to simply say the incredible period of success which followed is down to how players coped with the pressure is to ignore how absurdly gifted this Manchester United team was on an individual level and how that individual talent married to create what was as close to a perfect team as has ever been seen in the British game.

In Peter Schmeichel they had a goalkeeper who was the best in the world. For someone so dominating in stature, his ability to move and the speed of his reactions seemed almost superhuman; this didn't mean he was flawless but he made fewer errors than most and his size alone intimidated the opposition. At 32, he was moving into his peak years and it's no coincidence that whenever United struggled over the next few years, it would invariably be when the huge Dane was unavailable and, after 1999, when he was replaced by Bosnich and, later, Barthez.

Schmeichel was generally considered to be the best in the business anyway so it would be false and incredible to suggest that Tony Coton was responsible for the three and a half years of form and success which followed his arrival but his appointment had an impact; the short term benefit of Coton's arrival was the presence of a serious and senior competitor for the goalkeeper's jersey and, more importantly, Coton had a lot of experience to pass on. He had endured dips in form and knew how to cope with them. As a confidante, he would prove second to none for the great Dane.

Gary Neville blossomed into the best England right back of his generation but, at this point in his career, he was one of the many kids who were helped by Schmeichel's experience. Let it be said that the elder Neville was in fine form himself and played well at centre half and right back: he just found himself in the unfortunate situation that his brother Phil was playing as well as he ever would.

In the following season, Gary made that right back spot his own, helped by a fine showing in the European Championships. His fine form over two years had given him the edge over his brother and threw him back into the first team picture.

As for Phil Neville, he became a jack of all trades, a utility player called upon to play in either full back position or as a holding midfielder. Phil went on to play 386 times for United in their most glittering period before leaving for Everton in 2005, underlining his contribution with 11 trophies. As far as the Nevilles are concerned, the perception of them is generally one of hard workers who compensated for their lack of talent with effort. It is simplistic to simply dismiss them in this way; their defensive awareness were a major reason for United's success and their reliability is reflected in the pair's huge appearance tallies.

Honest toiler rather than talented artist was also a sobriquet that would dog David Beckham; as his star rose, it seemed as if the perception of his talent lessened in proportion; to many he was over-rated, only worth a place in the team because of his status as tabloid fodder, or even earning a career on the back of the goal that was to catapult him to stardom on the opening day of the following season. This does Beckham an incredible disservice; the half-way line shot against Wimbledon quite rightly earned plaudits but this was by no means the only outrageous goal scored by the midfielder in the first half of the 1996/97 season – it seemed as if he were running a one man goal of the season campaign. He had scored a wonderful chip in the 4-0 drubbing of Newcastle in the Charity Shield and followed up his Selhurst Park magic with a long range shot at Derby's Baseball Ground. Great goals at West Ham and Nottingham Forest were followed by another thirty yard effort against Tottenham at White Hart Lane. There was more to Beckham than boy band good looks. He spent hours on the training ground perfecting the art of crossing and free kicks. Beckham had an extraordinary talents, there was simply nobody who could deliver a ball like he could for years, but this was as a result of hours and hours of relentless dedication.

Beckham quickly became the most recognisable face in the sport over the next three years, the face of a new celebrity culture which carried football along with it. Alex Ferguson, who had notoriously sheltered Ryan Giggs from this sort of attention when he broke through, now had to embrace it as part of the game. It was perhaps no coincidence that when the manager wanted to get his message that 'no one is bigger than the club' across to the public, it was often done by dropping Beckham. Yes, the Londoner had limitations: he wasn't as naturally gifted at dribbling as Giggs, nor as technically outstanding as Cantona or Scholes but he compensated for this, like the Nevilles, with effort. If Beckham was left out of a game, it wasn't because he'd been found coasting in a previous match.

If Beckham's reputation overshadowed his talent then the same could be said for Nicky Butt. Classed as a tigerish, defensive midfielder to most neutral observers, Butt was a tremendous footballer with a natural instinct for the right pass or the smart movement to score a goal. He had that positional discipline that helped when defending and the professional attitude to accept he would be in and out of the side as and when required. Butt was seen as one of the most talented from that 1992 side and it was no coincidence that he was the first, after Ryan Giggs, to hold down a place in the first team. That he is often seen as the spare man in a central midfield is probably the consequence of Paul Scholes never quite fitting the role of a striker as well as Ferguson had hoped rather than anything negative to do with Butt himself.

In 1996, Paul Scholes posed a conundrum that Ferguson struggled to solve: was he a forward, a midfielder or somewhere in between? In an era before the 'false nine' became fashionable, Scholes was shunted forward and often replaced Andy Cole as a deep-lying striker. His key contribution spared the former

Newcastle man's blushes as he struggled to come to terms with life at Old Trafford and the increased scrutiny of press and public.

Considering that both Beckham and Gary Neville had always been earmarked as central players, perhaps it was simply a case of these players establishing themselves more quickly on the right hand side. In November 2001, Scholes would famously refuse to play further forward in a league cup tie at Arsenal: one of few public fall-outs with the manager but one that underlined the pair's difference of opinion over his role. Indeed, it wasn't only Ferguson who couldn't get it right; Sven Goran Erikkson famously picked Scholes on the left wing during the 2004 European Championships, a decision that now looks preposterous.

Paul Scholes has been venerated by a generation of fellow pros and, to most, he was the jewel in the crown of the 'Class of 92'. He is one of those rare modern footballers that peaked in their thirties; his goal return dropped from double figures in eight of his first eleven seasons to single figures after 2005. Later he found his niche: dominating games by lying deep, picking passes and orchestrating attacks. He was seemingly untouchable as a force in the domestic game and, with the likes of Rooney and Ronaldo at their peak, had willing runners to latch on to his pin-point delivery. Alongside Michael Carrick, there has probably never been a slower or more effective midfield pair in the history of the game. In essence, he became the central midfielder everyone had once hoped David Beckham would blossom into. The playmaker who could dictate terms against all opposition.

Having helped United to three consecutive league titles and another European Cup, Scholes retired in 2011 but made a dramatic comeback in an FA Cup against Manchester City in January 2012. United, trounced 6-1 by City back in October, slowly but surely clawed back the title deficit and led by 8 points with just 5 games to go in April. Sadly for United, fortune smiled on City that season but it has to go down as one of the greatest comebacks of all time;

by his very presence Scholes had transformed the title race.

One player who was not experiencing his first time in the limelight in 1996 was Ryan Giggs - for the Welshman was now considered an experienced hand, despite being in the same age group as those who were now celebrating their first championship. This was Giggs' third title and he had recovered from a dip in form which may have been the result of the weight of expectation and the extra physical attention that accompanied his growing reputation. There was now no denying his status as the best left winger at United - ahead of Lee Sharpe. Before, Giggs had been an exciting mishmash of speed and dribbling ability but, over the course of this twelve month period, there was a maturity and a technical proficiency that had not been seen before. Towards the end of the season, the number 11 was even used in central midfield. It would be Giggs who would be the leader in the following season: not in the traditional sense (in fact, if any player other than Beckham blossomed into their potential in the at-times difficult 1996/97 season, it was probably Roy Keane) but in terms of making an important and significant statement on the continent.

Manchester United relinquished their unbeaten European record in the following season (in fact, they lost three times at home in the campaign) and still made arguably their greatest impression yet in the Champions League. That was partly down to Giggs, who was the lone shining light even in a home group stage defeat to Juventus. Giggs had long been courted by Italian sides and it seemed as if with that respect came fear; he was by far the most menacing attacking force United had in a 0-1 reverse and that, perhaps encouraged the other youngsters to come out of their shells. United's 4-0 quarter-final victory over Porto was a true coming of age moment with Giggs again the star man - this time on the left side of a three man midfield.

Giggs would go on to break records for appearances and one club longevity. His personal collection of honours is greater than every English club bar Liverpool and United and he even took up the managerial reigns after David Moyes was sacked in April 2014. Often touted as a future United boss, Giggs' place in the history of the club is assured as the leader of the fabled 'Class of 92' if not, strictly speaking, one of them.

Andy Cole didn't get off to the best of starts in the 1996/97 season; a broken leg suffered early in the campaign left him sidelined until Boxing Day: by which time Ole Gunnar Solskjaer, a previously unheard of arrival from Norway, had staked his own claim for a first team place alongside Eric Cantona. However, Cole would rise against the threat of stiff opposition and, whilst not quite indispensible in the following season, he showed enough to suggest he had a future at Old Trafford.

That was no doubt helped by a suspension to Eric Cantona which rendered him unavailable for a game at Arsenal in February. United were forced to go into a tough game without their leader and, it must be said, put on one of their most impressive performances of the league season. Cole and Solskjaer were both on the scoresheet in a 2-1 win, suggesting for the first time that United could cope without their talisman.

There are differing accounts of what was going through Cantona's mind that ended up convincing him it was time to make the shock announcement and retire from professional football in May 1997. The most commonly accepted version of the story is that Cantona was dismayed at the Champions League failure against Borussia Dortmund in the Champions League semi-finals; the German side had won 1-0 in both semi-final legs: the second of which was at Old Trafford and could arguably have been decided in United's favour had Cantona been in sharper form.

The manager recalled in his first autobiography that he felt Cantona had been 'marginal' in the first leg and, the day after the second leg, the Frenchman had approached him to tell him of his intention to retire. "His answer was vague, amounting to little more than the suggestion that he had done as much as he could in the game and wished to take his life in another direction," said Ferguson when he asked his captain why. Ferguson asked Cantona to take some time to think it over but, privately, had resigned himself to losing him. After the final league game, the striker confirmed that he hadn't changed his mind. "When I asked him again why he felt that way, he was not as vague as he had been previously and specified two recent trends at Old Trafford that had left him disillusioned," said Ferguson, "he said he felt he had become a pawn of Manchester United's merchandising department and that he was not going to accept such treatment any longer. His second complaint was that United were not ambitious enough in the purchase of players. I had a lot of sympathy with him on both counts."

Considering that the manager was unable to convince Cantona out of retiring in these circumstances and that the blame was being placed on the club for their actions, it speaks volumes that Ferguson felt he was unable to appease his star man about player acquisitions and that this final account of Cantona calling it a day is at odds with the accepted story that he wistfully decided football was no longer for him and it was time to be an actor.

There simply has to be an element of truth to Cantona's lost enthusiasm for the game. This was a cataclysmic decision which shook football but Ferguson's following statement, "I pondered what he had said about the boardroom attitudes that limit my prospects of recruiting the biggest names in football. I have been severely handicapped by the club's insistence on a wage ceiling at Old Trafford" also gives the impression that the message was as much political as it was part of the chronological events in his life. Is it a coincidence that, shortly after bemoaning the spending restrictions, United broke their transfer record numerous times in a few years to bring in Ruud van Nistelrooy, Juan Sebastian Veron and Rio Ferdinand?

This is not to cast doubt on the content of the second conversation between Ferguson and Cantona but it suggests some playful manipulation in the recounting of it; from what we know, it seems at odds with everything that Cantona was so disillusioned with the transfer policy that it was one of the three major reasons he cited for retiring completely. If he had grown that frustrated with Manchester United, he could have simply requested a transfer.

It is more likely that Cantona's decision came down to a combination of falling out of love with the game and, perhaps, a little disappointment in himself. Though it ought to be said that the reports Cantona had been far from his best were a little unfair (there were plenty of moments of jaw-dropping extravagance in the 1996/97 season), there were also some unfamiliar indifferent moments. After an ineffectual game against Liverpool, the Frenchman reprimanded himself, saying "I forgot I could play so badly."

Cantona was also a victim of the manager's decision to deviate from his favoured system in Europe. One of the most compelling talking points from Alex Ferguson's era as Manchester United manager is the potential of the side that won the 1994 Double and what they could have done in Europe if the foreigner rules had been as relaxed as they were in 1996/97. This can never be known but it can be reasonably concluded that the reason they didn't do as well as they might have done in 1993/94 and 1994/95 is partly because they were never able to play their strongest side.

When they were finally allowed to do so, in 1996/97, Ferguson had decided that a tactical shift was needed and deployed a three man midfield and three man front line. Cantona became the spearhead of the front three, a completely unfamiliar role and, when it bombed so badly in Turin in a disappointing performance against Juventus, questions were naturally asked of the manager and the players. It isolated Cantona in a way that robbed him of the qualities he so often brought to the team; unable to float around the pitch and use his initiative to influence games, he was an easily identifiable spearhead and marked out of the game. Just because Cantona was not an off-the-shoulder forward doesn't make him any less of a player; it could be said that United's underachievements in Europe in 1996/97 were as much a reflection of the naivety of their manager as that of the players. The occasions it worked, it worked spectacularly but on the many occasions when it didn't, Manchester United were almost unrecognisable from the enthusiastic and energetic side which had been so successful in 1996, and had more or less coasted to the title in 1997.

But the effect these changes in formation would have on Cantona's state of mind cannot be underestimated; it is natural that he felt that tactics were shifting against his qualities. Against Dortmund, Cantona couldn't be solely to blame – despite a string of missed chances. The ball just wouldn't go in. But perhaps that evening was the first time Cantona had felt the anxiety; with glory so close, and that human need to succeed, the composure that would normally have made some of the chances almost second nature was gone: mostly due to the unfamiliar system in which he was being asked to play. It was no coincidence that United's success came when they reverted to their traditional 4-4-2 and played with two strikers. By that time, Cantona was off seeking pastures new.

Given what we know, it is difficult to consider the 'what if' of Cantona remaining a Manchester United player for the two or three years which followed his retirement. It is reasonable to say that the 1998 disappointment, which could just as easily be put down to a horrendous injury crisis, was partly due to some of the younger players' hesitation when it came to the crunch moments where Cantona would usually deliver. And, subsequently, that their 1999 success was due to their blossoming and maturing in no small part thanks to Cantona. It seems folly to compare the influence he might have had if present against the influence we can almost certainly determine he had in his absence.

As the youngsters came out of their shell and developed an assurance which riled opposition supporters up and down the country, the personality of Cantona was almost tangible. In truth, it barely matters who places him where on any poll of important players because the truth is, he had an influence on one of the greatest generation of players to have ever played in English football; Cantona's imprint was almost as influential on the Manchester United teams which followed his retirement as Alex Ferguson's.

There can be no comparison between Cantona and any other player who made an impact on a club in British football simply because the unparalleled era of success which followed his transfer in November 1992 transformed Manchester United at a time when the game itself was changing. It is almost incomprehensible to think that, when he was signed from Leeds, United weren't only eleven league titles behind Liverpool but three behind Arsenal, two behind Everton and level with Aston Villa. As United and Villa battled it out for the 1993 league title, they had every right to claim to be just as big a club when it came to trophy hauls at home and on the continent.

Sure, there were players who contributed to more league titles than Cantona and others who dominated the league for a period but none had quite the same influence on changing the culture of one club from perennial underachievers into unquestionably the most successful club in terms of trophies and the richest club in terms of revenue by 2003. It seems unlikely that there will ever be someone who has that kind of influence on the game in one country; these days transformations are dictated by financial takeovers, boardroom investments or the advent of a manager who guarantees success rather than by the fateful acquisition of a single player. In many respects, then, it would not be a stretch to identify Cantona as the most important player in the history of Manchester United.

There were prescient remarks in Ferguson's retelling of the Cantona retirement tale that cannot be dismissed. United's marketing department had grown exponentially and beyond all recognition over the following years. It had floated the idea of a subscription television channel over the season in a number of its official publications, suggesting the promise of first team games being shown live (though Red Issue showed prescience again themselves here in a spoof article, suggesting it would be more likely that every single youth and reserve game would be shown). Sky's deal with the Premiership was due to expire in 1997 and United sensed that there was an opportunity to cash in. We know how it turned out, but it is interesting to look back and see how the club were well positioned and prepared to capitalise and wonder 'what if'. Given the subsequent success United enjoyed, if they had had such a monopoly over their own television rights, we may well have been looking at the club celebrating its twenty-first consecutive league title. Back then, their foresight was seen as something of a major reason for Sky wanting to takeover in 1998. A fan protest and subsequent government enquiry ended that saga but it was clear that both Sky and United recognised the Red Devils as the eminent football brand in football.

United launched MUTV and it remains a popular service although they have never managed to acquire the rights to show competitive first team games live. Instead, it has served as a communication tool which has helped United define their commercial voice over the years. Gone are the days when official publications would deem it appropriate to comment on controversy involving players of other clubs. Instead, there is a sanitised and frustrating party line: PR driven to the point that, in the early days, former players who were too outspoken as pundits were never invited on again and it was one such outburst that saw the curtain famously fall on Roy Keane's United career.

That said, such a responsibly spoken outlet is perhaps the only way that the channel can exist; the commercial presence of the club means that every sentence is dissected, every word challenged. In the modern world of football such sanitisation is required. One only needs to look around British football and see that all clubs now follow that lead and all major clubs apply that same kind of media protection to their younger players. It may have created a game devoid of 'characters' but in 1995/1996 this was not so and perhaps, then, it was part of what made the difference; part of what gave Manchester United the edge.

It was an extraordinary cocktail of the right ingredients at the most opportune time; the way that football would become so popular might not have been anything anyone could have predicted but, despite the luck that was involved (United legend Gordon Hill refers to the "Class of 92" as a 'lottery win' for Ferguson), their development was intentional and geared towards success. The management of those stars was utter perfection. It can be lamented that the club should have won more than one European Cup in that period (if it is commonly agreed that 'that period' goes roughly up until the Glazer takeover in 2005) though, if we consider that 'one game from greatness' theory, it is difficult to think that Borussia Dortmund were truly a better team than Manchester United neither, for that matter, were Monaco who eliminated United in the 1998 quarter-finals.

The record books, however, do not have Manchester United's name as the winner of the Champions League in 1997 or 1998 and those regrets will remain with the manager and, possibly, some of the players. If what has been achieved is indisputable, though, then can it be seriously challenged that this Manchester United team matured into the best club side ever seen in the UK? It's a statement that carries tremendous weight but let us consider the alternatives.

Liverpool won eight titles between 1979 and 1990; United won eight between 1993 and 2003, taking one fewer. That in itself is not definitive; Liverpool fans would contend that their two European Cups won in that period tips it in their favour even if that theory disregards the change in regulations in the Champions League that meant, from 1997, it wasn't just league champions that qualified. The truth is that argument would linger for the ages, with the tribal merits of both sides being logically presented as impartial, conclusive evidence to support their point.

Even if one looks at the question of whether the 1999 team was the greatest Manchester United team ever, it is not straightforward. There are those who will not hear anything that suggests that the Busby Babes wouldn't have gone on to win everything the game had to offer year in, year out. There are others who feel that the team which won the club's first European Cup in 1968, with Sir Bobby Charlton, George Best and Denis Law as the front line, cannot be beaten and then there's the unknown continental potential of the 1994 side and the most recent European Cup winners in 2008. It's a completely subjective argument but let this record be the opportunity to state the case for the 1996 vintage which would ultimately form the backbone of successes up until 2003 and, in the case of some players, beyond that.

If we are to clinically look at these things, it can be observed that Sir Bobby Charlton won three league titles, George Best and Denis Law, two apiece, Bill Foulkes won four league titles, an FA Cup and a European Cup, Ryan Giggs won thirteen, Paul Scholes eleven, Gary Neville eight (he also featured in two more title-winning seasons, but didn't play in enough games to qualify for a medal), by himself Gary Neville won as many league titles as the 'Holy Trinity'.

Put in absolutely clinical terms, the only reasonable conclusion is that the 'class of 1992' (and friends) were the most successful group of players to have represented Manchester United, ably assisted, of course, by a stellar cast of international stars like Peter Schmeichel, Eric Cantona, Roy Keane and, a little later on, Cristiano Ronaldo. Whether they were the most gifted is a matter for subjective argument but it barely matters either way. It could theoretically be put forward in a discussion that Peter Schmeichel, by virtue of the commonly accepted opinion that he was the best goalkeeper on the planet for around six years, stands out as United's best ever player but, as we all know, goalkeepers are one breed and outfield players another. The merits of Cantona versus Giggs versus Scholes versus Ronaldo could be debated for hours but the bottom line is that Manchester United supporters have been fortunate and blessed to have witnessed all four.

Gary Neville is often quoted as saying that the achievements of the team he played in would not be truly appreciated until years after they had all retired. That could be a fair summary; after all, it was never the case, as far as the media were concerned, that they reported on history unfolding. They were too busy waiting for the fall of United or the rise of the next opponent to properly celebrate the achievements of the wonderful team they had the privilege to watch. In the UK it absurdly came to be that people enjoyed watching their stars fail more than they enjoyed watching them succeed. Success breeds jealously and so those who had found themselves a little annoyed by United's fantastic 1994 team cantering to a second title were given plenty of ammunition when Cantona made himself the bad guy in January 1995. There were neutrals who understood that Simmons was no angel but ask the majority of those who don't have a vested interest and they will only remember that Cantona kicked a fan. To supporters of teams other than Manchester United it wasn't a case of Cantona serving his ban and then coming back and succeeding but a case of Public Enemy Number One being back on the pitch when they thought he shouldn't have been. It was probably as much to do with fear of his ability as it was any concern that he would re-offend.

So it stands to reason that the confidence in this United team was perceived as arrogance and it is easy to see why when you look at David Beckham's outstretched-arms celebration against Wimbledon and Cantona's 'what else did you expect' chip against Sunderland later that same season. These iconic moments of bravado stuck in the throat of others. When Beckham was sent off in the World Cup of 1998, it was all the excuse many needed to unleash toxic vitriol which revealed more about their long-held emotions than it did the reflection of a nation's feeling about the red card against Argentina. Once Beckham was booed, the gloves were off; regularly in England games, the 'Three Lions' would routinely boo the Manchester United contingent. It must be fair to not dismiss the influence of an unsupportive crowd whilst at the same time not use it as an excuse for under-performance. The England crowd may have thought it was a bit of fun but how does it appear to the rest of the team when you are booing when your side has possession: whichever club the man with the ball plays for?

In the following years there was all the talk of a golden generation but during the time of Scholes, Beckham, Butt and the Nevilles, England truly had one and under utilised it by either wasting the talent of the players they had to accommodate lesser gifted players elsewhere in the team or by berating them unfairly in the stands. It came as an international shock when Nicky Butt was perceived as a star of England's 2002 World Cup campaign but it surprised nobody at Old Trafford. Butt had been overlooked in favour of players like David Batty, Rob Lee and Paul Merson in the 1998 World Cup squad and again for the 2000 European Championships for the likes of Dennis Wise and the pair of Gareth Barry and Steven Gerrard (with three caps between them and barely any club experience compared to the success Butt had enjoyed).

★

Of course it's not as simple as saying that the perception of United's success is denigrated by opposition jealousy – it wasn't as if Manchester United were without their supporters, even in the press and it's difficult to lay too much blame at the door of reporters who were used as part of Ferguson's siege mentality. Some of the truth, in fact, swings so far the other way as to level it out again. David Ginola was infamously named the PFA and Football Writers Player of the Year in the 1998/99 season but this was more to do with a split vote between a number of outstanding Manchester United players. If you were going to vote for a United star, would it be Roy Keane, who was insipring his team after coming back from a potentially career threatening injury, or Dwight Yorke, a striker who had surprised everyone by making the step up from Aston Villa to United with such comfort or David Beckham, fresh from the World Cup infamy of 1998? It wasn't an easy decision, and naturally, the vote would be split. In this instance, United's players were victims of their own success, though it is surely the case that if you asked any if they would trade their place in history in 1999 for an individual award in the same year, the answer would be a resounding and collective 'no'.

In a strange sort of way, it's probably more fitting that United achieved all they did in the mid to late 1990's without the universal love of the press. It made for a more unique matchday experience for supporters who were hated everywhere they went because the team were so good and, more often than not, United would score goals and turn teams over, home or away.

It has been twenty years since Manchester United became the first team to win the league and FA Cup double on two separate occasions. At the time of writing, it has only been five since most of them started to retire. To return to Neville's suggestion that it will only be when their time has been and gone that their achievements would be appreciated for what they were; it's probably about time now that the Nevilles are portrayed as more than competition winners, that Butt and Beckham are viewed as something more than workhorses and that the stature of Paul Scholes and Ryan Giggs as English football's most successful ever players is seen for what their medals represent.

There is no such danger of Sir Alex Ferguson's reputation going under the radar. The success of 1996 underlined his genius. Now Ferguson belonged in the same company as Busby, Shankly, Paisley, Clough, Ramsey, Stein and even Herbert Chapman. His subsequent successes in the seventeen years which followed cemented his place as the greatest of them all. In 1996, as has been documented in this book, Ferguson was still learning. He was adapting enthusiastically to the increased media exposure which he would quickly come to appear to detest. That *Manchester Evening News* poll and the knee-jerk reaction of United fans in the summer of 1995 was forgotten on the Wembley turf in May 1996.

There were some suggestions that his 2013 retirement was partly due to how dramatically the game was changing in terms of player power and profile; perhaps it would be understandable if a man who had been involved in the professional game since the 1950's felt somewhat alienated but back in 1996 he had his finger on the pulse of how to manipulate all these advances to his advantage and, as such, it is without question that there was no-one better in world football to have been the custodian for the careers of the young men who were dubbed his 'Fledglings'.

It was the perfect combination to create an almost perfect football team: one of the greatest ever seen, and without question the greatest Manchester United team of all time.

STATISTICS

OTHER SIGNIFICANT RESULTS

CHAMPIONS LEAGUE

Semi-finals

1st Leg

AJAX 0-1 PANATHINAIKOS
JUVENTUS 2-0 NANTES

2nd Leg

PANATHINAIKOS 0-3 AJAX (1-3 ON AGGREGATE)
NANTES 3–2 JUVENTUS (3-4 ON AGGREGATE)

FINAL

Stadio Olimpico, Rome - Attendance: 67,000

AJAX 1–1 JUVENTUS (AET)

Litmanen 41'   Ravanelli 12'

Juventus won 4-2 on penalties

UEFA CUP

FINAL

1st Leg

BAYERN MUNICH 2-0 BORDEAUX

2nd Leg

BORDEAUX 1-3 BAYERN MUNICH

Bayern won 5-1 on aggregate

CUP WINNERS' CUP

FINAL

King Baudouin Stadium, Brussels - Attendance: 37,500

PARIS SAINT-GERMAIN 1–0 RAPID VIENNA

N'Gotty 29'

MANCHESTER UNITED 1995-96

Date	Opponent	Venue	Competition	Score	Ground	Attendance	Scorers
Sat 19 Aug 1995	Aston Villa	A	League	1-3	Villa Park	34,655	Beckham 84
Wed 23 Aug 1995	WEST HAM UNITED	H	League	2-1	Old Trafford	31,966	Scholes 50, Keane 68
Sat 26 Aug 1995	WIMBLEDON	H	League	3-1	Old Trafford	32,226	Keane 27,79, Cole 59
Mon 28 Aug 1995	Blackburn Rovers	A	League	2-1	Ewood Park	29,843	Sharpe 46, Beckham 72
Sat 09 Sep 1995	Everton	A	League	3-2	Goodison Park	39,496	Sharpe 3,49, Giggs 74
Tes 12 Sept 1995	Rotor Volgograd	A	UEFA Cup 1R 1L	0-0	Central Stadium	33,000	
Sat 16 Sep 1995	BOLTON WANDERERS	H	League	3-0	Old Trafford	32,812	Scholes 17, 85, Giggs 33
Wed 20 Sep 1995	YORK CITY	H	League Cup	0-3	Old Trafford	29,049	
Sat 23 Sep 1995	Sheffield Wednesday	A	League	0-0	Hillsborough	34,101	
Tues 26 Sept 1995	Rotor Volgograd	H	UEFA Cup 1R 2L	2-2	Old Trafford	29,274	Scholes 59, Schmeichel 89
			Volgograd won on away goals				
Sun 01 Oct 1995	LIVERPOOL	H	League	2-2	Old Trafford	34,934	Butt 1, Cantona 70 (pen)
Tue 03 Oct 1995	York City	A	League Cup	3-1	Bootham Crescent	9,386	Scholes 7, 80, Cooke 14
			York won 4-3 on aggregate				
Sat 14 Oct 1995	MANCHESTER CITY	H	League	1-0	Old Trafford	35,707	Scholes 4
Sat 21 Oct 1995	Chelsea	A	League	4-1	Stamford Bridge	31,019	Scholes 3,9, Giggs 78, McClair 85
Sat 28 Oct 1995	MIDDLESBROUGH	H	League	2-0	Old Trafford	36,580	Pallister 43, Cole 87
Sat 04 Nov 1995	Arsenal	A	League	0-1	Highbury	38,317	
Sat 18 Nov 1995	SOUTHAMPTON	H	League	4-1	Old Trafford	39,401	Giggs 1,4 Scholes 8, Cole 69
Wed 22 Nov 1995	Coventry City	A	League	4-0	Highfield Road	23,400	Irwin 27, McClair 47,76, Beckham 57
Mon 27 Nov 1995	Nottingham Forest	A	League	1-1	City Ground	29,263	Cantona 66 (pen)
Sat 02 Dec 1995	CHELSEA	H	League	1-1	Old Trafford	42,019	Beckham 60
Sat 09 Dec 1995	SHEFFIELD WEDNESDAY	H	League	2-2	Old Trafford	41,849	Cantona 17,83
Sun 17 Dec 1995	Liverpool	A	League	0-2	Anfield	40,546	
Sun 24 Dec 1995	Leeds United	A	League	1-3	Elland Road	39,801	Cole 28
Wed 27 Dec 1995	NEWCASTLE UNITED	H	League	2-0	Old Trafford	42,024	Cole 6, Keane 53
Sat 30 Dec 1995	QUEENS PARK RANGERS	H	League	2-1	Old Trafford	41,890	Cole 44, Giggs 52
Mon 01 Jan 1996	Tottenham Hotspur	A	League	1-4	White Hart Lane	32,852	Cole 36
Sat 06 Jan 1996	SUNDERLAND	H	F.A. Cup	2-2	Old Trafford	41,563	Butt 12, Cantona 80
Sat 13 Jan 1996	ASTON VILLA	H	League	0-0	Old Trafford	42,667	
Tue 16 Jan 1996	Sunderland	A	F.A. Cup	2-1	Roker Park	21,378	Scholes 69, Cole 89
Mon 22 Jan 1996	West Ham United	A	League	1-0	Boleyn Ground	24,197	Cantona 8
Sat 27 Jan 1996	Reading	A	F.A. Cup	3-0	Elm Park	14,780	Giggs 36, Parker 56, Cantona 89
Sat 03 Feb 1996	Wimbledon	A	League	4-2	Selhurst Park	32,852	Cole 41, Perry og. 45, Cantona 71(pen)
Sat 10 Feb 1996	BLACKBURN ROVERS	H	League	1-0	Old Trafford	42,681	Sharpe 14
Sun 18 Feb 1996	MANCHESTER CITY	H	F.A. Cup	2-1	Old Trafford	42,692	Cantona 38, Sharpe 77
Wed 21 Feb 1996	EVERTON	H	League	2-0	Old Trafford	42,459	Keane 30, Giggs 81
Sun 25 Feb 1996	Bolton Wanderers	A	League	6-0	Burnden Park	21,481	Beckham 3, Bruce 15, Cole 70, Scholes 75,78, Butt 89

Date	Opponent	Venue	Comp	Score	Ground	Attendance	Scorers
Mon 04 Mar 1996	Newcastle United	A	League	1-0	St. James Park	36,854	Cantona 51
Mon 11 Mar 1996	SOUTHAMPTON	H	F.A. Cup	2-0	Old Trafford	45,446	Cantona 49, Sharpe 90
Sat 16 Mar 1996	Queens Park Rangers	A	League	1-1	Loftus Road	18,817	Cantona 90
Wed 20 Mar 1996	ARSENAL	H	League	1-0	Old Trafford	50,028	Cantona 66 (pen)
Sun 24 Mar 1996	TOTTENHAM HOTSPUR	H	League	1-0	Old Trafford	50,157	Cantona 51
Sun 31 Mar 1996	Chelsea	N	F.A. Cup	2-1	Villa Park	38,421	Cole 55, Beckham 59
Sat 06 Apr 1996	Manchester City	A	League	3-2	Maine Road	29,688	Cantona 7(pen), Cole 41, Giggs 77
Mon 08 Apr 1996	COVENTRY CITY	H	League	1-0	Old Trafford	50,332	Cantona 47
Sat 13 Apr 1996	Southampton	A	League	1-3	The Dell	15,262	Giggs 89
Wed 17 Apr 1996	LEEDS UNITED	H	League	1-0	Old Trafford	48,362	Keane 72
Sun 28 Apr 1996	NOTTINGHAM FOREST	H	League	5-0	Old Trafford	53,926	Scholes 41, Beckham 44,54, Giggs 69, Cantona 90
Sun 05 May 1996	Middlesbrough	A	League	3-0	Riverside Stadium	29,921	May 13, Cole 54, Giggs 90
Sat 11 May 1996	Liverpool	N	F.A. Cup	1-0	Wembley	79,007	Cantona 85

APPEARANCES 1995/96

PLAYER	LGE	FAC	LC	UEFA	TOTAL
Schmeichel	36	6	1	2	45
Giggs	30 (3)	7	2	2	41 (3)
Cole	32(2)	7	1	1	41 (2)
Butt	31(1)	7	0	2	40 (1)
Irwin	31	6	1	1	39
Bruce	30	5	1(1)	2	38 (1)
Keane	29	7	1	0	38
Cantona	30	7	1	0	38
Neville G	30 (1)	5 (1)	1	1	37 (2)
Beckham	26 (7)	3	2	2	33 (7)
Sharpe	21 (10)	4 (2)	2	2	29 (12)
Neville P	21 (3)	6 (1)	1(1)	1	29 (5)
Pallister	21	3	2	2	28
Scholes	16 (10)	0 (2)	1	1(1)	18 (13)
McClair	12 (10)	0	1	0	13 (5)
May	11 (5)	2	0	0	13 (5)
Parker	5 (1)	1 (1)	1	0	7 (3)
Pilkington	2 (1)	1	1	0	4 (1)
Davies	1 (5)	-	1	0 (1)	1 (6)
Cooke	1 (3)	0	1 (1)	0 (1)	2 (5)
Prunier	2	0	0	0	2
O'Kane	0 (1)	0	0	1	1 (1)
McGibbon	0	0	1	0	1
Thornley	0 (1)	0	0	0	0 (1)

GOALSCORERS 1995/96

PLAYER	LGE	FAC	LC	UEFA	TOTAL
Cantona	14	5	0	0	19
Scholes	10	1	2	1	14
Cole	11	2	0	0	13
Giggs	11	1	0	0	12
Beckham	7	1	0	0	8
Keane	6	0	0	0	6
Sharpe	4	2	0	0	6
McClair	3	0	0	0	3
Butt	2	1	0	0	3
Bruce	1	0	0	0	1
Irwin	1	0	0	0	1
May	1	0	0	0	1
Pallister	1	0	0	0	1
Cooke	0	0	1	0	1
Parker	0	1	0	0	1
Schmeichel	0	0	0	1	1
own goal	1	0	0	0	1

A TWO MAN SHOW?

Of Eric Cantona's 14 league goals, 5 came in single goal victories and another 3 were second half equalisers worth a total of 19 points.

Peter Schmeichel kept 12 clean sheets in 16 league games after he returned to the team in January following injury.

FINAL LEAGUE TABLE 1995-96

			Home					Away					Overall						
#	Team	Pl	W	D	L	F	A	W	D	L	F	A	W	D	L	F	A	Pts	GD
C	MANCHESTER UNITED	38	15	4	0	36	9	10	3	6	37	26	25	7	6	73	35	82	38
2	Newcastle United	38	17	1	1	38	9	7	5	7	28	28	24	6	8	66	37	78	29
3	Liverpool	38	14	4	1	46	13	6	7	6	24	21	20	11	7	70	34	71	36
4	Aston Villa	38	11	5	3	32	15	7	4	8	20	20	18	9	11	52	35	63	17
5	Arsenal	38	10	7	2	30	16	7	5	7	19	16	17	12	9	49	32	63	17
6	Everton	38	10	5	4	35	19	7	5	7	29	25	17	10	11	64	44	61	20
7	Blackburn Rovers	38	14	2	3	44	19	4	5	10	17	28	18	7	13	61	47	61	14
8	Tottenham Hotspur	38	9	5	5	26	19	7	8	4	24	19	16	13	9	50	38	61	12
9	Nottingham Forest	38	11	6	2	29	17	4	7	8	21	37	15	13	10	50	54	58	-4
10	West Ham United	38	9	5	5	25	21	5	4	10	18	31	14	9	15	43	52	51	-9
11	Chelsea	38	7	7	5	30	22	5	7	7	16	22	12	14	12	46	44	50	2
12	Middlesbrough	38	8	3	8	27	27	3	7	9	8	23	11	10	17	35	50	43	-15
13	Leeds United	38	8	3	8	21	21	4	4	11	19	36	12	7	19	40	57	43	-17
14	Wimbledon	38	5	6	8	27	33	5	5	9	28	37	10	11	17	55	70	41	-15
15	Sheffield Wednesday	38	7	5	7	30	31	3	5	11	18	30	10	10	18	48	61	40	-13
16	Coventry City	38	6	7	6	21	23	2	7	10	21	37	8	14	16	42	60	38	-18
17	Southampton	38	7	7	5	21	18	2	4	13	13	34	9	11	18	34	52	38	-18
18	Manchester City	38	7	7	5	21	19	2	4	13	12	39	9	11	18	33	58	38	-25
19	Queens Park Rangers	38	6	5	8	25	26	3	1	15	13	31	9	6	23	38	57	33	-19
20	Bolton Wanderers	38	5	4	10	16	31	3	1	15	23	40	8	5	25	39	71	29	-32

MANCHESTER UNITED RESERVES 1995/96 (PONTINS LEAGUE)

Date	Opponents	Res	1	2	3	4	5	6	7	8	9	10	11	12	13	14	15
16/08/1995	BOLTON WANDERERS	1-0	Pilkington	Casper	Clegg	McGibbon	May	Mulryne	Mustoe	Appleton	Tomlinson[1]	Baker	Thornley	Smith (7)		Twiss (10)	Hilton
30/08/1995	NOTTS COUNTY	2-2	Pilkington	Parker	O'Kane	Casper	McGibbon	Appleton	Cooke	Giggs[1]	Tomlinson	Davies	Thornley	Mustoe		P Neville (3)	Clegg (10)
02/09/1995	Liverpool	2-3	Pilkington	Clegg	O'Kane	Casper	Wallwork	Appleton	Cooke	Tomlinson	McClair	Davies	Thornley	Brebner		Baker	
06/09/1995	Blackburn Rovers	1-1	Pilkington	P Neville	O'Kane	Casper[1]	McGibbon	Appleton	Cooke	Mustoe	Tomlinson	Kirovski	Mulryne	Baker (9)		Wallwork[1] (8)	Clegg (3)
27/09/1995	Oldham Athletic	2-0	Pilkington	Clegg	O'Kane	Casper[1]	McGibbon	Mustoe	Cooke	Tomlinson[1]	McClair	Scholes	Tomlinson[1]	Baker	Gibson	Whittam	
07/10/1995	LEEDS UNITED	2-0	Pilkington	Clegg	P Neville	Casper	Clegg	Sharpe	Cantona	Cooke[1]	McClair	Kirovski[3]	Davies	Baker (7)		Mustoe (10)	Curtis
11/10/1995	West Bromwich Albion	4-2	Pilkington	Parker	Appleton	Casper	Clegg	Davies	Cooke[1]	Tomlinson	McClair	Kirovski	Davies	Baker[1]		Baker	
18/10/1995	BIRMINGHAM CITY	3-0	Pilkington	Clegg	Irwin	Casper	McGibbon	Baker	Cooke[1]	Tomlinson[2]	McClair	Davies	Thornley	Appleton (3)	Gibson	Mustoe (10)	
25/10/1995	Nottingham Forest	1-1	Pilkington	Clegg	P Neville	Casper	McGibbon	Sharpe[1]	Cooke[1]	Tomlinson	McClair	Kirovski[2]	Thornley	Appleton (6)		Mustoe	
01/11/1995	Sheffield Wednesday	3-5	Pilkington	Clegg	P Neville	Casper	Casper	Sharpe[1]	Cooke	Tomlinson	McClair	Kirovski[1]	Thornley	McGibbon		Appleton (11)	Thornley (6)
15/11/1995	SHEFFIELD UNITED	6-0*	Pilkington	P Neville	P Neville	May	May	Sharpe[1]	Cooke[1]	Beckham	McClair[1]	Appleton	Tomlinson	Beckham[1] (7)		Clegg (9)	Appleton 1 (6)
20/11/1995	WOLVERHAMPTON WDRS	2-0	Pilkington	Clegg	O'Kane	Casper	McGibbon	Appleton	Cooke[1]	Tomlinson[1]	McClair[1]	Kirovski[1]	Davies	Murdock (4)		Mustoe (6)	
29/11/1995	Tranmere Rovers	3-1	Gibson	P Neville	P Neville	Casper	McGibbon	Appleton	Cooke[1]	Kirovski	Tomlinson	Davies	Davies	Clegg (11)		Mustoe	Wood
06/12/1995	Leeds United	2-1	Gibson	Clegg	O'Kane	McGibbon	McGibbon	Appleton	Cooke	Davies	Tomlinson	Davies	Sharpe	Mustoe		Murdock	Casper
14/12/1995	OLDHAM ATHLETIC	2-2	Gibson	Keane	O'Kane	Casper	Casper	Appleton	Cooke	Baker	Tomlinson	Kirovski[1]	Mulryne	Murdock (9)		Baker 1 (2)	Brebner
20/12/1995	DERBY COUNTY	3-1*	Pilkington	Parker	O'Kane	Prunier	McGibbon	Appleton	Cooke	Kirovski[1]	Tomlinson	Davies	Mustoe	McGibbon		Baker (9)	Clegg
03/01/1996	Newcastle United	0-2	Culkin	Clegg	O'Kane	Casper[1]	McGibbon[1]	Davies	Cooke	Butt	Tomlinson	Scholes[1]	Mustoe[1]	Mustoe (10)		Baker (9)	Wallwork
09/01/1996	Everton	1-0	Pilkington	Parker	Clegg	Casper[1]	McGibbon[1]	Appleton	Cooke	Scholes	McClair	Scholes[1]	Sharpe	Appleton (6)		Mustoe (8)	Murdock
17/01/1996	LIVERPOOL	2-1	Pilkington	Clegg	O'Kane	Murdock	Murdock	Appleton	Cooke	Tomlinson	McClair	Scholes[1]	Sharpe	Mustoe		Wallwork (4)	Baker
24/01/1996	Bolton Wanderers	2-0	Coton	Parker	O'Kane	McGibbon	Wallwork	Beckham[1]	Cooke	Tomlinson	McClair	Scholes	Davies	Clegg (4)	Pilkington	Appleton (10)	
31/01/1996	BLACKBURN ROVERS	2-1	Coton	Clegg	Clegg	McGibbon	Murdock	Davies	Beckham	Kirovski	McClair	Kirovski[1]	Thornley	Appleton (7)		Tomlinson	Mustoe
15/02/1996	EVERTON	2-0	Coton	Clegg	Clegg	McGibbon	May	Appleton	Scholes	Tomlinson	McClair	Scholes	Thornley[1]	Mustoe (6)	Gibson	Brebner	
26/02/1996	Sheffield United	3-0	Coton	Parker	G Neville[1]	McGibbon	May	Beckham	Mustoe	Kirovski 1	McClair	Scholes	Thornley[1]	Tomlinson (8)		Clegg	
07/03/1996	SHEFFIELD WEDNESDAY	2-1	Pilkington	Parker	O'Kane[1]	McGibbon	Clegg	Beckham	Cooke	Kirovski	McClair	Davies	Davies[2]	Appleton	Pilkington	Clegg	Tomlinson
19/03/1996	Derby County	1-2	Coton	Clegg	O'Kane	McGibbon	Wallwork	Appleton	Cooke[1]	Scholes	Davies	Davies	Davies	Murdock		Baker (8)	
28/03/1996	Stoke City	1-1	Pilkington	Clegg	Clegg	McGibbon	McGibbon	Beckham	Cooke[1]	Kirovski	Scholes[1]	Wood 1	Mulryne	Appleton (9)		Mulryne (6)	Murdock (11)
04/04/1996	Notts County	1-0	Coton	Hall	O'Kane	Clegg	McGibbon	Murdock	Mustoe	Appleton	Davies	Scholes	Baker	Baker		Curtis (2)	Wallwork
10/04/1996	WEST BROMWICH ALBION	4-1	Coton	Parker	Clegg	McGibbon	Casper	Appleton[1]	Cooke[2]	Kirovski[2]	Scholes[1]	Davies	Cooke	Hall (7)		Baker	Mustoe (2)
20/04/1996	NOTTINGHAM FOREST	4-0	Coton	Parker	Clegg	Casper	McGibbon	Appleton	Mustoe	Kirovski[1]	McClair	Ford	O'Kane[1]	Baker		Hall (6)	
22/04/1996	Birmingham City	0-1	Pilkington	Parker	Clegg	Casper	Murdock	O'Kane	O'Kane	Kirovski	Baker[1]	Notman	Naylor	Wood (11)	Pilkington	McGibbon	
24/04/1996	NEWCASTLE UNITED	2-0	Pilkington	Parker	Clegg	Casper	Murdock	Mustoe	Cooke	Kirovski[1]	Baker[1]	Davies	Hall	Baker	Gibson	Byers (6)	
29/04/1996	STOKE CITY	1-0	Pilkington	Hall	O'Kane	Casper	Clegg	Appleton	O'Kane	Kirovski[2]	McClair	Davies	Baker	Cooke (2)	Gibson	Notman	
01/05/1996	TRANMERE ROVERS	2-3	Pilkington	Hall	Whittam	Casper	Murdock	Appleton	Cooke	Kirovski[1]	Baker	Davies	O'Kane[1]	Brown	Gibson	Notman	
06/05/1996	Wolverhampton Wtrs	2-3	Pilkington	McGibbon	Whittam	Casper	Clegg	Mustoe	Appleton	Davies	Cooke	Kirovski[1]	Murdock[2]	Murdock (2)	Gibson	Hall (3)	Wood (10)

1996 EUROPEAN CHAMPIONSHIPS

GROUP A

			Team	Pld	W	D	L	GF	GA	GD	Pts
England	1-1	Switzerland	ENGLAND	3	2	1	0	7	2	+5	7
Netherlands	0-0	Scotland	NETHERLANDS	3	1	1	1	3	4	-1	4
Switzerland	0-2	Netherlands	Scotland	3	1	1	1	1	2	-1	4
Scotland	0-2	England	Switzerland	3	0	1	2	1	4	-3	1
Scotland	1-0	Switzerland									
Netherlands	1-4	England									

GROUP B

			Team	Pld	W	D	L	GF	GA	GD	Pts
Spain	1-1	Bulgaria	FRANCE	3	2	1	0	5	2	+3	7
Romania	0-1	France	SPAIN	3	1	2	0	4	3	+1	5
Bulgaria	1-0	Romania	Bulgaria	3	1	1	1	3	4	-1	4
France	1-1	Spain	Romania	3	0	0	3	1	4	-3	0
France	3-1	Bulgaria									
Romania	1-2	Spain									

GROUP C

			Team	Pld	W	D	L	GF	GA	GD	Pts
Germany	2-0	Czech Republic	GERMANY	3	2	1	0	5	0	+5	7
Italy	2-1	Russia	CZECH REP	3	1	1	1	5	6	-1	4
Czech Republic	2-1	Italy	Italy	3	1	1	1	3	3	0	4
Russia	0-3	Germany	Russia	3	0	1	2	4	8	-4	1
Russia	3-3	Czech Republic									
Italy	0-0	Germany									

GROUP D

			Team	Pld	W	D	L	GF	GA	GD	Pts
Denmark	1-1	Portugal	PORTUGAL	3	2	1	0	5	1	+4	7
Turkey	0-1	Croatia	CROATIA	3	2	0	1	4	3	+1	6
Portugal	1-0	Turkey	Denmark	3	1	1	1	4	4	0	4
Croatia	3-0	Denmark	Turkey	3	0	0	3	0	5	-5	0
Croatia	0-3	Portugal									
Turkey	0-3	Denmark									

QUARTER-FINALS

Wembley - 75,440
Spain 0-0 England (aet)
England won 4-2 on pens

Anfield - 37,465
France 0-0 Netherlands (aet)
France won 5-4 on pens

Old Trafford - 43,412
Germany 2-1 Croatia
Klinsmann 20' (pen.); Šuker 51'
Sammer 59'

Villa Park - 26,832
Czech Republic 1-0 Portugal
Poborský 53'

SEMI-FINALS

Old Trafford - 43,877
France 0-0 Czech Republic (aet)
Czech Rep won 6-5 on pens

Wembley - 75,862
Germany 1-1 England (aet)
Kuntz 16'; Shearer 3'
Germany won 6-5 on pens

FINAL - WEMBLEY - 73,611

Czech Republic	1-2	Germany (aet)
Berger 59' (pen.)		Bierhoff 73', 95'